THE GLITTERING MOUNTAINS OF CANADA

THE TWINS
Looking down the Athabaska gorge from the Columbia Icefield. North Twin (12,085 ft.) is the third elevation of the Canadian Rocky Mountains

THE GLITTERING MOUNTAINS OF CANADA

A RECORD OF EXPLORATION AND
PIONEER ASCENTS IN THE
CANADIAN ROCKIES
1914–1924

BY
J. MONROE THORINGTON
B.S., A.M., M.D.

Fellow of the Royal Geographical Society. Member of the American, Canadian, French and Swiss Alpine Clubs and the Explorers' Club. Editor of the "Bulletin of the Geographical Society of Philadelphia." Co-author of "A Climber's Guide to the Rocky Mountains of Canada."

Victoria Vancouver Calgary

Copyright © 2012 Rocky Mountain Books
First edition 1925 John W. Lea

All rights reserved. No part of this publication may be reproduced, stored in a retrieval system, or transmitted in any form or by any means—electronic, mechanical, audio recording, or otherwise—without the written permission of the publisher or a photocopying licence from Access Copyright, Toronto, Canada.

Rocky Mountain Books
www.rmbooks.com

Library and Archives Canada Cataloguing in Publication

Thorington, J. Monroe (James Monroe), 1894–1989
The glittering mountains of Canada : a record of exploration and pioneer ascents in the Canadian Rockies, 1914–1924 / J. Monroe Thorington ; foreword by Robert William Sandford. — 1st RMB ed.

Includes bibliographical references and index.

Issued also in electronic format. (ISBN 978-1-927330-08-1)

ISBN 978-1-927330-07-4 (bound).—ISBN 978-1-927330-06-7 (pbk.)

1. Rocky Mountains, Canadian (B.C. and Alta.).
2. Mountaineering. I. Title.

FC219.T46 2012   917.11   C2011-908379-5

Printed in China

Rocky Mountain Books acknowledges the financial support for its publishing program from the Government of Canada through the Canada Book Fund (CBF) and the Canada Council for the Arts, and from the province of British Columbia through the British Columbia Arts Council and the Book Publishing Tax Credit.

This book was produced using FSC®-certified, acid-free paper, processed chlorine free and printed with vegetable-based inks.

To My Guides

EDWARD FEUZ JR.
CONRAD KAIN
JAMES SIMPSON

WITH THE AFFECTION WHICH HAS GROWN FROM
MUTUAL UNDERSTANDING AND RESPECT IN
DAYS ON THE HEIGHTS AND BY THE
CAMPFIRES OF THE NORTHLAND
THIS BOOK IS DEDICATED

"The first travellers called them the Glittering Mountains, on account of the infinite number of immense rock crystals, which, they say, cover their surface, and which, when they are not covered with snow, or in bare places, reflect to an immense distance the rays of the sun. The name Rocky Mountains was given them, probably by later travellers, in consequence of the enormous isolated rocks which they offer here and there to view."

GABRIEL FRANCHÈRE

"The more elevated portions are covered with perpetual snow, which contributes to give them a luminous, and, at a great distance, even a brilliant appearance; whence they derived, among some of the first discoverers, the name of Shining mountains."

WASHINGTON IRVING

CONTENTS

FOREWORD
All That Glitters Is Not Old   xv

PREFACE   xlvii

CHAPTER I
Lake Louise: The Entrance to the Northland   1

CHAPTER II
Trails of the Waputik   7

CHAPTER III
The Freshfield Group   19

CHAPTER IV
The Mountains of the Alexandra Angle   33

CHAPTER V
The Ascent of North Twin   45

CHAPTER VI
Mount Saskatchewan and Mount Columbia   57

CHAPTER VII
Passage of the Saskatchewan Glacier   65

CHAPTER VIII
Athabaska Pass and the *Voyageurs*, 1811–1827   71

CHAPTER IX
Athabaska Pass and the *Voyageurs*, 1846–1872   145

CHAPTER X
Nineteenth Century Speculation in Regard to Altitude at Athabaska Pass   157

CHAPTER XI
The Mountains of the Whirlpool 167

CHAPTER XII
Climbs from the Scott Glacier 183

CHAPTER XIII
The Ramparts and Mount Fraser 197

CHAPTER XIV
In the Shadow of Mount Robson 215

CHAPTER XV
Trail's End 233

APPENDIX A
Summary of Ascents, Between Kicking Horse and Robson Passes, 1922–24 237

APPENDIX B
Summarized Itinerary of Expeditions 241

APPENDIX C
A List of Some of the Loftiest Triangulated Peaks of the Rocky Mountains of Canada 247

APPENDIX D
The Freshfield Glacier, Canadian Rockies (By Howard Palmer) 249

APPENDIX E
David Thompson and the First Crossing of Howse Pass 267

APPENDIX F
The Panorama from Mt. Columbia 271

APPENDIX G
A Note on the Original Journals of David Douglas 279

NOTES 289

INDEX 301

LIST OF ILLUSTRATIONS

THE TWINS ii
FORDING BLAEBERRY RIVER BELOW HOWSE PASS 77
BREAKING CAMP, AMISKWI VALLEY 77
HOWSE PASS AND NORTH SASKATCHEWAN RIVER 78
CAMPGROUND AT BOW LAKE 79
BOW LAKE 79
PACK-TRAIN FORDING MISTAYA RIVER 80
UPPER WILDFOWL LAKE, MISTAYA VALLEY 80
THE FRESHFIELD ICEFIELD 81
APPROACHING CORONATION MT. 82
TONGUE OF FRESHFIELD GLACIER AND MT. FRESHFIELD 82
YOUNG ROCKY MOUNTAIN GOAT 83
HEAD BASIN OF FRESHFIELD ICEFIELD 83
THE FRESHFIELD GROUP FROM THE N. 84
HEAD BASIN OF FRESHFIELD ICEFIELD 84
MT. WALKER AND MT. PILKINGTON 85
CAMPGROUND ON NIVERVILLE MEADOW 85
MT. GILGIT AND MT. NANGA PARBAT 86
MT. TRUTCH AND MT. BARNARD 86
ON THE SUMMIT OF MT. NANGA PARBAT 87
EDWARD FEUZ ON SUMMIT CREST OF MT. BARNARD 87
VIEW S.E. FROM THE SUMMIT OF MT. FRESHFIELD 88
COL LEADING TO BUSH RIVER VALLEY 88
THE PEAKS OF CHEPHREN, AND HOWSE PEAK 89
THE GREAT FORD, FORKS OF THE SASKATCHEWAN RIVER 89

NORTH SASKATCHEWAN VALLEY   90
ALEXANDRA GLACIERS AND "TRIDENT COL"   90
CASTLEGUARD CAMP WITH WATCHMAN
PEAK AND THOMPSON PASS   91
CAMPGROUND ON CASTLEGUARD MEADOWS   91
ASCENDING MT. CASTLEGUARD   92
NEAR THE TOP OF MT. CASTLEGUARD   92
"LIKE LONELY SEA STACKS IN MID-OCEAN," THE TWINS   93
ON THE SLOPES OF NORTH TWIN   93
RETURNING FROM NORTH TWIN, ACROSS THE COLUMBIA
ICEFIELD TOWARD MT. CASTLEGUARD   94
MT. SASKATCHEWAN FROM THE SUMMIT
OF MT. CASTLEGUARD   94
EAST FACE OF MT. SASKATCHEWAN   95
TERRACE VALLEY AND S.W. FACE OF
MT. SASKATCHEWAN   95
MT. SASKATCHEWAN   96
SUMMIT OF MT. SASKATCHEWAN   96
THE BEND OF ALEXANDRA RIVER   97
MT. COLUMBIA AND COLUMBIA GLACIER BASIN   97
KAIN AND SIMPSON AT SUMMIT CORNICE
OF MT. COLUMBIA   98
COLUMBIA GLACIER AND MT. COLUMBIA   98
THE TWINS, FROM THE BASE OF MT. COLUMBIA   99
APPROACHING MT. COLUMBIA   99
VIEW NORTHWARD FROM THE SUMMIT
OF MT. COLUMBIA   100
VIEW WESTWARD FROM MT. COLUMBIA   100
HEAD OF CASTLEGUARD VALLEY   101
THE SASKATCHEWAN GLACIER   101
MARGINAL LAKELET OF SASKATCHEWAN GLACIER   102
PACK-TRAIN ON THE ICE BELOW MT. CASTLEGUARD   102
THE FIRST PASSAGE OF THE SASKATCHEWAN
GLACIER WITH HORSES   103
SASKATCHEWAN GLACIER AND MT. CASTLEGUARD   103

DAVID DOUGLAS 104

SIR GEORGE SIMPSON 104

ALEXANDER ROSS 104

WAITING TO BE PACKED 105

MT. EVANS AND MT. KANE 105

MEMBERS OF 1924 EXPEDITION 106

CON, JACK, AND DAVE PUT ON A DIAMOND HITCH 106

SCOTT GLACIER AND MT. HOOKER FROM CAMPGROUND ON WHIRLPOOL RIVER 107

SCOTT GLACIER AND MT. HOOKER FROM THE WHIRLPOOL VALLEY 107

HOOKER ICEFIELD FROM THE SUMMIT OF MT. BROWN 108

MCGILLIVRAY'S ROCK AND NORTHERN ENTRANCE TO ATHABASKA PASS 108

PACK-TRAIN ENTERING ATHABASKA PASS BELOW MT. BROWN 109

PACK-TRAIN ARRIVING AT THE COMMITTEE PUNCH BOWL, ATHABASKA PASS 109

NORTH FACE OF MT. SERENITY FROM MT. OATES 110

MT. ERMATINGER FROM THE N. 110

MT. ERMATINGER AND MT. HOOKER FROM MT. OATES 111

MT. HOOKER AND THE HOOKER ICEFIELD 111

SNOW PRECIPICE OF THE CONTINENTAL DIVIDE S.W. OF MT. HOOKER 112

IN THE SÉRACS OF SCOTT GLACIER 112

THE WALL BELOW MT. HOOKER 112

MT. HOOKER FROM THE N.W. 113

MT. HOOKER FROM THE S.W. 113

MEADOW CREEK APPROACH TO TONQUIN VALLEY 114

THE RAMPARTS FROM AMETHYST LAKES 114

SIMON PEAK FROM THE S.W. 115

SIMON PEAK FROM THE HEAD OF GEIKIE CREEK 115

VALLEY OF SIMON CREEK AND FRASER MASSIF FROM THE S. 116

MCDONELL AND BENNINGTON PEAKS FROM SURPRISE POINT 116

MT. RESPLENDENT FROM LYNX MT.   117
SUMMIT OF MT. RESPLENDENT IN STORM   117
MT. ROBSON FROM THE EAST END OF BERG LAKE   117
THE ARÊTE BELOW GREAT ICE-WALL OF MT. ROBSON   118
SUMMIT ICE-CAP OF MT. ROBSON   118
MAP OF FRESHFIELD GROUP   119
DOUGLAS' MAP OF ATHABASKA PASS   120
FACSIMILES OF HANDWRITING IN DOUGLAS' JOURNALS   120
LAST RESTING-PLACE OF DAVID DOUGLAS, ISLAND OF HAWAII   121
TONGUE OF FRESHFIELD GLACIER FROM MT. DAVID   122
NORTHERN PORTION OF GLACIAL BASIN   122
GATHERING BASIN OF FRESHFIELD GLACIER, LOOKING S.E.   123
GATHERING BASIN OF FRESHFIELD GLACIER, AS SEEN FROM PROMONTORY BELOW ADVANCED CAMP   123
SURFACE OF THE GLACIER-TONGUE NEAR ADVANCED CAMP   124
MT. NANGA PARBAT AND MT. TRUTCH, SHOWING UPPER ICE PLATEAU   124
PART OF LATERAL DEPRESSION   125
LATERAL DEPRESSION AND SECONDARY TONGUE   125
SÉRAC IN LATERAL DEPRESSION   126
ICE ADVANCING INTO LATERAL DEPRESSION   126
CREST OF THE ICE CASCADE   127
COLUMBIA ICEFIELD FROM SLOPES OF MT. BRYCE   128
ON THE SUMMIT OF MT. COLUMBIA   129
THE ROCKY MOUNTAINS FROM THE COLUMBIA RIVER   130
MAP OF TONQUIN VALLEY AND THE RAMPARTS   131
SECTION OF FRESHFIELD GLACIER   132
TONGUE OF FRESHFIELD GLACIER   132

FOREWORD
ALL THAT GLITTERS IS NOT OLD
JAMES MONROE THORINGTON
AND THE CANADIAN ROCKIES

By the time I began my life in the Rockies in 1970, *The Glittering Mountains of Canada* had already been out of print for more than forty years. While James Monroe Thorington was still alive and his climbing guides were still in use, limited editions of his other books were already rare and expensive. The eloquent articles he wrote in the *Canadian Alpine Journal* about his own early adventures in the Rockies, and his clear and carefully researched essays on the human history of the mountain West, were similarly hard to find. It appeared at the time that Thorington, for all he did to bring his experiences of Rockies to the world, was on the cusp of being forgotten.

The Glittering Mountains of Canada briefly emerged into popular consciousness again in 1978 when a memorable quote from it appeared on the back cover of *The Canadian Rockies Trail Guide,* by Brian Patton and Bart Robinson, which was and remains today the bible for hikers and backpackers throughout the mountain parks. Copies of the Thorington book itself, however, didn't become more available until some of the hundreds of libraries in the United States and abroad which stocked it began to discard some of their older materials. As *The Glittering Mountains of Canada* slowly came into the hands of later generations, its reputation as a classic in the mountain adventure genre started to quietly grow again, casting a warm and enduring glow on Thorington's larger contribution to the history of Canadian

XV

mountaineering and its literature. Hopefully, this elegant reprint will permanently secure Thorington's rightful place in that proud history.

To fully appreciate the understated eloquence Thorington invested into each of his books and to derive the greatest value from his careful telling of the history of Canada's mountain West, it may be useful to understand the milieu in which *The Glittering Mountains of Canada* was written. When the Alpine Club of Canada was formed in 1906, there was still enough unmapped wilderness remaining that the exploration and ultimate protection of it would become one of the club's visionary objectives. Even in the twentieth century, that most rapidly urbanizing of human epochs, there was still a place for explorers. Looking back historically, it was still a time of giants.

By 1920, much of the mapping of the southern Rockies, the Purcells and the Selkirks was complete. Though there were still many remote peaks that remained unclimbed, first ascents had been made of the last of the big peaks in each of the southern ranges. The bulk of the pioneering exploration in Thorington's time would be done north of the main line of the Canadian Pacific Railway. This is where the tallest mountains still lay, unclimbed, in the Rockies, in the Coast Ranges and in the "Canadian Himalaya" which formed the divide between Alaska and the Yukon in the remote north.

Following the First World War, climbing activity was concentrated north of the main CPR line at Lake Louise and south of the Grand Trunk Pacific line through the newly created Jasper Forest Park. Here, whole domains of unclimbed summits awaited those with the energy and means to break into the silence of remote and seldom visited valleys. During this time, a new generation of climbers, many of them Americans, had begun make Canadian mountains the centre of their activities. James Monroe Thorington was one of these. Over his lifetime, Thorington would make an especially important contribution to the esteem in which the world held the Canadian alpine.

James Monroe Thorington was born in Philadelphia, Pennsylvania, on October 7, 1894. Exploration of his family lineage reveals that his English ancestors belonged to the Bulkeley family descended from William the Conqueror. It appears it was Thorington's grandfather, a pioneer fur trader cum US senator from Iowa and foreign diplomat, who established the family name in the United States. Thorington's father was a successful physician, a calling young James also followed. Thorington received his undergraduate degree from Princeton in 1915, an institution with which he remained associated for the rest of his life.[1] He received his medical doctorate from the University of Pennsylvania four years later, where he later returned to teach ophthalmology.

Thorington's interest in mountaineering appears to have begun in his childhood. In his chapter on the fur trade era in *The Glittering Mountains of Canada*, he reports that the fabled alpine giants in the Athabasca Pass area near Jasper captured his imagination while he was still in grade school:

> When I was little; when you were a school-child, geography-books taught that the highest mountains of North America – Mt. Brown and Mt. Hooker – lifted their unsurpassed heights on either side of Athabaska Pass. You can still find these tremendous peaks, preserved in many a modern atlas; they have become a tradition among map-makers. In those school-days, of not so long ago, I had never seen anything higher than a city office-building; but the gargoyles and cornices, seen through the smoke and dust of street-canyons, seemed so impossibly high that the very thought of mountains loftier was incomprehensible. My curiosity was aroused; more often than anyone

knew, I would prop up that battered geography on my knees, and wonder at the sky-soaring propensities of those far-away mountains.

Despite this early grounding in the romantic though suspect history of the mountains of Canada, Thorington was first introduced to the alpine during what were to be many visits to the Alps during his youth. His interest in the Alps never waned and led to the publication of two books. The first, *Mont Blanc Sideshow: The Life and Times of Albert Smith*, was published in 1934. Dedicated to his wife, Christine, this book chronicles the extraordinary life of a British playwright who, after making an ascent of Mont Blanc, produced a musical of the same name which brought a great deal of attention in England to mountaineering.

Thorington's second book on the subject of climbing in Europe, *A Survey of Early American Ascents in the Alps in the 19th Century*, which he wrote after becoming president of the American Alpine Club, was published in 1943. By that time, however, Thorington had already made his way to the Canadian Rockies. Once he visited Canada, nothing stood in the way of his enthusiasm for its peaks. Throughout his life only his medical interests would occupy more of his time.[2]

Over his long and accomplished life James Thorington would spend fifteen climbing seasons in Canada, during which he would explore most of the Great Divide between Mt. Assiniboine and Mt. Robson. He would make nearly fifty first ascents in the Rockies and in the Purcells in British Columbia. It was not only summits, however, that burned in Thorington's mountaineering imagination. This fine climber was interested in maps, mountain literature and, above all else, the history of mountaineering in Canada and abroad.

Thorington was a collector of historical accounts by the early explorers of Canada's mountains. He was also a pioneer in recording the efforts of the country's first mountaineers. It is my opinion that nothing written to date can rival Thorington's history of early travels in Jasper National Park. Nor has any author, then or since, shed such precise light on the mountaineering history of the Athabasca Pass area. Thorington examined David Thompson's journals in careful detail to prove that it was Thompson, and not David Douglas, who first wrongly guessed the summit of Athabasca Pass to be roughly 10,000 feet in altitude. Thorington also went to Athabasca Pass to recreate Douglas's ascent, and in so doing made a convincing argument that the accepted history should be changed. In all of the controversy surrounding Douglas's purported first ascent of Mt. Brown, Thorington was the first to openly suggest that the British botanist probably didn't climb Mt. Brown at all.

Not only did Thorington become a scholar of Canada's alpine, he also became one of the best mountain writers of his time. Few such authors today rival the clarity, richness of description and subtle rendering of the most profound values of place that made Thorington's articles and books so important to the literature of Canadian exploration.

The year 1925 was a turning point in Thorington's life. It was the year he published *The Glittering Mountains of Canada*, one of the most referenced classics of exploration in the Canadian Rockies. It was also the year he married Christine Rehn, who was to accompany him on many of his extensive foreign travels. In 1935, following years of fond personal correspondence, Thorington translated and edited the journals of Conrad Kain and published them as *Where The Clouds Can Go*, without question one of the most enduring and valuable contributions ever made to mountaineering literature. In 1946 Thorington published *The Purcell Range of British Columbia*. Though now extremely rare, this book was the first compendium of early exploratory accounts and mountaineering expeditions in the Purcells.

In a more practical vein, Thorington also authored and co-authored edition upon edition of standard guidebooks on climbing in the Rockies and in the Interior Ranges of British Columbia. In this, he is owed a debt by many generations of visitors to these ranges. During his long life he also contributed extensively to the Geographic Names Board of Canada in efforts to record and name the country's western mountains.

Though James Monroe Thorington is principally remembered in Canada as a scholar of the Canadian alpine, his enthusiasms extended to mountains everywhere. He joined the German-Austrian Alpine Club in 1910, the Swiss Alpine Club and Mazamas in 1914, Le club alpin français and the American Alpine Club in 1918, the Alpine Club of Canada in 1919 and the Alpine Club (UK) in 1927. Thorington edited the *American Alpine Journal* from 1934 to 1946 and served as president of the American Alpine Club from 1941 until 1943. He was also an honorary member of the Appalachian Mountain Club and a fellow of the Royal Geographical Society. Thorington was active in many of his historical pursuits right up until the end of his long life. With his tireless fact finding and letter writing, combined with the organizational skills of a professional archivist, Thorington contributed almost as much to the formal history of mountaineering after his retirement from active climbing as he did while beating his way through the bush of the Great Divide.

For the purposes of this introduction, let us begin the story of James Monroe Thorington in the Rockies with the summer of 1922. It is easy to establish continuity in this story, for Thorington enjoyed many of his early experiences in the Rockies in the company of well-known local mountain guides and outfitters. His special relationship with them is made clear in his warm dedication of *The Glittering Mountains of Canada* to guides Edward

Feuz and Conrad Kain and to legendary outfitter and guide Jimmy Simpson.

Thorington's 1922 expedition was bound for the Freshfield Group, a cluster of mountains surrounding and surrounded by the Freshfield Icefield. Thorington was accompanied by Howard Palmer, a Boston climber who had made his reputation through exploration of the northern Selkirks between 1908 and 1912. The party's guide was Edward Feuz Jr., the Swiss who, with Palmer, had made the first ascent of Mt. Sir Sandford in the summer of 1912. Suffice it to say that the younger Feuz was already on his way to becoming even more famous than his pioneer father, who had come to Canada to work as a mountain guide for the CPR in 1899. The party's outfitter was Jimmy Simpson, the famous Bow Lake outfitter and hunting guide with whom Thorington would correspond for the next sixty years.

TO THE FRESHFIELD, 1922

It is July and twenty-seven-year-old James Monroe Thorington is at Lake Louise. He has made the steep but technically simple ascent of Mt. Fairview in order to see up the Bow Valley to the peaks of the Waputik Range and west into Yoho. The remote Rockies are calling him. His response – now one of the most quoted justifications for following the old trails into the grand Rockies, later appearing on the back cover of *The Canadian Rockies Trail Guide* – announces the second great wave of mountaineering in Canada, to the northlands, the fabled country north of the CPR:

> Beyond all this are other mountains, and still others, until all outline is lost and nothing left save delicate gradations of light, merging with distance. There was always a subtle mystery in those farther heights; clear delineation was denied by very space, exasperating and trying to the imagination. For there, in the north, was the region of the great icefields, of the

highest mountains, of the things that one wanted to see and could not; the clearest day was never fair enough. We have sat, tried companions and I, by the cairn of Fairview, blinking our eyes, attempting the impossibility of visualizing the thing that lay beyond that northern rim. Curiosity was ever present and insatiable; it mattered little whether the day was calm and luminous, crystal clear with a cold light that outlined crag and ridge; or whether grey-purple clouds clung low to a foreground of brightest green hills; or if the nearest things all disappeared in a white smother of driving snow-flakes – the wish to see into the beyond remained.

At last there was nothing to do but go; and go we did, into that wondrous land of far-off valleys where the great rivers of a continent come leaping down in little brooks and arching waterfalls from the ice-tongues; where rise, beyond the old horizon, the castellated crags and snowy spires we had read and dreamed of. ... We were not pioneers ourselves, but journeyed over old trails that were new to us, and with hearts open. Who shall distinguish?

On the 4th of July, Thorington met Feuz and Simpson in Field, the small but very pleasant capital city of Yoho National Park. Two days later the expedition set out with seventeen horses toward the head of the Amiskwi Valley en route to Amiskwi Pass. Bill Baptie was the horse wrangler and Tommy Frayne was the cook. "Mouse" Saddington, a fifteen-year-old apprentice wrangler and dishwasher, accompanied the expedition. The following day, the party crossed Amiskwi Pass into the Blaeberry River Valley. By July 9 they were at historic Howse Pass and were able to visit Conway Glacier. On the 10th the party descended Howse Pass and rode though Conway Canyon and up to the morainal terrace below Mt. Freshfield. The next day, they made their way beneath Mt. Niverville and camped in what would become one of the most highly regarded mountaineering camps in the Rockies, the Niverville Meadows. Thorington describes the ineffable mood of the place:

> On July 11th we reached a heather-covered alpland, below Mt. Niverville, pitching our tent beside a tiny brook, with banks of spring snow still remaining. There were trees, but dwarfed and twisted by storm. Flowers everywhere, as never seen at a lesser elevation; and, at sunset, the snowfields and mountain tops lighted by a procession of colours, ethereal and baffling.

With characteristic Thorington precision, a footnote tells us that Mt. Niverville was named for Joseph Boucher, Chevalier de Niverville, whose party went up the Saskatchewan River from The Pas to build Fort La Jonquière in 1751.

After making preliminary calculations of the rate of movement of the Freshfield Glacier, the expeditions sought routes for first ascents. On July 14, Thorington, Palmer and Feuz made the first ascent of Mt. Barnard. We join the party while they are on the glacier, if only to enjoy Thorington's developing literary style, a highly measured cadence that would soon disappear from mountain literature as climbers began to disassociate themselves from the Romantic writing traditions and align themselves with more self-centred ways of interpreting their experiences:

> Not many hours passed before we reached an elevation at which snow covered much of the ice, concealing the crevasses and making the use of the rope a necessary safeguard. We were soon in a labyrinth of crevasses, which we threaded, cutting steps, or crossing by firm snow-bridges from which hung shining icicles that dripped water into blue depths and darkness. No sounds save the bell-like tinkle of water dripping against the ice, and the faint whisper of an early morning breeze sweeping

up the slopes – a near silence broken by Edward, admonishing us to walk like cats and by no means to jump on the snow-bridges. There were places where we balanced like acrobats, on the crests – Edward dubbed them "garden-walls – between two crevasses. Huge things those crevasses were: some nearly a hundred feet wide, quite equal to that in depth; and, curiously enough, snowed up flatly and solidly at the bottom. One could have roped in and walked around for some distance.

By 10:45 that morning the trio had reached the summit of Mt. Barnard, the highest peak in the Freshfield Group. As the day was not far advanced, the climbers decided to make a first ascent of Mt. Trutch as well. The following day, Feuz led Thorington and Palmer up two more unclimbed peaks, both again over 10,000 feet. Nanga Parbat was first, then Mt. Gilgit. Two days later, their objective was Mt. Freshfield, the only peak in the group that had been climbed more than once. On July 20, Thorington and Feuz left Palmer to his glacial studies and ascended Coronation Mountain by a new route from Freshfield Glacier.[3]

If the number of peaks climbed in a new area were any type of measure, then Thorington's 1922 climbing season had to be rated an enormous success. The party knocked off six very fine 10,000-foot peaks in the remote Freshfield Icefield area. But motives far more important than mere summit bagging were inspiring Thorington's youthful climbing ambitions in the Canadian Rockies. The country was beginning to get inside him; he was being drawn to these peaks. His last words on the 1922 expedition belie a growing love for these mountains. He simply couldn't say enough about the Freshfields as they are accessed from the Niverville meadows:

> Nowhere in the Rockies can one reach such a tremendous ice-field with greater ease, and the possibility of establishing a high

camp will ever be an advantage when the more distant peaks are to be gained. There are problems for the student of glaciology; and, in this area, many are the unanswered riddles. The scenic magnificence of the upper basin is beyond all words: no description does justice to sunsets such as we saw night after night from the soft heather-carpet of the upper meadow, turning the icefield into a bowl of colours that would have puzzled an artist.

You should go there yourself to understand. Perhaps you will see the range as we did, one day when a layer of mist and fog hid all the mountains and left only the icefield and the lower cliffs visible in sombre hue. The sun broke through; a little breeze came up; there was a lowering of the mist-level; the snowy peaks appeared above in gleaming iridescence. The illusion could not have been bettered – it was as if another Universe were floating in space, close above our own.

Thorington later wrote an article – titled "Will Glaciers Disappear?" – on the "problems for the student of glaciology" which he encountered while contemplating the Freshfield Glacier from the vantage of the Niverville Meadows. The article drew attention from the popular press. A story in the Helena, Montana, *Daily Independent* for April 27, 1927, for example, quoted Thorington as being concerned by the pronounced retreat of glaciers in the Rocky Mountains. In "Will Glaciers Disappear?" Thorington explained the time lag between warming and glacial melt by using an analogy that is very interesting today, especially in the context of the current climate change debate. He observed that the advance and retreat of glaciers was the effect of climatic events long in the past. He likened these effects to the influence that words spoken by people in the past might have on future events. The actions of today, he said, may have consequences long after present generations have passed from the scene. Nothing in nature, he concluded, is ever lost.

THORINGTON AND WILLIAM LADD, 1923

The 1922 expedition to the Freshfields merely whetted James Thorington's appetite for the northlands. Throughout the following winter he and Dr. William Ladd spent hours poring over the few available maps and photographs of the region they called the "Alexandra Angle." This country which they considered "a land lost behind the ranges" included the peaks along the Great Divide between Howse Pass and Mt. Columbia, all of which were encompassed by the upper-most drainages at the headwaters of the North Saskatchewan River. Though some of the earliest expeditions, including those of James Hector, Norman Collie, Walter Wilcox, Jean Habel, James Outram and Mary Schaffer, had made brief incursions into this blank space on the map it was still, to a very large extent, virtually unexplored. Since the early expeditions, various Boundary Surveys had made preliminary maps of this region. But one could still very easily lose oneself amidst this ordered absence of human presence.

As was Thorington's way, the research done on the "Alexandra Angle" was thorough and included investigation of all the historical sources available at the time. Of especial value to Thorington were the accounts of the Palliser Expedition as recorded by Hector, who was the first to visit the Freshfields and the upper regions of the middle fork of the North Saskatchewan in 1860. In including Hector's account in those of his own expedition, Thorington offers interesting insight into just how much travel indigenous people did in the Rockies prior to European contact. In chapter 4 of *The Glittering Mountains of Canada*, Thorington quotes from Hector's notes of the discovery of Glacier Lake and the spectacular Lyell Glacier:

> "Two hours with the aid of the track the men had hewn, brought us to the west end of the lake, where there is a few

miles' extent of open grassy plain, fringed with wood, intervening between the foot of the glacier and the water's edge.

"Reserving the ascent of the glacier for the next day, I ascended the south side of the valley, and found it to be composed of deep blue lime-stone, full of iron pyrites in nodules. Start at sunrise to ascend the glacier, accompanied by Sutherland. The other men I sent off to hunt for sheep or deer, of which we found a few tracks....

"I wished Nimrod [Dr. Hector's chief hunter] to go with me, but he would not venture on the ice, but told all sorts of stories of sad disasters that had befallen those Indians that ever did so; how that, if they did not get lost in a crevasse, they were at least sure to be unlucky afterwards in their hunting."

Looking back from our vantage of history, we can see that Hector's almost off-handed remark says much. Clearly natives had not only travelled long enough in the Rockies to know the major passes over the Divide, but had experienced enough trial and error accidents on the glaciers to give the ice a wide berth in their travels. This awareness of the intimate knowledge natives had of this landscape makes it even more preposterous that for more than a century white North American history books celebrated "the discovery" of this landscape by their own heroes. They "discovered" little. The map of the West had already existed for centuries in the native mind. Thorington never disputed this.

Thorington's partner on this expedition was no stranger to the alpine, either. Dr. William Ladd had considerable mountaineering experience and had climbed in the Rockies with the likes of Conrad Kain as early as 1910. Ladd had been so impressed with Kain that he encouraged Thorington to use him as the guide for the 1923 trip. Ladd wrote to Kain to see if he would be available for an extended journey into the remote peaks beyond the

Columbia Icefield. Jimmy Simpson had already written Kain on the matter. Kain's response to Ladd, dated May 17, 1923, found its way into Kain's autobiography as edited by Thorington, and it says a great deal about Kain and the nature of his occupation in the years following the Great War. It didn't matter that Kain was the most famous mountaineer in the country; life was still not what he hoped it would be in Canada:

> Received your letter today and hasten to answer and explain matters to you. I received a few letters from James Simpson asking me to go along on your trip to Mt. Columbia. My life as a guide in the English-speaking countries was a complete failure from a financial point of view and as I love the great hills I had to turn my hands to something else to enable me to stay in the mountains. I have now a pack-train and follow up outfitting. I also climb mountains with people who hire me as a guide and outfitter.
>
> I will be leaving here tomorrow for a three week bear hunt. I also have a fishing party for two weeks in July. The latter will bring me about four hundred and fifty dollars. I could recommend another guide and outfitter for this fishing trip but no doubt it would be rather expensive for you and Dr. Thorington to pay me the above sum for thirty days. You can get one of the Swiss guides from the CPR for seven dollars per day.
>
> In case that you do not and you don't care to make your trip to Mt. Columbia without a third climber in the party I will go, but you would have to give me your decision not later than June 15th. If I come along I will act on the trail (from Lake Louise and back) as assistant packer to Simpson and so he would not need another man, as this would help to cut expenses down a bit.
>
> I know the country around Mt. Columbia. I was there with Mr. Wheeler and I also spent a winter trapping in that

country. I am sure you will like it. Mt. Columbia is a very long snow tramp....

I remember you and the climb of Mt. Fay with Mr. Mitchell. I believe Mr. Mitchell has not climbed a high peak since. I trust that you will get a Swiss guide from the CPR and that you will have a grand and glorious time in the great old hills.

Kain eventually agreed to join the Thorington–Ladd expedition, and "a grand and glorious time in the great old hills" is exactly what they had. The expedition of 1923 would in fact prove more exotic than anything any of them could ever have planned. It would be a journey that would connect James Thorington and Conrad Kain for the rest of their lives, and it would make for enduring history in the annals of exploration in the Canadian Rockies.

Plans for the expedition were finalized in the spring of 1923. The designated outfitter, Jimmy Simpson, wrote to Thorington to say that Tommy Frayne, who was cook for the 1922 Freshfields endeavour, would return to make the meals and run the camp. He added also that Ulysses LaCasse, who because of his broad grin was generally known as "Frog" would be the expedition's wrangler.

While tourists at the Laggan train station watched, the long pack string departed from Lake Louise on June 27, 1923. They reached Bow Lake the next day and by the first of July they had crossed the forks of the Saskatchewan and camped on Graveyard Flats below Mt. Coleman. The following day, they were at "Last Grass Camp" at the head of the Alexandra River. The idea of visiting the Columbia Icefield filled Thorington's every thought. Every landmark, every old camp they passed gave dimension to his waking dream of first ascents of peaks surrounding that great mass of ice.

After visiting the east and west Alexandra glaciers and the north basin of Mt. Lyell, the expedition reached Castleguard camp on July 5. The next day, the entire expedition, including Jimmy Simpson, Tommy Frayne and Ulysses LaCasse, climbed Mt. Castleguard. Thorington's account of this ascent gives dimension to the notion of "the glittering mountains of Canada." He touches on the timelessness on the summit moment in mountaineering:

> A little bergschrund is crossed and the summit reached in four hours from camp. The mountain dominates the Saskatchewan Glacier and presents a splendid over-look across the icefield, which stretches endlessly westward toward Mt. Columbia and northward to The Twins. Little misty clouds scud along in the breeze, their shadows wandering out across the snow and separated by splotches of sunlight. Mt. Bryce, in its sheer grandeur, is nearby, with range after range beyond the wooded depths of Bush Valley. Mount Forbes lifts a white fang in the south, while nearer are the flanks of Lyell and Alexandra streaming with glaciers.
>
> Jim and Conrad are lying flat on the shale, with a map spread out; there is a great pointing of fingers toward distant valleys, and the remarks which come to my ears indicate that fur-bearing animals next trapping season had best look out for themselves. Ladd and Frog are dividing the last piece of cheese, and Frog is not getting the best of it. Tommy and I sit with our backs against the summit cairn; one corner of it is decked with a mossy fringe of hoar-frost, which is dripping in the sunlight and falling into several cups to which we have constructed elaborate aqueducts of flat stones.
>
> Two hours on the summit flew rapidly, and we descended the northern Castleguard snow-ridge in spraying glissades to the icefield. Columbia seemed so near to us; it was early in the

afternoon and we walked some distance toward it before turning homeward. It was a day of enjoyment for all, although the momentary disappearance of Tommy through a snow-bridge was startling. We were fond of our cook, and our morale in those strenuous days depended much upon his oft-repeated bellow of "Come and get it." Four meals in a day never seemed too much!

On July 9, while Ladd unsuccessfully tried his luck fishing in the Castleguard River, Kain and Thorington made the first ascent of Terrace Mountain. The following day, they were ready for their first big ascent. At 3:20 a.m., they set out for the North Twin. As Thorington later explained, they come to know the scale of the Columbia Icefield on that day. At 6:00 the climbers were at last able to leave the shoulder of Mt. Castleguard at the head of the Saskatchewan Glacier and begin their long tramp over the icefield proper. Though it looked only half that distance to the Thorington party, the North Twin is a full twelve air miles from the shoulder of Mt. Castleguard. It took them several hours just to reach the head of the Athabasca Glacier and the base of Snow Dome. They were still only halfway to the North Twin. After circling widely to avoid crevasses at the head of the Columbia Glacier, Thorington began to see things that weren't there:

> Fatigue mirages – momentary illusions – began to appear; for an instant I was convinced that the dark line of a distant crevasse was a staff planted on the summit of North Twin; and I berated Conrad for bringing us so far only to let us be cheated of a first ascent.

Thorington's observations of mirages on the immense plateau were confirmed the following year by Osgood Field's expedition and have from time to time been reported by climbers right up to the present. Bushes and trees constantly seem to present themselves at various places all over the icefield as climbers pitilessly observe their own slow progress over the eternal snows. Only after the party stopped at 2:00 for lunch after nearly eleven hours of walking across the ice, had they reached their mountain. Before them was a stunning scene. The climbers peered in silent awe at the unclimbed, cliff-walled summit of giant Mt. Alberta, framed by the North Twin and ice-deep summit bulges of Mt. Stutfield. They reached the summit of the North Twin at about 4:20. Thorington tells us how it happened and what befell them next:

> Our own peak, immediately above us, its corniced summit ridge intermittently hidden by snow-flurries and wind-blown mist, rose in a slope of glistening snow, steep and unbroken. Conrad was leading, I was second and Ladd last on the rope. The wall of snow was ever before us as we went up; there was considerable step-cutting, not in hard ice, but in crusted snow, and our pace slowed before the top of King Edward came into view above the sharp arête of South Twin. We reached the summit just thirteen hours after leaving camp: fleeting glimpses of winding rivers in the west and of shining summits in the direction of Maligne Lake and Wilcox Pass were blotted out in the closing mist.

As too often happens in mountaineering, the climbers had reached the summit only to be greeted by dense cloud. Robbed of the view, the climbers had to be satisfied with the first ascent of the North Twin, the last of the unclimbed 12,000-foot peaks in the Columbia Icefield area, and the first traverse of the Columbia Icefield from the Castleguard Valley to the head of Habel Creek. As any climber will tell you, the summit is only halfway to the goal. The arduous return journey from the North Twin is one of the epics of early mountaineering in Canada. Thorington describes it as if it were a dream:

> Someone, following in our track, may one day understand that journey back across the icefield's vastness. For an analytical mind, it will at least afford insight of the psychology of fatigue: the half-hour in a blizzard, obscuring the trail and exhausting us; the clearing at sunset, with crimson and orange light banded against masses of lead-blue storm clouds behind The Twins; mist and snow-banners wreathed about and trailing from Columbia and catching up the light – we three mortals in the middle of the field, in all its immensity, struggling on in insufficiently crusted snow until the light failed.

Twenty-three hours after leaving camp, the climbers fell on the grass beside the campfire and ate breakfast as the sun rose on the peaks surrounding the Castleguard meadows. This had been the longest mountaineering ordeal to date in the Canadian Rockies. A long rest followed. The journey had even challenged the physical endurance of their guide:

> On awakening after our long and weary journey to North Twin, I found the sun high in the heavens. Tommy had the fire going and was putting together a tremendous lunch. From the teepee came intermittent strains of a harmonica, for which only Conrad could be blamed; and you have missed real music if you have not heard his orchestrations! This time, however, it sounded as if he were suffering from sunburned lips. In the direction of Ladd's tent there were no signs of life.

On July 12 Ladd and Thorington had recovered enough to follow Kain up the low saddle that connects the head of Castleguard with the Terrace Valley. Soon they were in the shadow of Mt. Saskatchewan, which, from that north-facing angle, reminded them of the Matterhorn as seen from Zermatt. Making their way up a series of chimneys and up the broken cliffs on the north side of the peak, they overcame the last steep pitches of snow to gain the arête. The summit required careful negotiation of several long cornices overhanging on the north. By about 3:00 in the afternoon they were constructing their summit cairn.

Two days later Thorington and his friends were off to Mt. Columbia. The usual trio was expanded for this ascent by the addition of Jimmy Simpson to the climbing party. Simpson had been the outfitter for the James Outram expedition of 1902 that saw the famous British climber make the first ascent of Mt. Columbia in the company of the Swiss guide Christian Kaufmann. Now, twenty-ones years later, Simpson was about to climb Columbia himself. It would prove to be a long slog. At 3:50 a.m. the climbers once again set out over the Castleguard shoulder. Unlikely as it may seem, the expedition had to stop en route to do a little entomology:

> Morning sun was gilding the ranges; the wind blew forcefully, and we turned toward Columbia, gleaming in the ice-blue of clear weather distance. Insects innumerable are carried up onto the ice by air currents from the British Columbia side; and, at 10,000 feet and above, we collected moths and beetles of many varieties. One might have some difficulty in obtaining such numbers at lower elevations; many were still alive, although torpid from cold. They form the food supply of snow-finches which one sees wheeling and darting about.

Though the snow conditions were better than when they made their way across the icefield to climb the North Twin, it was still a long way to Mt. Columbia. It was not until 1:30 p.m. that the climbers reached the peak of Columbia. Though it was cold, they stayed on the summit for forty minutes making photographs and trying to find words for the complex geography they were seeing. Just before they began their descent, Jimmy Simpson declared that the mountain was to become a habit for him and that he would, from now on, climb it every twenty-one years as was his wont. As the snow was hard, the return to camp took only six hours. But the night was not yet over:

> We had supper by the crackling logs, with the cross-lights from fire and western afterglow. The shadows lengthened, blue-black at the forest edge, and Conrad told us stories until there was no light remaining save that of the glowing embers, and the stars that peeped out above our heads.

Though time had run out for the Thorington–Ladd expedition of 1923, their adventure was not over. They climbed no more mountains on this trip, but they did do something that had never before been done in the Rocky Mountains of Canada. Jimmy Simpson had observed that the Saskatchewan Glacier could be accessed from the Castleguard Meadows by way of a low pass which he called Castleguard Pass. The glacier could then be accessed by a relatively flat moraine. Simpson had also observed that the glacier advanced at a gentle angle down to the outwash plains below. Though he was unsure of the conditions at the toe of the glacier, Simpson was confident that he could, with a little assistance from Ulysses LaCasse and the climbers, use the glacier as a descent route back into the Saskatchewan River Valley. Thorington describes the horses on the ice:

> Our horses on the glacier made an unusual procession; but, at first timid, they soon became accustomed to their surroundings and, like true mountaineers, hopped over the little cracks and crevasses. It was necessary, in avoiding a lateral glacier entering from the south, to take to the central ice for a short distance. The horses were taken down the glacier for more than four miles, with devious winding around the large transverse

crevasses. The steep terminal moraine, with treacherously balanced boulders and slippery glacial mud, was most troublesome, requiring some trail-building and considerable care to avoid damage to the pack-train. But before evening the last horse was safely off and camp finally made below the tongue on the flats toward the south side near a pleasant waterfall. Close by, the stream enters a narrow canyon, spanned by a natural bridge; apparently no one else, with horses, had ever stopped at our Glacier Camp.

At daybreak, without difficulty, we took the horses northward over a meadowed shoulder east of Mount Athabaska, about 7500 feet in elevation, whence we looked back and over the tremendous expanse of green ice to Castleguard. We could scarcely believe that the cayuses had come down such a place.

This mention of a "meadowed shoulder east of Mount Athabaska" is the first historical reference to this view of Saskatchewan Glacier from what is now called Parker Ridge. The ridge was likely named for the camp established on the other side of the ridge by Herschel Parker and Walter Wilcox during their visit to the Columbia Icefield in the summer of 1896.

By July 25 the expedition had returned to Lake Louise. But even as the eastbound Canadian Pacific passenger train bore Thorington and Ladd back toward Philadelphia, plans were already being laid for yet another expedition even farther into the northlands the very next year.

ENDLESS WEEKS ON UNCLIMBED PEAKS, 1924
Thorington spent much of the winter of 1923 planning an expedition beyond the Columbia Icefield into the Athabasca Pass area of Jasper National Park and to the ultimate peak in the northlands of the Canadian Rockies, Mt. Robson. The 1924 party was a different group of climbers than had tested themselves in

the Columbia Icefields the year before. Thorington was accompanied this time by Alfred J. Ostheimer and Dr. Max Strumia of Philadelphia. Once again the guide was Conrad Kain, but this time the outfitter was not Jimmy Simpson. The Canadian National Railway had recommended a local outfitter instead. And so it was that fourteen horses were supplied by Conrad Kain's old friend Donald "Curly" Phillips. In charge of the horses was David Washington Moberly, the grandnephew of Walter Moberly, the famous explorer and surveyor who had helped the CPR choose their route through the rugged mountains of the West. Jack MacMillan was the cook. With the blessing of Jasper Park superintendent Colonel S. Maynard Rogers, the expedition left Jasper on the 26th of June for Athabasca Pass. Their goal was to solve, once and for all, the mystery of mounts Hooker and Brown, a problem that had engaged Thorington since he first read about the Rocky Mountains as a child.

Thorington had studied everything he could find relating to the miscalculation of the heights of the legendary Athabasca pass peaks. His ambition was to climb Mt. Brown with the goal of comparing his observations of the ascent with those left behind in the journals of David Douglas.

By June 28 the expedition reached the junction of Scott Creek and the Whirlpool River. The next day, they reached Athabasca Pass and camped on Pacific Creek about a mile below the pass summit. Thorington could feel history welling up from every rock and patch of snow. But the history he expected did not coincide with the history described by David Douglas. Thorington was suspicious of the Douglas account from the moment he arrived at the pass:

> The lakes are desolate, lonely tarns, and in winter may be entirely covered. Of course there are no lofty mountains on either side, and one is almost at a loss to pick out Mount Brown,

for on the western side of the pass are several summits all about equal in height and resembling each other in outline. It is all so plain in Douglas' journal; a visit to the pass is the really confusing thing. A traveller of today, writing on the spot, could never describe the pass and its peaks in Douglas' words – the journal and the lay of the land simply do not agree.

On June 30, the day after they arrived at the pass, Thorington and his party set out at 5:30 a.m. with the hopes of ascending Mt. Hooker. But at 9300 feet the climbers found themselves cut off from Mt. Hooker's southern wall by an impossibly steep rampart of snow overhung with cornices. Realizing they were defeated, the climbers followed a ridge northward to the Kane–Evans col, from which they made the summit of Mt. Kane. Steeped in history as this part of the Rockies was, these mountains had been named earlier for explorers who used Athabasca Pass as the trade route connecting the northern prairies with the Pacific Coast. Mt. Kane had been named for Paul Kane, the artist who painted this continent from 1845 to 1848 under the auspices of the Hudson's Bay Company. From this summit Thorington had his first view of distant Mt. Robson, a peak he would visit at the end of the 1924 season.

The next day, July 1, 1924, Thorington, Ostheimer, Strumia and Kain effectively put an end to the mystery of David Douglas on Mt. Brown. In the most gentlemanly of mountaineering terms, Thorington pronounced that, in his mind at least, Douglas did not climb Mt. Brown. This is a critical juncture in the interpretation of mountaineering history. Had mountaineering advanced so much in a mere century that what was once an epic ascent was now just a stiff walk? Or did David Douglas invent this summit?[4] What follows now is James Monroe Thorington's account of that same climb, made ninety-seven years later after Douglas allegedly became the first mountaineer in North America. Readers are invited to judge for themselves whether Douglas really climbed Mt. Brown.

> On the following day we wandered up Mount Brown, past ice-glazed lakelets on benches of snow, like gigantic steps, above the Committee Punch Bowl. Then following the eastern margin of the Brown Icefield, we took what climbing we could find – the rope was unnecessary – and were soon walking up the long shale ridge to the top. The ascent took five hours, and we arrived at a quarter before three; the time was slow, but it was a blistering day and we were a lazy lot. Still, it makes one doubtful whether David Douglas, under winter conditions and with a limited time due to a late start, could have reached this particular summit.
> The Brown Icefield drains to Canoe River and to Wood River; the peaks on its western margin, all unnamed, are attractive and should preferably be reached from a camp at the head of Jeffrey Creek. The unnamed pass through the Divide, immediately north of Mt. Brown, deserves a visit. Three lakes, icy and varying in hue, form the sources of Robert Creek and drain to Canoe River. The Wood River and Columbia Groups are practically in line, Alberta and The Twins are visible, but Columbia hidden by square-topped Bras Croche. Two hours passed; cameras clicked busily, pipes were smoked; we snoozed in the sunlight. The view delighted us – we could not think of it as being "too awful to afford pleasure." In another two hours we had glissaded merrily back to the campfire, tracking in over the lower snow-patches just before seven o'clock.

After this thorough reconnaissance of the Athabasca Pass area, the Thorington expedition returned to the upper Whirlpool River to camp near Scott Glacier. It was thunder season and storms were in the air at night. It is not known whether there were more or greater storms in the Rockies in the early part of the twentieth century than there are now. Certainly, they were more talked about then, perhaps because travellers were in much more remote country than exists almost anywhere today:

> A night of thunder-storms; the morning of July 3rd clearing slowly after a threatening dawn. Such an electrical display and a pounding of thunder there had been – crashing and reverberating. During the flashes, white ghostly figures could be seen scurrying about, making the canvas secure. Now and then one would hear a muffled clanking on the gravel, indicating that the interior of a tent had been vacated by axes which might serve as impromptu lightning-rods. We believe this to be not entirely superstition; on the ridge of Mount Brown many pitted slabs of shale were found, with square-cut holes where metallic crystals had been cleanly destroyed by electrical agencies.

On July 5 the Thorington expedition embarked for the summit of Mt. Hooker on what would ultimately be known as one of the epic endurance tests in early mountaineering in the Rockies. It was one of those climbs where everything goes wrong, a real nightmare of serial calamities that can only be survived by strong, disciplined mountaineers.

As all substantial climbs do, the expedition to Mt. Hooker began early in the morning. Conrad Kain led the party out of camp at 4:45 a.m. The climbers took forty-five minutes to reach the ice and another forty-five to reach the rocks at the foot of the west wall of the glacier. It was the climbers' intention to use the rocks as a more direct route to the upper snows and the summit. This did not prove to be the best choice.

Two chimneys in the lower section of the wall took an hour. The climbers then traversed southward across and upward below a large waterfall in the centre of the wall. They then entered a gully, hoping they would be able to take advantage of the ledges in it to advance higher up the rock wall. It was at this point that the party was very nearly wiped out. It was only Conrad Kain's legendary cool-headedness that prevented a major disaster. Thorington explains:

> We had barely started when a whizzing, and Conrad's cry of "Stonefalls!" made us take what cover was available. It was the beginning of a raking fire in which we were all struck, but luckily without damage. Conrad, calmly saying "Gentlemen, we must move a little to one side," relieved the tension; we quickly got out of range, in time to avoid a heavy bombardment of larger boulders that came banging down over our intended path and would surely have done for us had we persisted. We realized afterward that in Conrad's cool leadership, in emergency, we had seen one of the finest things produced by mountaineering art.

This was only the first of many instances in which Kain's cool would be the key to survival on this climb. The party wisely decided to opt for a different route. The wall became steeper. In a narrow chimney above the gully, axes and packs had to be roped up. The last climber, looking up at an inopportune moment, caught the rope full in the face and lost a tooth. It was only after the ledges brought the climbers onto the upper glacier did they realize that the ice route would have been much preferable to the rock route they had unfortunately committed themselves to. Six hours had already passed and it was time for a second breakfast. They could now see Mt. Hooker directly in front of them. The northern cliffs, topped by a twisted and heavily corniced arête, did not appear to offer safe access to the summit. The eastern end of the mountain swept downward into a fearsome overhanging ice bulge they clearly wanted to avoid. Only the long western col seemed to offer any hope of achieving the summit. A long delay was necessary to cross the bergschrund of the glacier to reach the col. It was 2:30 before they reached the saddle.

Below a rock tower near the junction of the middle and western thirds of the summit arête, Thorington stopped to take a picture of the climbers advancing toward the summit beyond him. A tug on the rope pulled the camera from his grasp. It rolled a short distance on the shale before dropping out of sight. The camera was later recovered, and to Thorington's utter amazement the lens, shutter and bellows were still intact. Only the last picture he had taken was ruined.

Such was their luck that day; everything seemed to take twice as long to do and accidents plagued them. Still, they continued. It was 7:30 p.m. when they reached the summit.

Kain advised the climbers that they would not, under any circumstances, be following their ascent route down the mountain. Instead they started down a long snow shoulder to the west of the irregular pass that connects Mt. Hooker to Mt. Serenity. As they walked down the edge of the snow slope, about sixty feet of cornice broke away and sank silently to the valley far below. The arrival of the snow on the rocks below produced echoes that resounded all around them. After taking in a stunning sunset, the climbers resigned themselves to a night on the mountain. Just as they made their decision to camp, they stumbled upon a dry and roomy cave that just happened to have water near at hand. Expecting to be at their valley camp just after dawn, they ate the remainder of their food and stretched out to sleep. But the mountain was far from finished with them. During the night there was lightning and there was rain that turned to snow.

When the party awoke at 4:00 a.m. to complete their descent, they found dense fog obscuring everything. Rain and sleet continued to fall. They roped up and started their awkward descent. They reached the margin of the glacier. And there they stopped. The snow they expected to stop continued to fall. By

10:00 a.m. conditions were so bad that they decided to hole up on the moraine and wait for the storm to pass. It took six hours for the snow to stop. After they reached the glacier, the fog rolled in once more. The climbers' faces and clothes became coated with ice. Their rope froze. They did not reach their camp until 11:00 that night. They had been out for more than fifty hours.

When the climbers had not returned on the second day, Dave Moberly took it upon himself to ride to Jasper for help. He made the trip from the Scott Glacier to town in only nine hours. He dismounted, reported to Phillips that the climbers were missing, found fresh horses, remounted and immediately began the return journey with a rescue party. The party included Val Fynn of the Alpine Club of Canada, who abandoned his own climbing plans to join the rescue along with Oberland guides Alfred Streich and Hans Kohler. When the starving climbers arrived back at their upper Whirlpools camp, cook Jack MacMillan fed them, then got on his horse and rode downvalley. He was able turn the rescue party back at the Whirlpool tie camp, near the forks of the Whirlpool and Athabasca rivers.

Thorington's Athabasca Pass adventure had put to rest the David Douglas mystery and in so doing ended an era in Canadian mountaineering and exploration history. Thorington knew he had done this, too:

> The ascent of Mount Hooker was the fulfilment of a great desire. To see and to climb Mount Brown and Mount Hooker will perhaps not be thought of as a remarkable alpine ambition. They are probably not the peaks Douglas named; in fact we remain in ignorance as to precisely where he went, what he did, and what he named during his few hours at Athabaska Pass. The Interprovincial Survey has unquestionably done the best thing possible in perpetuating these classic names by applying them to a lovely peak on either side of the pass. But the

ambition to stand upon them is a deeper thing than it appears; for the naming of peaks by Douglas, and the over-estimation of altitude – no matter how strange and ludicrous the mistake may seem; no matter who was at fault in figuring – these things first led men in search of great Canadian heights. They came from the far corners of the earth, following pioneer trails, seeking beauty. And none there was who returned insensitive to the glory of that mountain vastness.

So we turned back from Athabaska Pass, on the Whirlpool trail toward the site of Jasper House, feeling that we too had come under the spell of this overland route of the long-ago, and, on Mount Hooker at least, had shared a little in its adventure.

In finally solving the mystery of mounts Hooker and Brown, James Monroe Thorington brought his life full circle. He had at last answered the question he posed to himself in grade school when he first read about the Canadian Rockies. He had put the problem of Athabasca Pass to rest, not just for himself but for the entire North American mountaineering community. And he had done so with perseverance and great respect for both history and place. Such was Thorington's nature.

In the end, the mountain life of James Monroe Thorington could perhaps be best encapsulated by the opening words in his own preface to *The Glittering Mountains of Canada*, in which he writes of an old prospector who, when asked to reflect on the sum of his life, declared that if nothing else his life had been worthwhile for having seen the Rocky Mountains.

Though we take such privilege for granted today, early adventurers and mountaineers did not. For them each day spent in the splendour of these mountains was unforgettable, a gift to be cherished as long as one lived. In his thoughtful, eloquent and respectful writing Thorington demonstrates why the creation of the mountain national parks matters so much to each subsequent generation. Because we have protected the parks, it doesn't matter that we were not the first to walk these trails. What matters, Thorington reminds us, is that we keep our hearts open as we journey over old trails that are ever new to us. In walking these trails we are connected by place to everyone before us who has ever been moved in their soul by the timeless grandeur of the Rockies. In the glittering mountains of Canada, the power of place never grows old.

ROBERT WILLIAM SANDFORD
CANMORE, ALBERTA
JANUARY 2012

NOTES TO THE FOREWORD

1. Thorington's papers are held at Princeton University Library, Manuscripts Division; contact information available at http://is.gd/OLf1fJ.

2. Thorington also wrote an influential textbook, *Refraction of the Human Eye and Methods of Estimating the Refraction, Including a Section on the Fitting of Spectacles and Eye-glasses*, published in several editions and reprints between 1916 and 1947.

3. In his account of the climb, Palmer notes that members of the 1918 Boundary Survey climbed from Bush Pass to a surveying station on the west ridge of Coronation Mountain only sixty feet from its summit. Though Palmer did not find a cairn on the peak, he assumed the surveyors had likely made the first ascent. Palmer's long association with the Canadian Alps is chronicled in his *Mountaineering and Exploration in the Selkirks* (New York: G.P. Putnam's Sons, 1914; full text available at archive.org, http://is.gd/JdUF8e) and his tribute to his long-time climbing partner, Edward W.D. Holway: *A Pioneer of the Canadian Alps* (Minneapolis: University of Minnesota Press, 1931). See also *The Freshfield Glacier, Canadian Rockies* (Washington, DC: Smithsonian Institution, 1924).

4. Douglas's own account can be found in *The History of Mountaineering in Canada*, vol. 1, *The Canadian Alps* (Banff: Altitude Publishing, 1990): 44–48.

PREFACE

There is told, in the Northwest, the story of an old prospector of whom, returning home after many years, it was asked what he had to show as the equivalent of so much lost time; and he answered only, "I have seen the Rocky Mountains." The desire to venture forth to the strange places of the earth is inborn in most of us and we can quite understand the reply. Yet time and opportunity seldom permit us to wander far from the beaten track.

Modern travellers, however, due to increased transportation facilities, are at a distinct advantage in comparison with the wanderers of a century ago, whose journeys were made under conditions of great difficulty. Even fifty years ago people were not found in the Rocky Mountains on pleasure bent. In the opening of land areas, mountain ranges are things to be passed by in the way most accessible; and not until a population becomes well established does it begin to acquire the aesthetic sensibility which enables it to devote a portion of its energy to the search after natural beauty. This has been true of all highland countries—the Alps, the Andes, the Himalaya, and the Rockies.

Thus, although travel across the Rocky Mountains of Canada began more than a century and a half ago, and the early fur-traders had considerable knowledge of the passes and river routes, description of the upland valleys, the great blue lakes, the vast icefields, has been reserved for wanderers of the last three decades.

The Canadian portion of the Rockies extends from the United States boundary at the 49th parallel of Latitude, near the margins of Glacier National Park, to a point near Latitude 54° where the 120th parallel of Longitude is crossed and the range becomes subalpine. For more than four hundred miles it stretches—a chain longer and less broken than the Continental Alps—and, in its primeval state, who in a life-time can know it all?

Yet today many of us do know something of it. For the tourist, passing through by rail, there are splendid glimpses into the mountain land of Canada. Its margins are accessible to everyone. Thousands of visitors have been to Emerald Lake and the Yoho Valley; to Lake Louise and the Valley of the Ten Peaks; to Banff and its delightful environs; and hosts of travellers, on a more northerly route, are becoming acquainted with the vast wonderland of Jasper Park. Engineers, however, being for the most part unimaginative as far as scenery is concerned, put railroads through by the lowest and easiest passes: natural beauty is incidental.

Hence it is that the main chain of the Continental Divide, practically uncrossed by low passes between the Canadian Pacific and the Canadian National railways, is a land never seen by the casual tourist. It is true that the Howse Pass and the Athabaska Pass were frequented in the days when the fur-trade flourished, and were later thought of as suitable for rail transportation routes; but, with the present locating of the roads, these pass areas have returned to the oblivion of more than a century ago.

Yet not quite. Alpine wanderers, few in number to be sure, have come with their pack-trains, have lingered a little while, and returned to tell of the marvelous grandeur of new horizons. A few have told their story well. Others, due to hardship and shortage of provisions, have come back with their goal just beyond a bend. So if one be asked to compare the Rockies of Canada with some other range, such as the Alps, it can only be said that we know too little of them as a whole to place them fairly in apposition with other mountainous regions.

If one realizes that the things which characterize alpine areas are often found below the snow-line, comparisons are not so difficult. In the Rockies of Canada one seeks in vain for cattle herds, châlets, or funiculars; and in their stead are found the pack-train, a bed of pine-boughs under an open sky, and old trails of the Indians. And so this book is written to tell you of the things beyond the margins; of natural wonders which will be the heritage of coming generations. In the light of more accurate topographical knowledge and established nomenclature, it seems not out of place that a new volume should be added to the small list dealing with mountaineering and exploration in the Canadian Rockies.

The author, with but few intermissions during the past decade, has been actively interested in the peaks and icefields at the sources of the Saskatchewan and Athabaska rivers. It is his desire to place on record the results of three major expeditions into the mountain area of the Continental Divide between the Canadian Pacific and the Canadian National railroads, together with less strenuous excursions among some of the beauty spots which every trans-Canadian traveller should see. In this way it is hoped that a volume will have been produced alike of interest to the leisurely excursionist and to the more strenuous climber of peaks.

The Expeditions of 1922 and 1923 were undertaken for the purpose of investigating the icefields and peaks at the headwaters of the North Saskatchewan River.

In 1922 the Freshfield Icefield was visited and its highest peak, Mount Barnard, with a number of others, ascended for the first time. A preliminary study of the motion in the Freshfield Glacier was undertaken at this time. During this season the upper Blaeberry, Howse, Mistaya, and upper Bow valleys were traversed.

In 1923 the author visited the remaining icefield sources of the North Saskatchewan along the Continental Divide. Alexandra River, the old "West Branch," was followed to its sources, and a base camp made on the margin of the great Columbia Icefield, Canada's tri-oceanic divide. The mountaineering results were of importance and extensive data regarding the details of the icefield were secured. The icefield was twice crossed, from Saskatchewan to Athabaska sources. First ascents were obtained of formidable Mount Saskatchewan, and of North Twin; the latter, 12,085 feet in elevation, being the third of triangulated heights in the Canadian Rocky Mountains. Mount Columbia, 12,294 feet, the second elevation of the range, was climbed for the second time. With horses a remarkable crossing was made, by way of the Saskatchewan Glacier, from the head of the "West Branch" to the sources of the Sunwapta; and, from below Wilcox Pass, Mount Athabaska was ascended.

The Expedition of 1924 deals with a more northerly section of the Continental Divide, situated at Athabaska River sources—the historic location of the earliest mountaineering in Canada. The narrative extends to the Mount Robson area, where the author had previously camped in years before the appearance of the "modern conveniences" that now exist.

This then is a book of mountaineering, not presenting the Canadian Rockies in their entirety—no single volume will ever do that—but including many of the finest things. It is also a book of mountain travel, under conditions such as perhaps the European traveller experienced in the Alps during the Eighteenth Century. Finally it is a book of mountain history; for here is Geography in the making, and with a tradition behind it—a story that has never been properly gathered together, and whose details, in part at least, are gone forever.

While our own performances have been thought worthy of the printed page, they can never mean to the reader quite what they mean to those who took part in them. You must go yourself to comprehend the daft enthusiasm which follows such a journey. No one but ourselves can ever be identified with those days of crag and precipice; of ice and snow in sunshine and storm; those days with the pack-train winding along northern trails; those nights—starlit nights in the country of fur-trade routes—with song and story beside the campfire. Those things are ours forever, while life lasts. Our guide, Conrad, and he is a philosopher, used to say, "It is good to have been once young, if only you have happy memories." A modern writer has paraphrased the thought in saying, "Memories are given us that we may have roses in December."

This is the record of our mountain memories, which may perhaps have the power of shedding afterglow, even though the light be dim in comparison to realities. And yet, if you glimpse but a bit of it, great indeed will be our reward.

A great deal of painstaking research was required in collecting the early historical material for the present volume, but as far as possible every source-book has been examined. The old narratives are exceedingly rare, and not to be had in every library. For this reason they have been more fully quoted than otherwise, in order that they may afford an available authentic record of events occurring within the mountain area before the advent of modern travellers.

A certain amount of topographical material has been inserted, and those who care to follow it in detail should secure the Atlas of the Alberta and British Columbia Boundary, Part II, containing maps which will be of service. The Atlas may be obtained from the Topographical Survey of Canada, Department of the Interior, Ottawa.

Not all that follows makes its appearance for the first time;[1] but the outlines of several chapters, published in the *Alpine Journal*, the *Bulletin of the Geographical Society of Philadelphia*, the *Canadian Alpine Journal*, and elsewhere, have been largely rewritten, amplified, and moulded to conform to a progressing narrative.

Acknowledgement is due to the many who, by their favors and suggestions, have made this book possible. The Topographical

Survey of Canada, comprising a group of gentlemen most cordial, has allowed the use of a selection of photographs obtained during the field-work of the Interprovincial Boundary Commission. The Smithsonian Institution has agreed to the reprinting of Mr. Palmer's paper on the Freshfield Glacier. Messrs. Osgood Field, Val. A. Fynn, Wm. S. Ladd, Howard Palmer, Harry Pollard and Max Strumia have permitted the use of photographs. Dr. James A. Morgan, of Honolulu, has kindly secured for me a photograph of Douglas' Tombstone. The editors of the *Alpine Journal, Appalachia,* and the *Canadian Alpine Journal* have loaned a number of the engraved blocks.

During 1922 and 1923, the pack-trains were in charge of James Simpson, a pioneer and hunter of wide experience, a powerful mountaineer, a man of resource and initiative, and withal, a true friend; to whom, in company with Conrad Kain and Edward Feuz—the leaders of the mountaineering—the author has taken pleasure in dedicating this book.

J.M.T.

2031 CHESTNUT STREET
PHILADELPHIA, PA.
DECEMBER 1925

CHAPTER 1
LAKE LOUISE: THE ENTRANCE TO THE NORTHLAND

"One of the Indians named Edwin, the Gold Seeker, said that the thunder came from a 'big snow mountain above the lake of little fishes.'"

WALTER D. WILCOX

It was a long time ago that I lost track of the number of times I had climbed from Lake Louise to the summit of Mount Fairview. From days of early June when spring snow still lay banked in the Saddleback until the flurries of late September; at many times between, and more than once in a season, in storm and sunshine, I have dallied along its trails.

When the Limited pulled out from Calgary, westward bound, on many a cool morning we sat on the observation platform—long before other passengers were about—waiting for the first glimpse of the Rockies. As the train swung along the windings of the Bow, we would crane our necks for that first glimpse of the misty jagged line, low down against the horizon, that meant high hills again. As we got nearer and the sun rose higher, the low-toned grey, resolving into purples and reds and the deeper hues of rock, contrasted sharply with the lead-blue patches of snow still untouched by morning light. Miles away still.

Then Canmore, with the Three Sisters—how much higher they always looked than we expected—and the broad avenue of rocky peaks, with strangely twisted strata, that leads to Banff. "We seldom stopped at Banff on the way out; it was reserved for the homeward journey, after the days of trail, when nothing was quite so enjoyable as the warm water of the swimming-pools. How many last-days of vacations we remember—basking lazily on the grass, wet bathing-suits warmed by the sunlight, as we strove vainly to fix in our memories the detail of that lovely panorama of the Bow, its falls and foaming canyon, stretching toward the far distances of shadowed cliff and lighted ridge!

But when the train had passed the square-topped tower of Pilot Mountain, it was always Fairview that we looked for. We learned to recognize its outlines far away; long before Storm Mountain and the wooded saddle of Vermilion Pass were near; long before the opening of the Valley of the Ten Peaks drew our eyes to the towering heights of Deltaform and Neptuak and Temple. Perhaps it was only because we knew the little mountain so well; but little heights always affect the mountain-lover in such fashion. A small peak as a rule is the best view-point because there is still something left to look up to. Panoramas from the very highest levels, lacking definite fixation points, are apt to confuse all but the trained observer; the outlook from a lower point often charms because of the uplift of form and outline which delimit it. And so it is with Fairview. Year after year we have come back to it; perhaps as a convenient training walk, but more likely on account of the sheer beauty with which it is surrounded.

The little motor-railway to Lake Louise[2] winds upward through the trees, along a road-bed bordered with iceland poppies, red, white and yellow, and with a final effort and a long-drawn whistle reaches the Château. You will stand spellbound at the startling view of Lake Louise, with the pure, icy heights of Victoria soaring beyond the long expanse of deep-blue water—a lake, iridescent as a chameleon's skin, with sudden, pulsating changes of colour to brilliant green or dull grey as sunlight strikes or shadow dulls.

But if you are following with us the upland paths, a long stop will not be made on the lake-shore; but, with a pack full of lunch, you will be out on the trail that zigzags up the forested slopes of Fairview. If it is early in summer, snow-banks, discoloured and half hidden by twigs and pine-needles, still remain in shadowed nooks along the way. The mountain side will be alive with springs and rivulets formed by melting snows above. In places the trail has become a stream bed, which must be circumvented by devious balancings on unstable boulders and slippery logs.

It is good to stop and look back at a peacock-blue corner of the lake, seen through the pine-tops. Our gaze wanders to the Bow Valley, with its strip of silver river, and the bare peaks of the Richardson Group beyond. The whistle of a locomotive is heard, shrill and strangely near; but only a thin wisp of smoke, far below, indicates an Express from the west. Sometimes the whistle utterly deceives and it is only a friendly marmot, just around the bend; you can see the fat little beasts sprawled out on the rocks, sunning themselves, ever ready to pop down into their burrows if an over-curious human should approach too closely.

Up on the trail, heavy timber thins out and gives way to soft-needled larch and scrubby, wind-blown pine. A lumbering porcupine, crossing the path, climbs a stump to watch as we go by; a pebble tossed and he scuttles off indignantly. A walk of two hours has brought us up the curving path near the Saddleback; snow patches become more frequent, and before reaching the cabin the corniced summit of Mount Temple is in view. Pleasant it is to while away an hour on the nearby ridge of Saddle Mountain;

it is only a short scramble up the bouldered crest to the edge of a tremendous precipice above the valley called Paradise. Perhaps an eagle, flying below the cliff edge, will be trying to your sense of balance—it may be sadly lacking on the first day—but you will have much to distract your attention. Almost below is the winding stream that comes from the melting ice of Horseshoe Glacier; and, across the valley, tiny Lake Annette nestling like a blue jewel below Mount Temple. Highest of the Lake Louise mountains is Temple, its elevation of 11,626 feet, nowhere seen to better advantage than in its stupendous, rock-ribbed northern wall, crowned by a glistening cap of pure white, corniced snow, from which thundering avalanches fall on warm summer days. An avalanche does not have to look very big to produce a tremendous roar, and the spattering snow-blocks and clouds of spraying flakes are often visible long after the noise has died away.

Northwest from Saddleback a shaly trail leads upward in diminishing zigzags toward the summit of Fairview. Just one foot over nine thousand feet it rises, a barren cone with larger slabs and boulders as the top is neared. There are strange little things about those rocks if you but look closely: tiny short-stemmed flowers, pink and white, in flat masses of colour against a background of brilliant green leaflets; moths, light-blue and brown, hovering on the trail; small jumping-spiders, with filamentous homes protected by the clefts of stones. Sometimes, in late June, on the margins of the long western snow slopes where we so often glissaded downward, we have seen grouse, with white winter plumage partially retained, in striking contrast to the dark rocks on which they perched. And once, on the very top of the mountain, a lonely squeaking pika came bravely out to investigate the straps of our pack-sacks.

How many carefree, sunlit hours we have spent there! In the south is the precipitous wall, with cliff and hanging glacier surmounted by rising heights from Sheol to Lefroy,[3] flanking the valley that contains Lake Louise. And here one is able to appreciate the magnitude of that valley more than from the lake-shore by the Château. Symmetrically angled Victoria, at the valley's head, sweeps airily downward in a gleaming ice-face that rests on the edge of bold cliffs and promontories. Here one may see avalanches occasionally breaking from the line of green ice-front and toppling down with trailing banners of snow to the lower glacier. Down the steep northwestern wall of Fairview are the waters of Lake Louise, arrowy, and dark as lapis save for the brief silver wake of a tiny skiff. Beyond, as a far retaining wall, are forested slopes, with terraced benches that hold the Lakes in the Clouds,[4] rising to timber-line and adorning the bases of little bastions and turrets that fortify the heights of Whyte and Niblock.

After that, it is into the north that you will be looking; into a north that begins just across the Bow Valley,[5] with the far peaks of Yoho and broad snowfields gleaming in the afternoon light. Northeastward is the wide valley of the Pipestone, with trails, used rather infrequently, to the unexplored rock-peaks at the head of the Clearwater and Siffleur rivers. Mount Hector's bold breadth of cliff and two-fanged Molar separate the Pipestone from the upper valley of the Bow, which leaves the railroad and curves into the north country, close below the eastern escarpment of the Waputiks. There are peaks of the Continental Divide, continuing the wall that borders Yoho, and supporting a vast snow-plain, partially seen—the Waputik Icefield—whose eastern tongues form headwaters of the Saskatchewan. Through a visible break the glaciers of Mount Balfour stream down to the delta of Hector Lake; there is a glimpse of distant blue-green water in an angle of the valley where Bow Peak, a landmark of the pioneers, lifts its broadly rounded heights.

Beyond all this are other mountains, and still others, until all outline is lost and nothing left save delicate gradations of light, merging with distance. There was always a subtle mystery in those farther heights; clear delineation was denied by very space, exasperating and trying to the imagination. For there, in the north, was the region of the great icefields, of the highest mountains, of the things that one wanted to see and could not; the clearest day was never fair enough. We have sat, tried companions and I, by the cairn of Fairview, blinking our eyes, attempting the impossibility of visualizing the thing that lay beyond that northern rim. Curiosity was ever present and insatiable; it mattered little whether the day was calm and luminous, crystal clear with a cold light that outlined crag and ridge; or whether grey-purple clouds clung low to a foreground of brightest green hills; or if the nearest things all disappeared in a white smother of driving snowflakes—the wish to see into the beyond remained.

At last there was nothing to do but go; and go we did, into that wondrous land of far-off valleys where the great rivers of a continent come leaping down in little brooks and arching waterfalls from the ice-tongues; where rise, beyond the old horizon, the castellated crags and snowy spires we had read and dreamed of. It was the valley of the Bow and the trails of the Waputik that led us onward to unvisited corners of the northern ranges. We were not pioneers ourselves, but we journeyed over old trails that were new to us, and with hearts open. Who shall distinguish?

Lake Louise was in the door-yard, and Fairview the house-top from which we descended to seek the fields beyond the bounding sky-line.

CHAPTER II
TRAILS OF THE WAPUTIK

(Emerald Lake, the Blaeberry and the
Bow. Traverse of Mount Gordon)

"Snow-draped peaks we passed by, and turquoise lakes set amidst the old pinewoods and ringed round by gaunt precipices, and above, the snow. Wonderful waterfalls that plunged sheer for hundreds of feet into rock-cut canyons where the wild waters raged in fierce tumult. Sometimes the whole undergrowth amidst the black stems of the burnt forest would be aglow with the many coloured 'painter's brush,' or a mass of gold orange daisies would have their colour set against the black satin stems of the charred trunks and a sapphire blue sky. The lure of the wilds always called us onward."

J. NORMAN COLLIE

Emerald Lake is a Happy Hunting-ground for the traveller who has not the time or the experience for wandering far from the railroad. When the train comes down from Lake Louise, across the Great Divide at the pass of Kicking Horse, and has puffed through the spiral tunnels, below the peaks of Cathedral and Stephen,[6] with a glimpse of far-flung mountains in Yoho Valley; when you have come to Field and been driven across the river and through that glorious arcade of slender jack-pines to the

Châlet beside the rippling, green water, with a shining mountain-range beyond—then only have you found the threshold of true contentment.

Perhaps as you came over the Divide, at Kicking Horse summit, you noticed a small monument at the water-parting. It is dedicated to the memory of Sir James Hector, physician and explorer with the Palliser Expedition, sent out by the British Government, in 1857, to explore the country for possible railroad routes. The pass (5329 feet), was discovered by Dr. Hector in 1858, after he had set out from Bow Fort, crossed the Continental Divide through Vermilion Pass, and reached the headwaters of the Kootenay. Thence, he tells us, they traversed a height of land, and descended the Beaverfoot to its mouth, "a large flat, where the wide valley terminated, dividing into two branch valleys, one from the northwest and the other to the southwest. Here we met a large stream, equal in size to Bow River where we crossed it. The river descends the valley from the northwest, and, on entering the wide valley of Beaverfoot River, turns back on its course at a very sharp angle, receives that river as a tributary, and flows off to the southwest through the other valley."

Hereabouts occurred an incident of near-tragedy. Hector goes on to state:[7] "One of our pack-horses, to escape the fallen timber, plunged into the stream, luckily where it formed an eddy, but the banks were so steep that we had great difficulty in getting him out. In attempting to recatch my own horse, which had strayed off while we were engaged with the one in the river, he kicked me in the chest, but I had luckily got close to him before he struck out, so that I did not get the full force of the blow. However, it knocked me down and rendered me senseless for some time. After travelling a mile along the left bank of the river from the N.W., which because of the accident the men had named Kicking Horse River, we crossed to the opposite side. We passed many small lakes, and at last reached a small stream flowing to the east, and were again on the Saskatchewan slope of the mountains."

There is another approach to Emerald Lake, quite as interesting and even more spectacular. In a short hour one may motor from Field to the charming bungalow-camp at Takakkaw, stopping for a moment where the glacial Yoho River makes a foaming junction with the Kicking Horse. You will know when camp is near by the roar of water—Takakkaw Fall, coming from the Daly Glacier more than two thousand feet above. Winding and twisting in an age-worn groove, it makes a little leap toward the brink of the precipice and drops its plunging volume sheerly for a thousand feet, arching outward again in a great curve of spray and falling five hundred feet more to Yoho River. It is the highest waterfall in the Canadian Rockies, and one may spend hours watching the play of colours on the brilliant spray—the shimmering rainbows at the river's edge, that cling in the rising mist.

From Takakkaw, a well-kept trail rises to Yoho Pass and leads down again to Emerald Lake which is spread out below. If the day be still young, it is pleasant to stroll about on higher levels—the height of Takakkaw becomes apparent, and its glacial sources are in view. The Yoho Valley is revealed, with peaks of the Continental Divide beyond—Balfour, Gordon, and all the rest—mantled in the icefield of the Waputik. Across the basin containing Emerald Lake, in the west, is the Presidential Range; its rising summits and glacier-hung cliffs are constantly in view if one follows the trail toward Burgess Pass. Mount Burgess is the rocky peak so conspicuous from the lake shore, and flanks the low, wooded saddle which itself is right above the Kicking Horse and Field village. To reach it, the trail leads along the cliffs of Mount Wapta and affords splendid distant views into the south, where rise the mountains of the Ottertail. It will perhaps be late in the day and the sunset a thing to remember: the sun-flickering gone from the lake and the green turned to a dull, filmy blue; the cliffs of Burgess rosy with light; the Presidential Range a silhouette against an orange sky. In the long shadows of gathering twilight, the trail leads down to Field or toward the lighted windows of Emerald Lake Châlet.

Immediately north of Kicking Horse Pass, the Waputik Range continues the Continental Divide to Howse Pass. Only a little of it is seen from Yoho Valley, but, in its northern portion, the icefields mantling the range have a combined area of more than forty square miles,[8] draining chiefly to Bow River, a South Saskatchewan headwater.

We ate our lunch in the Yoho Valley, Howard Palmer and I, beside the river's bank at Takakkaw. It was July 4, 1922, and we walked the Burgess Pass trail back to Field as a bit of training before leaving for prospective climbs in the Freshfield Group. It was a calm, warm day, and we were not yet in the best of condition; still we were down in the village in five hours and thought well of ourselves.

At Field, we were joined by our guide and friend Edward Feuz Jr., well known for his many first ascents in the Alps of Canada. Two days later found us on the trail, our pack-train of seventeen horses being under the care of Jim Simpson, who for more than twenty years has pioneered these mountains. Bill Baptie was the horse-wrangler, and Tommy Frayne our cook. Saddington—we never did learn his first name, as he answered always to the nickname of "Mouse"—a youngster of fifteen, came along to wash dishes and help keep the straying horses in line.

On the first day we went only as far as Amiskwi[9] River, tributary to the Kicking Horse, through heavy timber, but on a good trail which demanded no cutting. It is the beginning of the western approach to Howse Pass, seldom travelled, but forming one of the few routes which permit progress close in on the western slope of the main range. For the most part, the steep British Columbia side, with heavy undergrowth stimulated by the great precipitation on the western slope, serves as an efficient barrier to travel with horses. We crossed Emerald and Kiwetinok creeks, with bits of steep work in their canyon beds; and from our camp-ground, in the evening, looked across the river to ridges and rocky summits of the northern Van Horne Range.

It took us all the next day to reach Amiskwi, or Baker, Pass. There are heavily timbered stretches where one rides for many minutes with no view save patches of blue sky and slants of sunlight in the tree-tops; then a sharp descent to a rushing stream: the horses splash through the milky glacial water, and one catches a glimpse of snow-peaks far up the valley. Northland trails are ever thrilling, with a prospect that changes constantly. We gazed up at peaks bordering on Yoho Valley, and at the flying buttresses of Mount McArthur, so conspicuous for miles along. The forest is dense; in places there are windfalls, the tree-trunks piled up and interlaced like gigantic jack-straws. If they lie across the trail, packs may be caught or snagged awry, and the axe comes into play. Jim would be off his horse—he was in the lead—making the chips fly and the woods resound with the echo of his chopping. The way is soon clear, the horses urged into line—there is a trail vocabulary especially designed for wayward cayuses—and the outfit swings along, with sunlight shafting down as through clouds after a summer storm.

Amiskwi trail parallels the western wall of the Waputiks; the pass (6535 feet) is not a useful one for mountaineering as it is scarcely possible to penetrate the range from this side. In the evening we ascended the high ridge east of the pass—Ensign Station—whence we obtained a magnificent view of the entire area. Across the deep valley of Trapper Creek, apparently impassable for horses, we looked to the summit of Mount Baker (10,441 feet), and to Mount Ayesha (10,026 feet), with its little blue lake high in a rock-bowl. Mount Collie (10,315 feet) adjoins it closely and connects its southern ridge by a glacier-saddle with the peak once named for the German explorer Habel but known since the war by the more cumbersome title of Mount des Poilus. It is possible that climbers might cross to the Collie–Habel col;[10] but cliffs and timber would cause much delay if horses were taken into Trapper Creek. To the west, we had vistas of Mount Laussedat (10,035 feet) and the high peaks along Blaeberry River; while, farther north, the southern walls of the Freshfield Group rose grandly, tinged with the deep rose and purple shades that precede twilight.

The descent from Amiskwi Pass to the Blaeberry is over one of the steepest trails in the mountains. For a short distance from the pass summit, one zigzags up a side-hill of open woods whence an impressive view is had of Mount Mummery (10,918 feet), a white giant, rising across the valley into two splendid peaks, above a curling green glacier cleft by dark morainal lines. Mount Cairnes (10,120 feet), with its massive ice-crown, stands out prominently in the southern Freshfields. Then comes the down-trail, steep and muddy, slippery for beast and man, three thousand feet to the river below. A black bear preceded us, and from his uneven, sprawling track we concluded that he was in somewhat of a hurry; at least we never caught up with him and our pace was by no means slow and dignified.

We forded the Blaeberry, our long procession of horses trailing neck-deep through the water, and camped in the meadows beyond. All afternoon, a second bear—perhaps a neighbour of the Amiskwi traveller—wandered about our campground, and we could see the tips of his ears above the scrub bush as he cautiously raised up to investigate our presence. One of the boys chased him; he clambered up to the top of a tall pine and sat disconsolately on a limb, whimpering.

Our way to Howse Pass[11] lay up the Blaeberry Valley, crossing and recrossing the diminishing stream as we neared the summit. There are sharp little rocky peaks to be seen at the head of

Cairnes Creek, and a waterfall in a canyon farther along. Much of the trail is washed out by the shifting river; what is left becomes a tangle of undergrowth and obstructive timber, keeping Jim out of his saddle and axes flashing. Camp was made below Mount Conway, in a beautiful meadow not far from the pass summit, and we spent the afternoon in making a visit to the cirque[12] below Conway Glacier. On the very summit of Howse Pass a stop was made to photograph a fat grey owl that sat sleepily on the lowest limb of a fire-killed tree and hissed at us when we reached toward him.

We were just at the base of Howse Peak (10,800 feet), the highest of the Waputiks, a serenely beautiful snow peak which had been in view as we came up the Blaeberry and which flanks the pass on the eastern side. The range of the Waputiks here diverges from the main watershed, and extends into Alberta the peaks of Chephren—the western summit usually known as the "White Pyramid"—Kaufmann, and Sarbach, which fill the Howse–Mistaya river angle. From the pass we ascended the timber cutting, marking the Divide, through the forest for about a mile, and then spent a difficult hour in the dense bush working out to the basin of Conway Creek above the deep canyon into which the stream descends. The basin is a large one, extending into the heart of the Freshfield Group; a precipitous hanging glacier cascades down from the north face of Conway, while the main tongue curls over a terminal cliff several hundred feet in height and sends down slender waterfalls to the cirque in which we stood.

Evening by the campfire; crystal, with the last rays of sunshine back of the spire of Mount Forbes. Summer evening is a long twilight, never growing dark, and on this night a full moon rises, shedding its silvery glory over the meadow. We can hear the distant jingle of bells as the horses move slowly through the marsh-grass. The guides tell stories of old explorers who passed this way in the long-ago; tales so fantastic that if the shade of David Thompson or of Dr. Hector had walked in to listen, we should have been unsurprised. If spirits return to haunt the best-loved places may they not have joined us as invisible guests?

Next day was July 10th, and we descended the canyon of Conway Creek to its junction with Freshfield and Forbes brooks; with many little fords, and fine glimpses of the snowy Waputiks behind us. We emerged into a spacious amphitheatre of joining streams, from which flows Howse River. A hotel would have been here, had original plans matured and the railroad come this way; but now there are only gravel-flats, with magenta fireweed, and game tracks crossing and recrossing. South is the entrance to the Freshfield Group, while westward, the massive outlines of Coronation Mountain, the green saddle of Bush Pass, and the grim towering peak of Forbes, complete a delightful and impressive panorama.

We were riding leisurely along, admiring the beautiful prospect, when suddenly Jim, ahead of me, began to urge his horse into full gallop. We followed closely, and on a small gravel-cliff had the unusual experience of catching a baby goat, that apparently had strayed from home. The little animal was headed off by a horse on each side and a stream in front. When several of us approached, the kid gave a frightened leap, fell in the water and was rescued, kicking and struggling in the arms of Tommy. It really was only coincidence that the cook should have made the catch, but the wee beast no doubt expected immediate consignment to the pot. It was interesting to see that the animal remained limp, as if dead, as long as it was held tightly; but ready to stiffen like a steel spring and bolt if the chance offered. We soon released it, and in our last glimpse it was proceeding with all speed, but with a damp and injured air, down the Saskatchewan gravel-bars.

As the Freshfield Group, where we spent the days following, is described later,[13] we shall here continue on the Waputik trails.

It was July 21st when we descended Howse River to a point below the Glacier Lake stream. Alpine flora gives the river-flats a gay appearance and game tracks are everywhere—moose, bear, deer, and goat trails winding back and forth. Every evening we had watched, through binoculars, the big billy-goats come out to feed on the high alpland above the cliffs. And once, as we came late into camp, a cow moose with her calf plunged back into the timber.

Since crossing the Divide, at Howse Pass, we were again in Alberta. Next morning, rounding the base of Mount Sarbach, we reached Mistaya[14] River not far from the main Forks of the North Saskatchewan. It was a chilly day, with fog and showers, one of the few on which we travelled in the rain. A trail on the west bank of the stream avoids the old difficult fords, and, at evening, camp was made at the base of Chephren. Clearing weather cheered us, and we fairly revelled in the gorgeous spectacle presented by the Kaufmann Peaks and the towers of Murchison, all agleam with new snow, sparkling above the violet-tinted cliffs of a shadowed valley.

The headwaters of the North Saskatchewan—North Fork and Mistaya rivers—parallel the Continental Divide, in a broad, heavily forested trench which continues, across Bow Pass, to the upper Bow Valley, a South Saskatchewan tributary. Perhaps nowhere else in the world can be found such a number of large and beautiful lakes as those which are found here, directly below the escarpment of a great mountain chain. Close to camp, the Wildfowl Lakes reflect the rocky pinnacles that rise on the eastern side of the Mistaya, and which give way to slightly lower and more separated summits which buttress Bow Pass. Howse Peak and the Waputiks form a stupendous, unbroken wall on the west. Trail to Bow Lake was followed on the next day; a trail of gradual rise, with undulant, pine-crested hillocks, whence one obtains glimpses into sequestered nooks, corners of sapphire lakes, and occasionally, northward, the expanse of one of the most extensive valley views of the Rockies—from Bow sources to peaks near Nigel Pass and Brazeau headwaters. There are a few gaps in the Waputik wall, through which we could see distant snowy peaks, beyond the precipices of Mount Patterson (10,490 feet) with their slender, interlocking icefalls.[15] From the summit of Bow Pass it is but a short walk to a rocky bluff above the ultramarine expanse of Peyto Lake, with a view of the glacier and its ice-arch; one follows the course of Mistaya River to the Saskatchewan Forks—spread out like a map—with the snows of Mount Wilson (10,695 feet) visible beyond.

Bow Lake is the most pleasant of camping places. Our tents were in a grove of old trees near the water's edge, where white-tailed deer came down to drink, heedless of our presence. Just opposite, Bow icefall cascades downward through the gap between Portal and St. Nicholas peaks, the broken ice-snout coming almost to the lake. Trout abound in the lake, big Dolly Varden, but the larger ones always ruined our primitive tackle: a splash, a bit of line flicking skyward on the end of a green pole, a man sitting down with unexpected suddenness, and language usually reserved for private conversation with the horses! Across the lake a wall of cliff, beginning at Bow Peak, supports the Crowfoot Glacier; and, through a gap farther east, the snow slopes of Mount Hector rise to a sharp peak.

The distance from Bow Lake to the railroad, twenty-six miles, is broken by a camp on Hector slide, north of which looms the jagged ridge of towers making up Dolomite Peak. Down the valley one sees the peacock-blue water of Hector Lake, and the delta made by the entering streams from the glaciers of Balfour. And finally, through a rift in the clouds, the groups above Lake Louise burst into view, Mount Temple and the Victoria ridge rising above all the rest. The home-corral is near; the cayuses sense it, and shy skittishly as the long-drawn whistle of a locomotive is heard far down the valley.

From Bow Lake a year later, in 1923, we reached rail by a decided variant of this route and succeeded in annexing one more adventure of the Waputik trail. We had come back from the Columbia Icefield, Dr. Ladd, Conrad Kain, and I, and wished to avoid a repetition of the final day's ride. So, deciding to penetrate the mountain group and climb across to Takakkaw, we left the horses, on July 24th, Simpson taking the pack-train by trail to Lake Louise.

In an hour we had rounded the lake to the gloomy canyon below the Bow icefall. So narrow is the stream-cut gorge that not far from the glacier a single gigantic stone forms a bridge, on which one may sit and look down into the roaring cauldron of water below. Ascending the rocky ledges beside the ice, we quickly gained height and eventually were able to cut our way across the top of the fall to the Wapta névé.[16] It presents a broad expanse, somewhat crevassed, with long-ridged peaks rising from the snow. Across the long slopes behind St. Nicholas and Olive we tramped, to Vulture Col—its curious summit blocks suggesting an enormous bird rising from a nest—and thence up the smooth, slanted slabs to the summit of Mount Gordon.[17] The weather was cloudless, but in the soft snow we had taken nearly eight hours from our lake camp. From our elevation of 10,336 feet, we again paid our respects to old friends in the north, from Freshfield to Columbia. Across the Balfour Glaciers we looked down to Hector Lake, with cloud shadows moving lazily across; to the Ottertail Group, and the peaks of Yoho.

We entertained the audacious idea of going on to ascend Balfour, and actually started for it; but a rumble of thunder, when we had glissaded to Balfour Pass, warned us that we had accomplished enough for one day. Leaving Diableret Glacier we ran down past two lovely waterfalls at the head of Waves Creek, the lower fall foaming and spraying through a series of basins worn in the sandstone. We were not to go free. A violent electric storm, with pelting hail, overtook us. The retreat of Yoho Glacier makes it impossible to cross the ice-snout as in former years. We made vain attempts to ford Yoho River; even when roped together, the current was too swift for us. Conrad went clear under, and came up looking like an alpine Neptune arising from the deep—still holding his pipe between his teeth!

Finally we crossed the canyon, lower down, making the passage roped, over a slanted log, with serious damage to soaked clothing. Water rose and bridges went out. The stream from Twin Falls, although one of the twins gave up the ghost some years ago, was a raging torrent. We built a rickety structure from logs and got over somehow; then wandered through the drenched brush to find the trail, and finally arrived at Takakkaw as daylight was fading. A last flash of lightning and a peal of thunder, resounding toward Little Yoho, was as if Jupiter Pluvius and the witches of the Trolltinder were having a final laugh at us. But we had defied these evil spirits and had attained to knowledge of the fairy-like splendor of the Waputik.

CHAPTER III
THE FRESHFIELD GROUP

"The man who can drag himself up a vertical rock face when he can just get the finger-tips on to one little ledge, will be of far less use in an exploring party than the man who can judge quickly the state of snow."

CLINTON DENT

The Freshfield Group was the goal of the Expedition undertaken, in 1922, by Howard Palmer, Edward Feuz, and myself. We had come from Field with Jim Simpson, over the Howse Pass trail; a route followed by David Thompson[18] of the North-West Company as early as 1807—Joseph Howse, clerk of the Hudson's Bay Company, did not begin to use the pass until two years later—and for four years ensuing, until hostile Indians of the western slope forced the traders to turn to Athabaska Pass in crossing the Continental Divide.

There seems to be no mention of the Freshfield Group until 1860, when it was visited by Dr. Hector, of the Palliser Expedition, while searching for the northern approach to Howse Pass. He writes,[19] "At daylight I started with Beads to see where the valley leads to, and after five miles through very thick woods, we suddenly emerged at the foot of a great glacier [Freshfield Glacier] which completely fills the valley, and showed us that there was no hope of getting through with horses by this route. We ascended over the moraines, and had a slippery climb for a long way to reach the surface of the ice, and then found that it was a more narrow but longer glacier than the one I visited the previous summer [Lyell Glacier]. The upper part of the valley which it occupies expands considerably, and is bounded to the west by a row of high conical peaks that are completely snow-clad. We walked over the surface of the ice for four miles, and did not meet with many great fissures. Its surface was also remarkably pure and clear from detritus, but a row of large angular blocks followed nearly down its centre. Its length I estimated at seven miles, and its width at one and a half to two miles. By three p.m. we had returned to our halting-place of yesterday, and now proceeded to try Beads' valley.

"For three miles we followed up the stream to the south, until we found that it suddenly rose from a glacier [Conway Glacier] in a high valley to our right. However, as the valley before us continued to look wide and spacious, with a flat level bottom covered with dense forest, we left the river and continued a southerly course, sometimes seeing little swampy streams, which showed us that the water was still flowing to the Saskatchewan. After about three miles we observed a small creek issuing from a number of springs, to flow in the direction in which we were travelling; but we could hardly believe it to be a branch of the Columbia, and that we were now on the west slope of the mountains, seeing that we had made no appreciable ascent since leaving the main Saskatchewan, and had encountered nothing like a height of land. We camped here beside a small lake and beautiful open woods, where the timber is of very fine quality."

The Freshfield Group is situated on the Continental Divide, in latitude 51° 39′ 51″, between Howse (5010 feet) and Bush (7860 feet) passes, an air-line of some ten miles; although, due to the southwesterly bowing of the watershed between the two passes, the actual crest of the group is much longer. Howse Pass lies nearly a hundred and twenty miles south of Yellowhead Pass; and in 1881, the year of chartering the Canadian Pacific Railroad, it had been decided to abandon it in favour of the Yellowhead route, since the latter afforded a lesser gradient. It was felt, however, that a more direct route to Kamloops could be found; and, when in the following year the practicability of Rogers Pass across the Selkirks' summit was ascertained, the railroad was finally diverted to its present location in Kicking Horse Pass. The Howse Pass is perhaps forty miles from Kicking Horse, but the distance by trail from Field to the Freshfield tongue is more nearly sixty-five miles. Between Howse and Athabaska passes—less frequented than in olden days—there is no intervening gap in the Divide through which horses can be taken; the western slope is steep and heavily forested, while the valleys, draining to the Columbia, through Bush River, are unsuitable for travel paralleling the main range.

On the western side of the Freshfield Group, the Campbell Icefield forms a chief source of the south fork of Bush River, draining to the Columbia. The Freshfield Icefield itself, some twenty square miles in extent, fills the eastern cirque, and discharges by a single tongue, three miles long and three-quarters of a mile wide, its stream being an ultimate source of Howse River.

The chief peaks of the group lie on the Divide, subsidiary ridges extending east and southeast to enclose large glacier cirques, of which the Conway, Lambe, Cairnes, and Mummery are the most extensive. In the group are approximately thirty peaks of importance, of which at least twenty-four exceed 10,000 feet in altitude. The watershed summits are chiefly snowy peaks; those on the subsidiary ridges of the eastern wall are scarcely of lesser height, but generally more rocky in appearance.

Climbing parties in this region have been infrequent, chiefly because of the distances involved. In 1902,[20] an Anglo-American party consisting of Messrs. Collie, Outram, Stutfield, Weed, and Woolley, with the guides Hans and Christian Kaufmann, made the first ascent of Mount Freshfield (10,945 feet). In 1906, with Gottfried Feuz and Christian Kaufmann, Messrs. Burr, Cabot, Peabody, and Walcott ascended Mount Mummery (10,918 feet), from a camp in the upper Blaeberry Valley. Eaton and Marocco, with Heinrich Burgener, came out from England in 1910, and, from camp at the Freshfield tongue, traversed mounts Dent (10,720 feet) and Freshfield, over the intervening, unnamed snow-dome. They likewise made first ascents of Pilkington (10,830 feet), Walker (10,825 feet), and a snow peak on the Divide, south of Pilkington, for which the name "Burgener" was suggested, but which has since been named Mount Bulyea (10,900 feet). During 1917, the Interprovincial Survey occupied a number of high ridges and summits, including Bergne (10,420 feet), and Lambe (10,438 feet). In 1920, Messrs. Eddy, Fynn, and Mumm, with Rudolf Aemmer and Moritz Inderbinen, made the third ascent of Freshfield. Other climbers who have reached the group accomplished little or nothing because of bad weather.

In 1922, Howard Palmer and I had the good fortune to visit the group, with Edward Feuz as guide, and make a number of ascents. On the new map of the Survey, we discovered that there was a peak on the Divide—Mount Barnard (10,955 feet)—higher than Freshfield and, therefore, the loftiest of the entire group. Barnard lies south of and hidden by the Pilkington–Bulyea ridge and is quite invisible from the glacier-tongue. The difference in height between it and Freshfield is not great, and these facts explain in part why the mountain had for so long remained unattacked. We determined to make it our objective.

We had come from Howse Pass on July 10th, a short ride down Conway canyon to the lower flats, and thence up trail through forest, rising sharply and emerging on a morainal terrace with the broad ice-tongue close at hand and Mount Freshfield, southward, rising to a slender peak. A grassy slide nearby, gay with columbine, paintbrush, and forget-me-nots, affords a welcome feeding ground for the horses. Strangely enough, good grass is exceedingly scarce between Field and the upper Blaeberry, and there had been many long morning searches for wandering cayuses.

A glacier never fails in its fascination. The snout where the milky stream begins, is the balancing point in the battle between onward motion and dissipation. Most glaciers are retreating, slowly but steadily, although such changes are cyclic and advance may someday begin. About the tongue are blocks and boulders, weighing tons, carried down from higher points, in moraines,[21] and left behind as the ice retreats. Were it not for their slow motion, glaciers would be among the greatest of natural transportation agents. The glacier surface is often flat and easy to walk on; but ice is not perfectly plastic, and, where it moves over declivities, crevasses and chasms are formed, with blue walls and toppling pinnacles. Little surface streams from melting ice rush down, banking and swirling in their frozen canals, eventually to disappear in the depths of crevasse[22] or moulin.[23]

It is not difficult to step over a few boulders and scramble out on the glacier. The same stone blocks, which Dr. Hector noticed, are scattered about, although they have moved some distance in the intervening time; the snow-covered conical peaks—Walker, Pilkington, Freshfield, and Dent—remain unchanged. The huge upper snow-basin, from which, as from the neck of a bottle, the glacier-tongue extends, is not seen in its entirety until one travels some distance up the ice. The basin receives snow from the magnificent curve of watershed peaks: there are broad, undulating slopes from the peaks eastward toward the Blaeberry; a higher level of icefall and plateau from the south, from Nanga Parbat to Dent; and, from the direction of Bush Pass, smaller glacier-tongues, which, in retreat, have disconnected from the icefield.

From a few of the peaks, rocky buttresses with peninsulas of meadow push out to the glacier margin. It is quite easy, as we found, to back-pack up the ice and make camp on such a spot. On July 11th we reached a heather-covered alpland, below Mount Niverville,[24] pitching our tent beside a tiny brook, with banks of spring snow still remaining. There were trees, but dwarfed and twisted by storm. Flowers everywhere, as never seen at a lesser elevation; and, at sunset, the snowfields and mountain tops lighted by a procession of colours, ethereal and baffling.

The icefield may be roughly divided into three sections: an icefall basin, descending between Dent and Walker; an upper snow-basin, rising high up on Walker, extending southward to Mount Barnard and eastward to the snowy dome of Gilgit (10,300 feet), where it drops off in cornices and cliffs; and a lower head-basin descending from the slopes of Mount Barlow (10,320 feet), and adjoining peaks, and connecting with the other divisions in a series of icefalls and flat ice-areas that eventually form the Freshfield tongue. From the minor peaks on the south side of Bush Pass, the Niverville and Pangman glaciers descend into the Freshfield basin, but are at present only loosely connected with the icefield. The Niverville stream runs under the Freshfield ice, while a subsidiary pressure tongue of the Freshfield basin actually faces up-stream toward the Niverville tongue. Much of the upper ice is stagnant, with surface drainage incomplete, and in the late afternoon the ice is covered with water, in some places to a depth of six or eight inches. Our high camp was a fine place from which to see the long, sinuous medial moraines, trailing back for several miles to the promontories in which they originate.

Climbs from the high camp were made on the days that followed, with intervals during which we occupied ourselves with a survey of the glacier-tongue and a rough study of the ice movement.[25] On July 11th, Edward and I put out a line of stones, 1100 yards above the ice terminus, Palmer lining them up with the transit and signalling to us from a station on the western lateral moraine. The width of the glacier is here 1000 yards; our fourteen stones, at one-hundred-and-fifty-foot intervals, were remeasured on the morning of July 19th, after a time period of six full days. We calculated the motion as being between four and five inches per day, which is in agreement with the July movement of other glaciers on the main chain.

On the first medial moraine east of the central axis of the glacier, Jim and I found a small area, near the base of Mount Skene (10,100 feet), where there are curious clusters of iron pyrite, many of them larger than a golf-ball, riding free on the ice surface. This deposit was observed in no other location except for a small bit picked up in the Garth–Coronation gully just below the hanging glaciers. The immense boulders in the medial moraines are remarkable for their average large size. Some are as big as a bungalow, and afford amusing climbs. The largest of all on the ice was ascended by Edward, who built a little cairn on top. The occurrence of such enormous boulders appears to be related to the so-called "Block Moraine," supposedly due to ancient seismic disturbance.

On the southern wall of the icefield were situated our objective peaks. On July 14th, we were successful in making the first ascent of Mount Barnard,[26] loftiest summit of the group. With an early start, we descended slopes of grass and shale between our little camp and the ice. We were in shadow, but rosy light, striking through the mist-bands clinging to the cliffs of Mount Solitaire, diffused across the upper snows and came down to meet us as we walked along.

Dawn, on a glacier, often comes silently. Streams have almost vanished, and resume their turbulent rushing only when sunlight again falls on their sources. The crags and buttresses, from which trail long, winding moraines, seem close at hand. But distance, on snow and ice, is deceptive. The moraines are here flat and compact, yet not so royal a road as the level ice. We advanced four miles without difficulty, jumping over smaller crevasses and deviating for larger ones.

Not many hours passed before we reached an elevation at which snow covered much of the ice, concealing the crevasses and making the use of the rope a necessary safeguard. We were soon in a labyrinth of crevasses, which we threaded, cutting steps, or crossing by firm snow-bridges from which hung shining icicles that dripped water into blue depths and darkness. No sounds save the bell-like tinkle of water dripping against the ice, and the faint whisper of an early morning breeze sweeping up the slopes—a near-silence broken by Edward, admonishing us to walk like cats and by no means to jump on the snow-bridges. There were places where we balanced like acrobats, on the crests—Edward dubbed them "garden-walls"—between two crevasses. Huge things those crevasses were: some nearly a hundred feet wide, quite equal to that in depth; and, curiously enough, snowed up flatly and solidly at the bottom. One could have roped in and walked around for some distance.

Then, from a higher plateau, we gazed upon our long-hidden mountain. White and gleaming it was, lifted up in the haze of distant forest-fires in British Columbia, until it seemed to touch the sky. Crossing a mile of flat snow, we reached its base at the eastern end. The northeast face is snowy and broken by large schrunds, and here was the only visible point where they were sufficiently bridged to allow of crossing. We tackled a wall of steep, soft snow, above a tiny bergschrund,[27] moving cautiously and anchoring deeply, slowly but surely to the main arête.[28] It was not done in a moment.

A high wind tugged at the rope as we walked along the ridge, and we were glad enough to pull our caps down over our ears. Vast ice-basins lay below us, snow slopes falling steeply on the north; while unbroken couloirs,[29] partially ice-filled, curved giddily to the southern and western glaciers. Far ahead, rising above an ascending succession of lesser snow-blown crests of the ridge, gleamed the slender, highest point. Two hours were spent in following the ridge; the ice-axe came more frequently into play; speed lessened. A last bit of cutting in the ice of a couloir-head brought us to the base of the snow-spire, and in a few minutes we were on a summit scarcely big enough for the three of us at once. It is good to be alive at such a moment, and, for a time only too short, stand as the little monuments of such a glorious pedestal.

The highest summit of the Freshfield Group was ours. At a quarter to eleven we had attained its respectable elevation of 10,955 feet, in a little less than seven hours. While distant views were somewhat obscured by smoke, the sheer drop on the south and west to the Campbell Icefield was always spectacular. We built a little cairn and ate our lunch; then retraced our steps back along the ridge until the sharp arête descending northward toward Mount Bulyea could be reached. The snow was in good condition and we made our way rapidly downward. A sudden gust of wind snatched Palmer's hat and sent it sailing through the air. For a thousand feet it went before touching the snow, finally spinning down a steep slope and coming to rest. We soon glissaded down to the basin eastward, finding the hat almost in our path; not often is head-gear blown down from a mountain-top into a glacier basin and found again!

The day was not far advanced, lacking still a half-hour until noon. Finding ourselves close to the base of Mount Trutch (10,690 feet), we decided to ascend it as well. Peculiarly wedge-shaped, this fin-like peak of the Divide had attracted our attention from camp. Like Barnard, this mountain is named for a past Lieutenant-Governor of British Columbia;[30] and so there is a mixed nomenclature superimposed upon a group that Collie, its first visitor, had attempted to preserve for prominent names of the Alpine Club. On the northeast face of Trutch is a steep hanging glacier, while on the southwest a cliff descends to the snow-basin. A single northwest arête rises like a ridge-pole to the summit, followed by a sheer drop to the ice. The arête itself is of shale and snow, presenting no great difficulty; but the last four hundred feet, invisible from below, turned out to be a knife-edge of rock, which had to be straddled and took a good hour to negotiate. On the summit, at two o'clock, we piled up a few stones to commemorate our visit. Ten hours had elapsed since starting; not often does one make two first ascents above 10,000 feet, in a single day! There was no alternative route but to retrace our steps; so we faced about, reached the snowfield, and tramped back to camp feeling that our day had been a successful one. We had travelled about fifteen miles on the ice.

To the east of Trutch rises the symmetrical, snowy peak of Nanga Parbat (10,780 feet), and farther eastward, the dome of Gilgit (10,300 feet), heavily corniced on the northeast where it falls off to the lower head-basin of the icefield. On July 16th, we left the high camp at a quarter of four—at least we think so, although our clock had been set by the average of three guesses and did not agree with the rising sun! Crossing the lower ice, our way lay through the crevassed draw just west of the conspicuous moraine and rock-ridge swinging down from Gilgit. Reaching the upper basin, which is uncrevassed and sloping just enough to make a fine ski-ground, we crossed to the base of Nanga Parbat, working across a little schrund and up the shaly northwestern buttress, which from camp looked like an enormous black gendarme. Here there was a bit of climbing. I was the middle man on the rope and Palmer last—Edward having jokingly remarked that he wanted a good anchor on the end, in case he should unexpectedly plumb the depths of a crevasse—and for a short stretch my view was entirely obstructed by our guide's boot-soles, scratching their way upward.

The morning mist was rising; everything became hidden except the foreground, but we were soon on the crest and followed a steepening snow-ridge to the summit. Clouds continued to blow in, so after a short rest we descended to a warmer corner, along the southeastern rocks, where slopes on the west allowed us to cut down to the bergschrund. This we jumped—the slope was steep, and our form most execrable—and skirted the base of the mountain to our old track on its northern side. Keeping high on the slopes, we crossed to Gilgit, and ascending from the west were on top a few minutes after noon.

The weather, which had been smoky, cleared suddenly. The icefield below us in unbroken whiteness is the southerly terminal source of the North Saskatchewan. That tiny green island at the ice margin is our meadow camp—absurdly far below, as if on a different planet. Howse River is seen on its northern course. Mount Forbes (11,902 feet), the fifth elevation of the Canadian Rockies, towers across the valley; a grim, snow-powdered spire it is, worthy of comparison to the Matterhorn or the Dent Blanche, although from few points can these Swiss peaks equal their Canadian rival in sheerness of line. Beyond, in the north, distant peaks are visible—Lyell and Columbia—with bits of icefield that seem like great white birds soaring afar. To the south and west, one gazes across glaciers and towers from which descend streams to the Bush and Columbia valleys; and across the ranges to peaks of the Selkirks, rising dimly in the haze. The southeast ridge of Nanga Parbat curves brokenly and rises in dizzy heights to the spires and pinnacles of Mount Mummery, whose black precipices wall the head of Waitabit[31] Valley.

But it was always the icefield itself that held our attention; we were never tired of admiring the prospect, perhaps because its contrasts made it one of the most picturesque landscapes we had ever seen. The vast field of ice, at its terminus, is in close apposition to the dark green of fir-trees, beyond which is a flat of gravel-islands through which runs the river, a silvery line, into the north. Distant patches of yellow meadow cling to the bases of dark, shattered towers; range after range is seen, in relief intensified by sunshine and shadow; snowfields are glittering, in light which might in a moment be cut off in the blue shadow of moving cloud.

In just five hours from the high camp, on July 18th, we were on top of Mount Freshfield (10,945 feet), the only summit of the group that has been climbed more than once. The route up a broad snow-filled gully, just east of the Freshfield–Dent icefall, leads in interesting fashion to the slopes opposite Pilkington. Ascent was then made obliquely to the south and the summit gained over an easy rock crest. The day was smoky and we had no distant view; so a glissade was made homeward, camp being reached in many minutes under three hours. Edward soon had a bowl of erbswurst soup ready, and after lunch we struck the tent and packed our belongings down to the Freshfield tongue.

All this time, Jim had packed bread—and an occasional ptarmigan—up to the high camp for us. Bill and Tommy down below had been getting restless, although they spent part of every day on the glacier, prospecting in the moraines.

On the last day, July 20th, Edward and I made the ascent of Coronation Mountain (10,420 feet) from the Freshfield Glacier.[32] It is the imposing, massive peak named by Collie, and is well seen from the mouth of Forbes Brook as a broad-based rock mountain with a steep glacier on its northern face. Leaving camp at four o'clock in the morning, we ascended the ice for more than a mile and took to the bush on the north side of a gully sloping down between Mount Garth and Coronation. At timber-line, steep grass slopes and loose rocks led up to morainal débris below two small hanging glaciers; the tongue to the north was reached without delay and the snow above ascended, a sharp watch being necessary because of occasional stones falling from a wall nearby. It was not altogether easy; the slopes became steep and hard, requiring some cutting before the arête was reached east of the pyramidal summit. Two rocky gendarmes were traversed below the top, the sheer drop to Forbes Brook making it an exciting performance. Mount Forbes was directly opposite, its superb ridges looming grandly through the smoke, and we could trace out the difficult route by which it is ascended. But we had no distant view, and a chilling wind compelled us to beat a retreat as soon as a cairn was built. Glissades on the steep slopes made descent rapid, and we reached camp shortly after noon, quite ready for lunch.

Forest-fire smoke, occasionally a drawback in Canadian mountaineering, continued, so on the following day camp was broken. We had climbed six lovely peaks, each exceeding 10,000 feet in elevation, and were inclined to be quite content with our luck. But let no one think that the climbs have been exhausted; more than half the peaks of the group remain virgin, Freshfield being the only one of all that has been visited more than once. Several of the unclimbed peaks—Garth[33] (9970 feet), Pangman[34] (10,420 feet), Helmer (10,045 feet), and Solitaire (10,800 feet), to mention only a few—appear difficult enough to keep strenuous climbers out of mischief for at least a week or two.

Nowhere in the Rockies can one reach such a tremendous icefield with greater ease, and the possibility of establishing a high camp will ever be an advantage when the more distant peaks are to be gained. There are problems for the student of glaciology; and, in this area, many are the unanswered riddles. The scenic magnificence of the upper basin is beyond all words: no description does justice to sunsets such as we saw night after night from the soft heather-carpet of the upper meadow, turning the icefield into a bowl of colours that would have puzzled an artist.

You should go there yourself to understand. Perhaps you will see the range as we did, one day when a layer of mist and fog hid all the mountains and left only the icefield and the lower cliffs visible in sombre hue. The sun broke through; a little breeze came up; there was a lowering of the mist-level; the snowy peaks appeared above in gleaming iridescence. The illusion could not have been bettered—it was as if another Universe were floating in space, close above our own.

CHAPTER IV
THE MOUNTAINS OF THE ALEXANDRA ANGLE

(Mistaya and North Fork Valleys. Pinto Pass and Lyell Glaciers)

"There are none the less moments of irrational passionate revolt, moments in which one would buy back with a year of the life that is left one solitary hour among the untroubled mountains of youth."

ARNOLD LUNN

It was the unfrequented region surrounding Mount Columbia, a land almost "lost behind the ranges," which lured Dr. William Ladd and myself into joining forces on our Expedition of 1923. During winter days we had spent hours in poring over available maps and photographs, familiarizing ourselves as best we could with the geography and history of North Saskatchewan headwaters. We were to visit an area much less compact than the Freshfield Group, with peaks carved on a vaster scale and more widely separated. It was plain that the Columbia Icefield must be crossed, in part at least, before climbs could be made; we knew that the distances were very great. A further incentive was the fact that the mountains were situated near the limits of journeys made by earlier explorers, whose observations had frequently been made under conditions that precluded satisfactory results. There would be work for us to complete.

The terminal branches of the North Saskatchewan, as our map-dissection revealed, find their sources chiefly in the eastward drainage of the Continental Divide, between Howse Pass—in the northern Waputiks—and Mount Columbia. Mistaya River, locally known as Bear Creek or the "Little Fork," flows northward from Bow Pass, receiving streams from the Waputik ice through Peyto Glacier, and joining the main Saskatchewan between mounts Sarbach and Murchison. Howse River, the "Middle Fork," flows from the Freshfield Group, and also receives streams from Bush Pass, as well as from the Lyell Icefield through Glacier Lake. The third branch, the North Fork, comes from Sunwapta Pass, which, in the north, separates Saskatchewan from Athabaska headwaters. The North Fork has its chief source in the Saskatchewan tongue of the Columbia Icefield, but its volume is soon increased by Alexandra River, its old "West Branch."

Howse River and the North Fork meet from almost opposite directions, and, turning abruptly eastward, receive Mistaya River in a sharp angle from the south, the combined stream finding exit to the plain through the portals between Wilson and Murchison.

Something of the trails in these valleys I had learned from the journey to the Freshfield Group; but beyond the Saskatchewan Forks it was a vast unknown—although Ladd and I, from peaks near Lake Louise, had seen the far mysterious mountains of the north and had wished to make their closer acquaintance. It seemed a shame that these beautiful snowy summits should have no admirers but themselves.

Following the Divide from Bush Pass, in a northward air-line of twenty miles, one reaches Thompson Pass, crossing the Forbes–Lyell Group *en route*. There is no magic carpet equal to a map for doing such a thing; in reality it would be extremely difficult, for the Lyell Icefield system is a large one and the glaciers of the Lyell massif[35] alone occupy more than thirty square miles. The icefield was discovered, as were so many other topographical features of the region, by Dr. Hector. He had gone there in behalf of the Palliser Expedition, in 1859, the year preceding his visit to the Freshfield Group. Encamped at Glacier Lake, he tells us,[36] "Two hours, with the aid of the track the men had hewn, brought us to the west end of the lake, where there is a few miles' extent of open grassy plain, fringed with wood, intervening between the foot of the glacier and the water's edge.

"Reserving the ascent of the glacier for the next day, I ascended the south side of the valley, and found it to be composed of deep blue lime-stone, full of iron pyrites in nodules. Start at sunrise to ascend the glacier, accompanied by Sutherland. The other men I sent off to hunt for sheep or deer, of which we found a few tracks." Then follows a paragraph, entertaining, and preserving for us one of the few instances of superstition of Canadian Indians regarding a mountainous area: "I wished Nimrod [Dr. Hector's chief hunter] to go with me, but he would not venture on the ice, but told all sorts of stories of sad disasters that had befallen those Indians that ever did so; how that, if they did not get lost in a crevasse, they were at least sure to be unlucky afterwards in their hunting.

"I saw now that the glacier I was upon was a mere extension of a great mass of ice, that enveloped the higher mountains to the west, being supplied partly through a narrow spout-like cascade in the upper part of the valley, and partly by the *resolidifying* of the fragments of the upper *Mer de Glace,* falling over a precipice several hundred feet in height, to the brink of which it was gradually pushed forward. A longitudinal crack divides the glacier throughout nearly its entire length, sharply defining the ice that has squeezed through the narrow chasm, from that portion of the glacier that has been formed from the fallen fragments, the former being clear and pure, while the latter is fouled by much débris resting on its surface and mixed in its substance.

"The blue pinnacles of ice, tottering over the brink of the cliff, were very striking, and it was the noise of these falling that we had mistaken for thunder a few days before when many miles down the valley. On coming fairly in view of the precipice, when about two miles from the front of the glacier, I found, by watching the fall of these pinnacles, and observing the interval till the crash was heard, that I was a little more than four miles distant, so that the lower part of the glacier is about six miles in length. After examining the surface of the glacier, and arriving at its upper end close to the precipice, we struck off to the north side of the valley, to ascend a peak that looked more accessible than the other.

"Here we found traces of where a bear had been digging roots of alpine plants. We started an old goat, and got quite close to him, but not having a gun could do him no harm. We had a splendid view over the *Mer de Glace* to the south and west, the mountain valleys being quite obliterated, and the peaks and ridges standing out like islands through the ice mantle."

Mount Forbes was unnamed in those days, but Dr. Hector saw it and recognized its pre-eminence; for he goes on to say, "The mountains to the north are very rugged, but not so high as those to the south of the valley. In that direction there is one peak which has a pyramidal top completely wrapped in snow, and at least double the height of where I stood."

Dr. Hector's narrative is so accurately and clearly written that we found it quite worth while to continue our delving. We learned that, after the pioneers, alpinists came searching for these great mountains of the north. But they too were forced to become explorers, since information was incomplete, and, in many cases, incorrect. Coleman, in 1892, rediscovered Fortress Lake, and, in the following year, visited Athabaska Pass. Wilcox, in

1896, starting from Laggan, was the first white man to journey up the North Fork and cross to the Athabaska. Collie and his companions had come out from England, in 1897 visiting the Freshfield region, and in 1898 discovering the Columbia Icefield itself. Habel, the German explorer, to whom we are indebted for calling attention to the beauty of the Yoho Valley, in 1901 made an extensive study of the western sources of the Athabaska, penetrating to the northern base of Columbia, calling it "Gamma." Sir James Outram, in 1902, with the guide Christian Kaufmann, and accompanying Collie during a part of the season, accomplished a series of great climbs, including first ascents of Freshfield, Forbes, Lyell, Alexandra, Bryce, and Columbia. Reasonable enough that we too should have been attracted by these stories of such an alpine Wonderland!

It was early in the spring when we arranged our plans. Our outfitter, of course, would be no other than Jim Simpson, who had taken Palmer and myself to the Freshfield Group during the season preceding. Jim was quite keen to go again into the north-country which he knows so well. He wrote to say that Tommy, best of cooks, would be with us again; and that one, Ulysses LaCasse—because of his broad grin more conveniently known as "Frog"—would come as horse-wrangler. Finally, and luckiest of all, we secured the promise of Conrad Kain, super-guide and philosopher, whose stories have since quieted our nerves over many a day of bad weather, to lead us up the icefield peaks.

No one, for many years, had visited the Thompson Pass area with climbing purpose; and, as there remained an untouched twelve-thousand-foot peak on the Columbia field, we could scarcely be expected to control our excitement. It was July 27th when we left Lake Louise with our procession of horses. We had quite an audience, for the start of a pack-train is a thing not seen every day. Such a commotion! Boxes and saddles; duffle bags and pans. Squealing horses tethered in the scrub-pine, breaking loose now and then and galloping through the clearing, bells clanging and pack-covers flapping. The cayuse that is being packed—how sleepily he stands, with belly forcibly distended lest the rope be too tight; the shrewd look in his eye as an uncovered axe touches his rump. A heave and a buck; profanity and the operation repeated ... off at last with the horses fighting for their place in line.

Bow Lake, where tumbling icefalls and sparkling water afford a setting in which many an Izaak Walton has become oblivious of his sport, was reached on the second day. Jim has a fine camp there now; a comfortable boat, brought in from the railroad by pack-horses, a snug boat-house on the sandy beach, and a regular block-house of logs where one could spend the most restful sort of vacation. We recommend it.

On the day following, we rode through the meadows leading in gentle slope to the summit of Bow Pass, and down the Mistaya to campground on the Wildfowl Lakes. There we pitched our tents, the nest of a ruby-throated humming-bird above our door, and wandered along the lake shore where we could watch the antics of sandpiper, wheeling and darting in broken flight, and harlequin duck diving and rippling the calm-mirrored images of jagged ridge and ice-hung peak.

Simpson and Ladd walked down to the lower lake to investigate a cache of provisions in a little cabin. I went part way along the lake to photograph and sat down to admire the majesty of Howse Peak and the wall of the northern Waputiks. A stiff breeze was blowing, catching up the water and whirling the surface spray up into curious, transient waterspouts six and eight feet high over a circle twenty feet in diameter. The boys were soon back, reporting that a wolverene—the nightmare of winter trap-lines—had got into the cabin, and made things the worse for his visitation.

Our next day of travel was a delight. Between the lakes Mistaya River is forded, trail leading to the Forks of the North

Saskatchewan. We pass through Pyramid Camp, where we had stopped a year before, our blaze still legible on the big tree under which we had slept. The river foams and boils in a misty canyon, far below; towers of Murchison rise across the valley like shattered cathedrals; pack-horses are splashing through pools and sloughs whose borders are riotous in flower colours. The trail is cut and broken by turbulent glacial brooks, with soaring ice-clad peaks above. An eagle soars from the cliff shadows, into blue space, guiding us to the Saskatchewan.

At the Forks, instead of turning up Howse River, the entrance to the Freshfield Group, we crossed the long ford and camped on the far bank below Mount Wilson. If one is unlucky, at high water there will be swimming and wet packs. The river flows between Murchison and Wilson, past the Kootenay Plain and, continuing as Nelson River, connects Lake Winnipeg with far distant Hudson Bay. Here, however, it is broken by gravel-bars into shallow rapids, through which the horses struggle, while their riders make futile attempts to remain dry-shod. Camp is splendidly situated on a terrace, at the junction of the North Fork, Howse and Mistaya rivers, where in the long-ago the Indians came to tan and cure hides after their hunting trips. The panorama is one of great beauty, strangely suggestive of the Oberland peaks from Grindelwald—sky-soaring Chephren with its pure white snow-saddle, ice-hung Kaufmann Peaks, and the rock-wall of Sarbach, massed in the Howse–Mistaya angle. A glimpse of the Lyell Icefield through the gap of Glacier Lake, and the spire of Forbes, add to a scene whose foreground is a river, lighted by the afternoon sun, with horses grazing on the flats, and smoke rising through gnarled and ancient trees.[37]

The Forbes–Lyell Group of mountains is separated into southern and northern divisions by the Mons and Lyell icefields, lying on the Continental Divide. The chief peaks of the southern area are Forbes (11,902 feet), east of the Divide, and Bush

Mountain—Rostrum Peak (10,770 feet), and Icefall Peak (10,420 feet)—in British Columbia. Peaks of the Divide, north of Bush Pass, Cambrai (10,380 feet), Messines (10,290 feet), and Mons (10,114 feet), show what part the late war played in the nomenclature of the Northwest.

The northern division extends from Mount Lyell to Thompson Pass (6511 feet), in the splendid range encircling the head of Alexandra River. Lyell possesses five peaks, all above 11,000 feet, from the central one of which the Divide continues northward over Farbus, Oppy, and Douai, and rises to the abrupt, snowy summits of Alexandra—11,214 feet, and 10,990 feet—whence it crosses Fresnoy (10,730 feet), Spring Rice (10,745 feet), and descends to Thompson Pass from the summit of Watchman Peak (9873 feet).

Morning came; daffodil glow preceding a succession of delicate colours, and leading us up the North Fork Valley. Bars of sunlight relieve the shadowy recesses of primeval forest—cottonwood, poplar, and cedar—through which winds the trail. Close to the cliffs of Mount Wilson, meandering streams, suggesting lines of a jig-saw puzzle, gleam through the meadows. Tiny fish dart in the shallows; and all the toads seem to be amphibious, hopping into the water as our horses pass. Mount Saskatchewan, mirrored in many a quiet pool, stands guardian of the entrance to Alexandra River.

"Graveyard," because of ancient hunting relics which adorn it, is the name given to the camping place opposite the mouth of Alexandra River. A bit of buffalo skull, white and friable, recalls the days when these huge animals ranged even into the remote valleys of the north. Pinto Pass, with an old Indian trail leading over the Cline[38] River, may be reached in a few hours; Ladd and I strolled out above it to the bench-land below Mount Coleman for a far-reaching view of the Saskatchewan Valley. We sat down among the forget-me-nots; Bow Pass could still be seen, a dim grey-blue saddle on the southern skyline. We looked into Alexandra Valley where brilliant light outlined the distant range. The sun was setting behind the outlying pinnacles of Mount Saskatchewan—antique towers and air-castles—while purple shadows lengthened in the gorge below, and against this glorious background we watched three sheep, in silhouette row, walk up a nearby ridge and disappear.

With the exception of a few travellers and Indian hunters, there have been but few visitors to the valley of Alexandra River. Locally known as the "West Branch," the first white men to gain even a partial view of it were Wilcox[39] and Barrett, who, in 1896, *en route* to Fortress Lake, ascended a spur of Mount Saskatchewan and looked up the river to its bend. Based on information from Tom Wilson, of Banff, that there was an Indian trail across the pass at the valley-head, Mr. C.S. Thompson, an enthusiastic mountaineer, in 1900, travelled as far as the pass now bearing his name. He took one packer with him, and although no climbing was attempted because of bad weather prevailing, they explored the pass and visited the northern glaciers of Lyell.[40]

There is still a faint trail, with many crossings of the stream which divides and wanders between little green islands, where birds hide and disclose their presence only when one approaches closely. Alexandra and its tumbling glacier-falls loomed ahead. Several deer bounded away when they got wind of the horses. Little drab buffalo-birds followed us; friendly fellows who like nothing better than a ride on the back of a cayuse. There are many game tracks, but in the heat of the day the larger animals—deer, moose, and sheep—are high up near timber-line where cooler breezes drive off the flies. Just as the Freshfield area was the home of big goats, so this and neighboring valleys form the territory of the sheep; for sheep and goat are on unfriendly terms and do not range together.

We passed by Camp Content, where Outram had stopped years before, and, crossing an angle of the river, placed our tents close to the Alexandra Glaciers, naming our stopping place—the reason was obvious—"Last Grass Camp." Mount Oppy (10,940 feet), with its gabled ice-crest, rises with Alexandra above this spot, with the northern Lyell basin close at hand. It was our intention to attack this basin in the hope of attaining the Lyell–Farbus col and the unclimbed Divide peak of Lyell (No. 3; 11,495 feet), just equal in height to the central peak ascended by Outram. There also one might traverse the arête of Farbus (10,550 feet), and across a steep little ice-col reach Mount Oppy itself, peaks well guarded by icefalls above the Alexandra Glaciers.

But weather was ever unkind. We visited the glaciers, scarcely half a mile distant; enormous, with flat tongues spreading below broken séracs so placed that one can only with difficulty reach the upper snows. The western Alexandra Glacier is conspicuous with its regular, parabolic dirt-bands, differentiating the seasonal variation between winter and summer snows.[41] On our first walk over the ice, a little shower passed, followed by an entrancing double rainbow which arched from the ice-tongue to our camp in the woods below.

Next day the peaks were again shrouded in mist. It was July 4th, and we ascended, in three hours, into the northern Lyell basin. Crevasses and the icefall of the eastern Alexandra Glacier soon forced us to the moraine, a direct ascent to which is made unpleasant by muddy cliff and running water. By a little fire, kindled on an upper meadow, we sat and watched for momentary glimpses into the upper ice-world as the snow-tops played hide-and-seek in the fog. So many times from the viewpoints above Lake Louise we had seen the triple-headed snow-mountain clear, against an azure northern background; now to be on its very slopes and find it hidden. Still it was not an unpleasant place to be, there beside our smouldering fire. Although the heights were often invisible, we could always gaze downward on those marvelous glaciers. The masses of ice were softened here and there by the interposition of thin vapors, drifting back and forth; towers and pinnacles of ice seemed on the verge of splitting and crumbling; sea-green arches, transparent as our finger-tips seem when held before a strong light, were all luminous with the pale yellow glow that came through a distant snow-saddle beyond Rice Glacier. Then, as we descended, rain drenched us. But a roaring fire at camp, and a bit of bear-steak that Simpson brought in—I think he said he found it growing on a tree—made us quickly forget the weather.

A few days later we rode to Thompson Pass. It had cleared off, and we followed the trail up Castleguard River—the name given to the stream above the Alexandra angle—and through dense forest to the broad grassy levels leading to the summit lakes. Watchman Peak is charmingly reflected in the lower lake, while from the pass summit, below Spring Rice, we could look far into the gloomy depths of Bush Valley with the unbroken wall of Mount Bryce (11,507 feet) descending into it. This western country is wild in its appearance and looks nearly impossible for horses.

It must have been about this time that Jim, apropos of nothing in particular, remarked that his birthday was about to recur. Tommy and I made secret plans. When the day arrived, Tommy concocted a gigantic doughnut, liberally powdered with sugar and mounted on a pedestal of heather. We stood the candle from our folding-lantern in the centre and the result was almost artistic. At lunch-time it was brought in with all ceremony and presented to "Chief Nashan"—for Jim is known as the Wolverene among the Stoney Indians, because of his uncanny ability as a hunter. Jim was much surprised; but we were still more so when he confessed that although the date was right he had been a whole month short on time! Still, we had had our fun and the monotony of a day of showers was broken. After all, time on the trail is an impossible thing to keep track of.

CHAPTER V
THE ASCENT OF NORTH TWIN

(Columbia Icefield and the Glaciers of Castleguard)

"Our course lay, for the most part, over vast fields of snow, but the early portion of it presented scenery of surpassing beauty, far more magnificent and dazzling than that of the day before. There were broad and bridgeless chasms, whose depths the eye, from their dizzy edges, vainly sought to ascertain;—towering masses, in forms that, from their strangeness, seemed unreal;—spires of brightness, grottos and palaces of frost,—here recent, soft, of snowy whiteness,—there older, hardened, passing into crystal azure,—sprinkled with frozen dew, festooned with silver fringe; their inmost caverns dark,—vast stalactites of ice, in line, guarding the portals."

DR. MARTIN BARRY

The continent of North America possesses two hydrographic apices which are remarkable for the river systems extending therefrom. In each of these areas occurs a watershed of the triple-divide type whose streams form great and lengthy rivers, flowing enormous distances to terminate in widely separated bodies of water.

The southerly of these interesting regions is found, near Latitude 43°, in the Wind River Mountains of Wyoming, south of Yellowstone National Park. Here rises the Snake River, flowing to the Columbia, its waters carried through British Columbia and emptying into the Pacific at the northwest corner of Oregon. Not many miles distant are sources of Green River, flowing southwest to the Colorado and reaching the Gulf of California. Eastward, branching headwaters of the Missouri find their way to the Mississippi basin and the far-off Gulf of Mexico.

Less well known is the Canadian watershed to be found in Latitude 52°. There, in a region extensively glaciated, are sources of river systems whose waters make their way for hundreds of miles, by winding, devious routes to three separate oceans.

The Rocky Mountains of Canada form the Alberta–British Columbia Boundary and extend northward, from the Montana line, at the 114th Parallel, until the 120th Parallel is reached, near Latitude 54°, and the range becomes subalpine. Great icefields mantle the Continental Divide between the Canadian Pacific and the Canadian National railroads, the scenic grandeur culminating in the Columbia Icefield, in Latitude 52° 12′.

This icefield, the largest known in Canada, containing approximately one hundred and fifty square miles, forms an unusually compact triple divide. From its snows, on the Continental Divide, attaining an elevation of 10,000 feet over a large area, are formed the headwaters of the Athabaska, which, by way of Great Slave Lake, joins the Mackenzie system, whose delta is beyond the Arctic Circle. Western ice-tongues supply Bush River, tributary to the Columbia and reaching the Pacific. From many converging streams on the eastern slope is formed the Saskatchewan River, emptying into Lake Winnipeg, whence the Nelson River continues the drainage to Hudson Bay and the North Atlantic.

Thus do two mountain uplifts form the drainage sources for much of continental America between Mexico and Alaska.

The two water-partings possess no little of historic interest. In 1805, the Lewis and Clark Expedition, reaching the forks of the Missouri, pioneered the Jefferson River and crossed to the Clearwater branch of the Columbia on their way to the Pacific Coast. Only a little later, Canadian fur-traders, in 1807, made use of the Howse Pass in travelling across the Rocky Mountains, from the North Saskatchewan—the Kootenay Plain—to the Columbia Valley. In 1811, the Athabaska Pass was opened by David Thompson of the North-West Company and served for many years as a much-frequented route between Athabaska trading posts—Fort Edmonton, Henry House, and Jasper House— and the Columbia Loop.

Anyone who has even superficially examined the map of a continent will realize that rivers of any length possess sources in elevated portions of the earth's surface. It is the land uplift, usually a mountain region, in which occurs the greatest precipitation; the ranges and inland table-lands, or even lofty plateaus, serve the further purpose of providing the potential energy, the *vis a tergo*, for stream flow. It will be further understood that such a region is topographically more complex than an area of coastal plain; and that, to unravel the complex features which a mountain range often possesses and which are frequently hidden, it is quite essential for a field observer to attain lofty ridges—if not the very summits themselves—in order to discover what may lie beyond.

The Columbia Icefield, one of the largest subarctic fields, was first seen, in 1898, by J. Norman Collie,[42] who described the view from the summit of Mount Athabaska as follows: "A new world was spread at our feet; to the westward stretched a vast ice-field probably never before seen by human eye, and surrounded by entirely unknown, unnamed, and unclimbed peaks. From its vast expanse of snows the Saskatchewan Glacier takes its rise, and it also supplies the head-waters of the Athabaska; while far away to the west, bending over in those unknown valleys glowing with the evening light, the level snows stretched, finally to melt and flow down more than one channel into the Columbia River, and thence to the Pacific Ocean. Beyond the Saskatchewan Glacier to the southeast, a high peak (which we have named Mt. Saskatchewan) lay between this glacier and the west branch of the North Fork, flat-topped and covered with snow, on its eastern face a precipitous wall of rock. Mount Lyell and Mount Forbes could be seen far off in the haze. But it was towards the west and northwest that the chief interest lay. From this great snow-field rose solemnly, like 'lonely sea-stacks in mid-ocean,' two magnificent peaks, which we imagined to be 13,000 or 14,000 feet high, keeping guard over those unknown western fields of ice. One of these, which reminded us of the Finsteraarhorn, we have ventured to name after the Right Hon. James Bryce, the then President of the Alpine Club. A little to the north of this peak, and directly to the westward of Peak Athabasca, rose probably the highest summit in this region of the Rocky Mountains. Chisel-shaped at its head, covered with glaciers and snow, it also stood alone, and I at once recognised the great peak I was in search of; moreover, a short distance to the northeast of this mountain, another, almost as high, also flat-topped, but ringed round with sheer precipices, reared its head into the sky above all its fellows. At once I concluded that these might be the two lost mountains, Brown and Hooker."

The high rock-peak, which Collie thought might be Mount Brown, was later named Mount Alberta, while the glacier-clad mountain was christened Columbia. Two fine peaks, one rocky, the other snow-covered, which from the level of the icefield hide Alberta, became known as The Twins.

From Thompson Pass, the Continental Divide swings northward across the eastern shoulder of Bryce (11,507 feet), and, traversing the centre of the icefield, rises to the summit of The Snow Dome (11,340 feet), the hydrographic apex of the Saskatchewan, Athabaska, and Columbia river systems. Almost doubling on itself, the Divide then turns sharply southward and westward to the summit of Mount Columbia.

This splendid peak, attaining the elevation of 12,294 feet, according to measurements of the Interprovincial Survey, is the second peak of the Canadian Rockies and is overtopped only by Mount Robson (12,972 feet), the highest of the entire range. Robson is situated on the Continental Divide, there a Pacific–Arctic watershed, north of Yellowhead Pass; but it rises from no icefield comparable to the Columbia.

North Twin, a near neighbor of Columbia, reaches the height of 12,085 feet, making it the third elevation of the range and the loftiest summit entirely in Alberta.

From Mount Columbia, the Divide crosses Mount King Edward (11,400 feet), and Chaba Peak (10,540 feet), and peaks along the crest of the Chaba basin, gradually descending to Fortress Lake Pass (4388 feet).

In the deep valley north of Mount Bryce, and below Columbia, three crevassed glacier-tongues supply Bryce Creek, which joins with Rice Brook from Thompson Pass and the glaciers west of Mount Alexandra to form the North Fork of Bush River and drain to the Columbia Valley. From Mount Castleguard (10,096 feet), the Castleguard Glacier tongues form northern sources of Alexandra River, while to the east of Castleguard Valley minor, separate snowfields supply Castelets and Terrace creeks. Above Terrace Valley rise the shattered, forbidding cliffs of Mount Saskatchewan (10,964 feet), filling in the angle between Alexandra River and the North Fork.

The northern margin of the Columbia Icefield is bordered by the broad snows of Mount Kitchener (11,500 feet), and The Twins—South Twin, 11,675 feet; North Twin, 12,085 feet—the latter, as we have seen, the third of triangulated peaks in the Canadian Rockies. Between The Twins and Mount Columbia a magnificent precipitous cirque contains the plunging, banded

Columbia Glacier and the tongue from The Twins, draining to the main Athabaska River. The Twins and Mount Kitchener, grouped with peaks farther north—Stutfield (11,320 feet), Woolley (11,700 feet), Diadem (11,060 feet), and Alberta (11,874 feet)—make up the gigantic massif, as yet but partially mapped, between the Sunwapta and Athabaska rivers.

To see these things we had come up-trail, past Outram's old "Camp Columbia," with its surprising waterfall, to campground above 7000 feet in the meadows below Mount Castleguard and its ice-tongues. Here, indeed, is the spot of which wranglers dream: plenty of water, wood everywhere, horse-feed for months; and the horses can't get away! Castleguard Camp fulfills one's idea of Alpine Paradise. A meadow, acres of it, with a heather carpet and flowers beyond description; little cascading streams; a tiny canyon, where leaps an arching waterfall. Can you imagine it at evening? Smoke from the campfire rising through tall trees beside the tents; horse-bells tinkling in the distance, as they might on a foreign alpland; snow summits of Lyell turning heliotrope and violet; shadowed walls of Castleguard Valley seen to the Bend; Watchman Peak, with Thompson Pass patched by sunlight, and glimpses of far-away ranges in the west; Mount Bryce, stupendous, its icy peaks silhouetted and incandescent; the low southern Castleguard tongue brilliant with light reflected from the Columbia Icefield; Mount Castleguard itself, and Athabaska, at the valley head, old-rose and golden. One despairs in the telling of it. It is a place to which one will return.

From camp, one is but a short distance from Thompson Pass. Two hours' walk to the valley head leads over a low divide to the Saskatchewan tongue, whence Mount Athabaska could be climbed. East of camp, a range of minor peaks, of which Terrace (9750 feet) is the chief, separates Castleguard from Terrace Valley. It is easy to cross a low snow pass below the southern slopes of Athabaska South station, and reach meadows below

Mount Saskatchewan. Finally, in two hours one may ascend the Castleguard Glaciers to the eastern ridge of Mount Castleguard, at 9000 feet, whence a route to the summit is obvious; or, what is of equal interest, one may circle to the northwest and attain the Columbia névé without having crossed a single crevasse of any size. As many of the icefield climbs are of great length, the gaining of altitude and the avoidance of icefalls is an immense advantage over Outram's route to Columbia by the low southern Castleguard tongue or Collie's attempted route through the crevasses of the Athabaska Glacier.

Mount Castleguard, of which we made the first traverse, on July 6th, affords the finest near views of the Columbia Icefield. Our entire party went up, including Simpson, our cook, and our wrangler. Above the eastern ridge, which we attained by way of the easy central glaciers, are short stretches of steep snow. A little bergschrund is crossed and the summit reached in four hours from camp. The mountain dominates Saskatchewan Glacier and presents a splendid overlook across the icefield, which stretches endlessly westward toward Mount Columbia and northward to The Twins. Little misty clouds scud along in the breeze, their shadows wandering out across the snow and separated by splotches of sunlight. Mount Bryce, in its sheer grandeur, is nearby, with range after range beyond the wooded depths of Bush Valley. Mount Forbes lifts a white fang in the south, while nearer are the flanks of Lyell and Alexandra streaming with glaciers.

Jim and Conrad are lying flat on the shale, with a map spread out; there is a great pointing of fingers toward distant valleys, and the remarks which come to my ears indicate that fur-bearing animals next trapping season had best look out for themselves. Ladd and Frog are dividing the last piece of cheese, and Frog is not getting the best of it. Tommy and I sit with our backs against the summit cairn; one corner of it is decked with a mossy fringe of hoar-frost, which is dripping in the sunlight and falling into several cups to which we have constructed elaborate aqueducts of flat stones.

Two hours on the summit flew rapidly, and we descended the northern Castleguard snow-ridge in spraying glissades to the icefield. Columbia seemed so near to us; it was early in the afternoon and we walked some distance toward it before turning homeward. It was a day of enjoyment for all, although the momentary disappearance of Tommy through a snow-bridge was startling. We were fond of our cook, and our morale in those strenuous days depended much upon his oft-repeated bellow of "Come and get it." Four meals in a day never seemed too much!

Next morning a climbing party of four again ascended to Castleguard shoulder, hoping to reach Mount Columbia; but cold wind and snow-squalls prevailed, and drove us ignominiously back to camp where we made short work of a fresh batch of Tommy's biscuits. Our labor was not entirely useless, for we packed up to the ridge a supply of clothing, condensed fuel, and a small tent, to serve as a high camp in emergency.

July 9th was a day of threatening weather. Ladd went down-trail toward the Castleguard stream and tried the fishing, but with indifferent success. Conrad and I made a little first ascent of Terrace Mountain (9750 feet), by its southern glacier and the col at its head. The glacier is small, but offers an array of wavy, wind-blown ridges of snow, in whose hollows we counted no less than twelve lakelets, interconnected by ice-tunnels. The mountain, situated between Castleguard and Terrace valleys, is without difficulty, three hours bringing us to the corniced summit, whence one obtains a map-like view of the Columbia Icefield with its glacier-tongues extending out, like tentacles of some monster of pre-history. Altogether it is one of the most satisfactory views in the vicinity, and the overlook to Mount Saskatchewan served us well a few days later.

To ascend the unclimbed North Twin (12,085 feet) had been

the great prospective of our journey. On July 10th we attained this goal. With an early start (3.20 a.m.), in two hours we were high on the Castleguard ridge and off on the margin of the icefield. New snow had fallen during the days preceding; bands of mist raised fingers, swirling skyward, as if to warm them in the glow of morning. Columbia and The Twins, afar, showed only their upper heights above the undulating snowy wastes.

We came to know the Columbia Icefield on that day. It was six o'clock when we left the ridge. Soft snow and distance: North Twin is twelve miles in air-line from Castleguard shoulder, but looks less than half of that. One descends, above the head of Saskatchewan Glacier, into a broad, nearly level basin, whence the slopes rise gradually along the base of an unnamed snow-crest adjoining Athabaska on the west. Just this much takes hours; and, on rounding the head of Athabaska Glacier to the base of The Snow Dome, one is but half way to North Twin.

The Snow Dome does not rise conspicuously from the icefield; it is broad-based, situated west of the Athabaska Glacier, and slopes gradually up to a summit slightly more than a thousand feet above the main field. It is more attractive when seen from Wilcox Pass, in which direction it presents gigantic ice-crowned cliffs and terraces, with a spectacular icefall ending near the Athabaska tongue. The chief interest of the mountain is in its position as hydrographic apex of the region. From its slopes, melting snow flows to the North Saskatchewan; to the Athabaska, through the Sunwapta River; to the Columbia, by way of Bush River headwaters. These rivers, flowing to three different oceans, spring from one of the greatest of continental watersheds.

As we skirted the western slopes of The Snow Dome, North Twin loomed apparently close at hand; but distances are as deceptive as on the ocean, and nearly level snow hides many deep depressions. We circled widely to avoid crevasses at the head of Columbia Glacier, which slopes to the Athabaska Valley. The

Twins are an isolated pair, ringed by cliff and icefall, North Twin alone being connected with the icefield by a snow col—a ribbon of snow—leading down toward Habel Creek. And after weary hours,[43] when one has crossed the last long slopes and plateaus, it is necessary to lose altitude in crossing this deep saddle to gain the peak.

Here we made the first stop, for lunch, at two o'clock. Over the head-cirque of Columbia Glacier rise mounts Columbia and King Edward, above icy terraces and benches of cliff. South Twin is close at hand, with grim, pinnacled walls, towering to a sharp ice-peak, difficult in appearance, and only to be attacked by the col connecting it with its northern relative. Framed by North Twin and the snow-humps of Stutfield, the valley of Habel Creek is a foreground for cliff-ringed and unclimbed Mount Alberta.[44]

Our own peak, immediately above us, its corniced summit ridge intermittently hidden by snow-flurries and wind-blown mist, rose in a slope of glistening snow, steep and unbroken. Conrad was leading, I was second, and Ladd last on the rope. The wall of snow was ever before us as we went up; there was considerable step-cutting, not in hard ice, but in crusted snow, and our pace slowed before the top of King Edward came into view above the sharp arête of South Twin. We reached the summit just thirteen hours after leaving camp: fleeting glimpses of winding rivers in the west and of shining summits in the direction of Maligne Lake and Wilcox Pass were blotted out in the closing mist.

Still, it was warm enough—just a moderate breeze blowing—and we remained twenty minutes on the summit; but the view we hoped for never came. The descent to the col was without incident (4.40–5.40 p.m.); we had made the first traverse of the Columbia Icefield, from Castleguard Valley to the head of Habel Creek—from the Saskatchewan to the Athabaska slope—and the last untrodden twelve-thousand-foot peak of the Rocky Mountains of Canada had fallen to us.

Someone, following in our track, may one day understand that journey back across the icefield's vastness. For an analytical mind, it will at least afford insight of the psychology of fatigue: the half-hour in a blizzard, obscuring the trail and exhausting us; the clearing at sunset, with crimson and orange light banded against masses of lead-blue storm clouds behind The Twins; mist and snow-banners wreathed about and trailing from Columbia and catching up the light—we three mortals in the middle of the field, in all its immensity, struggling on in insufficiently crusted snow until the light failed.

We had brought some portable fuel and a small kettle with us and left it on a snowy hummock far out on the icefield against our return. It was dark when we approached it, but we soon had some water melted to slake a burning thirst. While Conrad and Ladd were attempting to make tea, I walked on alone to the slopes below Castleguard. The unbroken snow was hardening a little, the air comfortably cool, and only a gentle wind stirring. I sat down to wait for the others. Beyond Athabaska dark clouds hung and lightning flashed; in another direction, above Mount Bryce, stars appeared in all the glory of high altitudes; in the western horizon there was still a pale afterglow, and bits of mist floated about on the surface of the icefield, as if earth and sky were mingled in one.

The rest of the party came up; I had seen the flickering lantern, and located them by their shouts. We roped up together and went on through the night, over the Castleguard shoulder and down the long slopes beyond. It is not easy to thread crevasses in the dark—lucky that we knew the way, but how we cursed that lantern! When we pulled into camp, it was three o'clock, and morning was on the hills as it had been when we departed.

Twenty-three hours we had been out; we were very tired, and the grass beside the campfire seemed luxurious in its softness as we sat there breakfasting in the light of the rising sun.

CHAPTER VI
MOUNT SASKATCHEWAN
AND MOUNT COLUMBIA

"Now the violet tint was upon us, but the summit of the mountain was still burnished with a line of bright gold. It died away, leaving a lovely red, which, having lingered long, dwindled at last into the shade in which all the world was enveloped, and left the sky clear and deeply azure."

JOHN AULDJO

Filling the great angle between Alexandra River and the North Fork, a thing of towers and battlements, rises Mount Saskatchewan. Formidable in appearance, and long sought by climbers, it had never failed to attract the attention of those who came into the region. A symmetrical monolith on the jagged northeast ridge is well known as the "Lighthouse," and serves as a landmark in the valley of the North Saskatchewan.

We knew the mountain well by this time. From the east, on the slope of Mount Coleman, we had gazed upon its unclimbed heights, wondering at its sheer forbidding face of snow-powdered cliff. The bounding ridges are broken with deep gaps below the summit and bristle with gendarmes. On the icefield we had again seen this sky-cleaving wedge and examined its southwestern face, which, although formidable, offered a more feasible approach. It was always challenging.

On awakening after our long and weary journey to North Twin, I found the sun high in the heavens. Tommy had the fire going and was putting together a tremendous lunch. From the teepee came intermittent strains of a harmonica, for which only Conrad could be blamed; and you have missed real music if you have not heard his orchestrations! This time, however, it sounded as if he were suffering from sunburned lips. In the direction of Ladd's tent there were no signs of life.

A day in camp put us in good shape again and we were ready for further work. Early on July 12th, we started up the gradually rising slopes behind camp and made our way to the low snow-saddle connecting the head of Castleguard with Terrace Valley. It was just five o'clock; and descending the meadows on the far side, we were soon in the shadow of Mount Saskatchewan, which rose above us in outline suggestive of the Matterhorn as seen from Zermatt. We approached the southwestern face, above Terrace Creek, where a slanting, subsidiary ridge descending, north of the summit, breaks the face into an eastern and a western cirque.

Entering the smaller cirque, which is also the more precipitous, over scree and winter snow, we came close to a "jolly little company of goat"—five old ones, with several kids—who scuttled off across a subsidiary ridge to the east and showed us a route thither. A deep couloir, snow-filled, afforded access to the ridge; but the goat arrived much more gracefully and rapidly than we.

We were now on the crest between the two cirques, and followed it up to the first cliff belt. Far away through Terrace Valley rose the white, north face of Forbes and the glaciated range from Thompson Pass to Lyell and Alexandra. Snow, mist, and sky; partially hidden in cloud, with sunlight breaking through: the Columbia Icefield revealed itself. We turned for a moment to watch the goat; after attempting to dislodge stones on us in the couloir, they had crossed some higher ledges to the north and were soon out of sight. A big billy remained behind on guard. High on a cliff ledge was poised an enormous boulder; behind this he went and was quite hidden. But every once in a while we could see his bearded face poke out through a crack; he was quite curious about us and we found him very amusing, the entertainment undoubtedly being mutual.

Through slabby chimneys, where little showers of icy water came down; up bits of broken cliff, traversing eastward, we found cracks which led upward. The first belt, about forty feet high, was surmounted at a point nearly a hundred yards east of the rock crest between the cirques, and we crossed some steep bits of snow on the way thither. Under the second line of cliff, we again traversed eastward before finding a suitable break. On a small buttress we built a direction cairn to guide our return, and as a possible service to future climbers. A short distance farther east, we reached 10,000 feet at a point below and north of the summit. Then followed long slopes of wet, down-tilted scree and shale, leading to steep pitches of snow by which the arête was eventually gained. It was hard work, but the cliffs were well covered, and only once or twice did small superficial avalanches go down behind us.

In the Italian valleys of Monte Rosa, there is an ancient legend of a "Lost Valley"; and, just as the peasants of days gone by may have looked over to the unknown meadows of Switzerland, so we gazed from the precipitous north face of our mountain. It was 2.40 p.m., and it became apparent that the point we had aimed for was not the highest, but that the true summit lay several hundred yards farther east. To reach it, due care and attention were given to the cornices overhanging on the north; but with some step-cutting and a final bit of rock scrambling we reached the top.

North Fork and Alexandra River meet in a broad sunlit angle; with care, we looked down the wall to the lighthouse pinnacle, now almost under us. Peaks, icefields, and glaciers were all about us. We built small cairns, leaving a record of our North Twin ascent as well—there had been no visible rock outcrop on its summit—and started down again at just half-past three.

On descending, we had scarcely gotten off the steep snow, when a thundershower overtook us. We crouched in a corner until its violence had passed, and then with speed were down the rocks and glissading in showers of spray to the meadows below. We stopped and finished what remained of our provisions, and strolled homeward over the snow pass. All the western peaks were aglow with the radiance of sunset; we were refreshed, carefree, and happy. Without hurrying we arrived in camp at nine o'clock, satisfied beyond expression that we had been the first to ascend a mountain whose impressive and imposing architecture had for years excited our admiration.

Mount Columbia, the despotic, white monarch of the icefield, on occasion—with an oft-worn crown of storm and mist removed—assumes an aspect more benign, although always serene and majestic. From the north, in the gorge of the Athabaska, its elevation is best appreciated. It was from the depths of this valley that the German explorer Habel, in 1901, saw it and named it "Gamma." He was misled by its appearance as a rock-pyramid, and failed to identify it as the rising, soaring snow-peak which Collie had described.

Even from the level of the icefield, at 10,000 feet, Columbia merits its proud position as the second elevation of the chain. It had seemed so far above our heads when we were on Castleguard, we wondered if we should ever reach it. But on July 14th we started out. The climbing party derived added pleasure from the presence of Simpson; Jim had been with Sir James Outram and the guide Christian Kaufmann, but had not climbed, at the time of the first ascent, in 1902, just twenty-one years before. Reaching Castleguard shoulder (3.50–5.30 a.m.), we found the snow in fine condition and rapidly traversed the tracks made some days previously.

Morning sun was gilding the ranges; the wind blew forcefully, and we turned toward Columbia, gleaming in the ice-blue of clear weather distance. Insects innumerable are carried up onto the ice by air currents from the British Columbia side; and, at 10,000 feet and above, we collected moths and beetles of many varieties. One might have some difficulty in obtaining such numbers at lower elevations; many were still alive, although torpid from cold. They form the food supply of snow-finches which one sees wheeling and darting about.

Although favorable conditions of snow made travel more easy than on our *tour de force* to The Twins, we again had to cross many gaps and deceptive, crevassed hollows. Far out on the icefield, shortly after ten o'clock, we had lunch on the flat snow above the head of Columbia Glacier. The snow cirque of the glacier is encroaching on the head of the basin dropping to Bush Valley; a deep, broken snow pass is formed, which, in years to come, may isolate Columbia from the icefield. In similar fashion, The Twins are being cut away from the field through the "plucking" of the Columbia Glacier basin against the glaciers descending to Habel Creek.

Sun-glare, reflecting from the high snowfields, may produce severe burns equal to any resulting at the seashore, and we were glad enough to protect our eyes with goggles and cover up blistered faces. Thirst is unquenched by the eating of snow; there is practically no water on the entire icefield, and, on this climb, we had learned the lesson to carry a small amount with us.

We were soon at the bergschrund, a narrow chasm easily crossed, and on steeper snow beyond. At 11,000 feet we halted by a rocky outcrop where water trickled; we were in the centre of and more than half way up the great eastern snow-face, practically treading the Continental Divide. We wondered what the other outfitters would have said if they could have seen Jim with an ice-axe, roped in a climbing party? The pitch steepened; steps were occasionally cut; a stinging, relentless wind tore up the snow-crust until the air seemed full of whirling white shingles. We toiled upward for some time in the gale, in some danger of having snow-glasses broken by bits of flying ice. Traversing slightly to the north, we were more sheltered, and, cutting through a narrow bit of cornice, soon were shaking hands on the summit. It was half-past one.

Words fail, and time was insufficient to grasp the complex geography of all that we overlooked.[45] The taking of a dozen photographs occupied many minutes and left one worn out and wondering where the time had flown. High wind made it difficult to stand upright; the rope whipped out in the icy gale, and fingers became numb. Our thermometer registered 23°.

The immediate foreground was the immense icefield, stretching in all directions, bounded by splendid peaks, which, from our more lofty position, seemed far below. We were above the sources of four mighty rivers: Saskatchewan, Athabaska, Columbia, and, not far away, the Fraser. To gaze down on the Columbia Glacier and the icefalls of The Twins pouring to the Athabaska gorge was as if one peered into the Bottomless Pit. Contrasting with the misty, low-toned colouring of distant river-flats and meadows—meadows with pale, silvery lakes—was the vivid green of foreground crevasse and chasm. Here was a panorama, cloudless, extending from peaks of Jasper Park to summits of the Bow Valley; from the northern Selkirks, across the Loop, and groups bordering the valleys of Wood and Canoe rivers, to eastern, nameless ranges on the Brazeau[46] and the Cline. Above our nearest neighbor, King Edward, Mount Clemenceau loomed in the Wood River area; across the haze of the Athabaska Valley, beyond South Twin, the mountains toward Yellowhead lifted in splendour undiminished by distance. In the direction of Maligne Lake, jagged peaks, of lesser elevation, were dazzling in the gleam of new snow. Mount Alberta and Mount Bryce, respectively north and south of us, were things of primitive beauty, distracting attention from all the rest: Bryce, rising in snowy heights one above the other, with avalanches falling from its savage northern face; Alberta, cliff-ringed and austere, its head aloof and wreathed in cloud. Lyell, Forbes, Freshfield, and a host of others towered gloriously.

The wild gorge of Bush River can be traced nearly to the Columbia; the Saskatchewan, across the icefield, flows eastward between mounts Wilson and Murchison to find exit to the plains; into the north, one follows the course of the Athabaska. One retains of it all, chiefly a memory of river valleys—streams sparkling in the sunlight—winding on their long journeys to distant oceans.

Forty minutes we spent on the summit, and fifteen more, out of the wind, on a level spot below the cornice. The top of Gamma! Let no one think that Columbia is a mere snow-hump rising from a névé; it is a distinct peak in every sense, looking its height and quite worthy of its place. Simpson intends to climb it every twenty-one years from now on!

Softened snow permitted a rapid though cautious descent, a final long glissade carrying us to the icefield. Return to the Castleguard shoulder was made in good time, although we delayed in watching the sunset. The icefield was an empire of silent purity, brilliant in golden sheen; a rosy haze filtering down through the Selkirks, lifting them to unearthly heights.

In a little while we were back at the campfire; just six hours from the summit. We had supper by the crackling logs, with the cross-lights from fire and western afterglow. The shadows lengthened, blue-black at the forest edge, and Conrad told us stories until there was no light remaining save that of the glowing embers, and the stars that peeped out above our heads.

CHAPTER VII
PASSAGE OF THE
SASKATCHEWAN GLACIER

(The Ascent of Mount Athabaska)

"The scenery we were entering was at once strange and exciting. The common features of Alpine landscapes were changed; as if by some sudden enchantment we found ourselves amongst richer forests, purer streams, more fantastic crags."

DOUGLAS FRESHFIELD

For many years there had existed, among the outfitters, the desire to find a direct route practicable for horses between the heads of Castleguard and Sunwapta rivers. If this could be done, it would shorten the transportation time between Thompson and Wilcox passes. We had had a good look at the glacier from the summit of Castleguard, and, while the climbing party was occupied with Mount Saskatchewan, Jim had been prospecting for a way down.

Two days after our ascent of Columbia, on July 16th, we broke camp at Castleguard. It was the loveliest day imaginable, and we hated to go; the peaks stood out against a turquoise background, so beautifully sharp and clear, with filmy wisps of multicoloured, diaphanous mist clinging to their lower slopes. The tents were down and the last horse packed; we knew that some day we would come back.

The ultimate sources of Castleguard River head in a low divide,[47] with meadows which we crossed to a tiny marginal lake by the Saskatchewan Glacier, nearly opposite Mount Athabaska. A shore of flat moraine permitted the pack-train to progress to level ice. Our horses on the glacier made an unusual procession; but, at first timid, they soon became accustomed to their surroundings and, like true mountaineers, hopped over the little cracks and crevasses. It was necessary, in avoiding a lateral glacier entering from the south, to take to the central ice for a short distance. The horses were taken down the glacier for more than four miles, with devious winding around the large transverse crevasses. The steep terminal moraine, with treacherously balanced boulders and slippery glacial mud, was most troublesome, requiring some trail-building and considerable care to avoid damage to the pack-train. But before evening the last horse was safely off and camp finally made below the tongue on the flats toward the south side near a pleasant waterfall. Close by, the stream enters a narrow canyon, spanned by a natural bridge; apparently no one else, with horses, had ever stopped at our Glacier Camp.

At daybreak, without difficulty, we took the horses northward over a meadowed shoulder east of Mount Athabaska, about 7500 feet in elevation, whence we looked back and over the tremendous expanse of green ice to Castleguard. We could scarcely believe that the cayuses had come down such a place. The descent to Sunwapta Pass was direct, through grassland and open timber to the river, whence we followed trail across the true Saskatchewan–Athabaska divide to camp not far from the tongue of Athabaska Glacier.

It was a place to remember. The valley-flat, bordered by ancient timber—from whose dusky shadows rushing brooks emerge—is sparsely covered by thickets of scrub-evergreen and willow. We spent delightful minutes in watching the antics of gopher: furry little beasts, and childishly curious. Franklin grouse, the "fool-hen" of the Northwest, were abundant; the hens often paraded close to the tents, bringing several chicks for our inspection and showing not a trace of fear. Several lakelets on the Athabaska moraine are remarkably deep and blue for their size; their shores are a salt-lick, crossed and recrossed by game tracks; four sheep bounded away when we first walked there. Several days later the cook served up a savory dish which tasted very much like mutton. None of us could guess where it came from; but, from the grin on Jim's face, it is barely possible that he might have solved the riddle.

The Athabaska Glacier is the chief source of Sunwapta[48] River, the Sunwapta Pass, some four miles southeast of Wilcox Pass, dividing ultimate sources of North Saskatchewan from Athabaska drainage. Wilcox Pass is really not a pass at all, but a detour on the Sunwapta, by which the eastern meadows of Wilcox Mountain are rounded to avoid a deep canyon below the Athabaska tongue. The glacier itself is spectacular enough; it descends in three icefalls, from the Columbia field, through the gap between Mount Athabaska and The Snow Dome. The tongue flows for more than five miles and spreads in an enormous uncrevassed fan close to the trail. The headwater of the Sunwapta is augmented by the fall of Dome Glacier, plunging down between The Snow Dome and Mount Kitchener. Nowhere else did we observe a greater quantity of falling ice; scarcely an hour passed without resounding crashes announcing a streaming avalanche.

By the north glacier and the northwest arête we made, on July 19th, the third ascent of Mount Athabaska (11,452 feet). It is such a radiant, dazzling mountain when the sun shines on its unbroken northern snow; and it was a pity that we had wretchedly bad weather. The route, above timber-line, was entirely on snow until the final crest was reached and an occasional rocky outcrop found. There are several steep slopes where one must traverse laterally for short distances under a bit of hanging glacier; some enormous blocks lie frozen high up in the slope, and here only were we glad that the day was not too bright. Less than six hours brought us to the summit, a rising snow-wedge, without cornices. It was snowing hard, and through holes in the fog we had just occasional glimpses of the Saskatchewan Glacier. There was little to indicate the presence of the Columbia Icefield, and although it was discovered from this very point it would have been unseen if the first ascent had been made under weather conditions such as we experienced.

The northwest glacier, by which we descended, is a variant of former routes, but interesting and repaying because of a tumbling icefall which one may safely approach. On the moraine we picked up a large trilobite fossil, quite different from the small shell-fossils which load the strata below the summit of Nigel Peak (10,535 feet) across the valley. There is a fine view over the Athabaska Glacier to the peaks of Diadem and Woolley beyond; but lowering clouds prevented our seeing very much of it, although the sun came out again as we reached the lower moraine and walked back to camp.

We had now completed our northern program as far as weather had permitted. North Twin, Saskatchewan, Columbia, Athabaska, and lesser peaks had fallen. The distances covered had been great: we had made two journeys across the Columbia Icefield—North Twin a round trip of more than thirty miles; Columbia but slightly less. North Twin, Saskatchewan, and Columbia had been captured within five days, perhaps constituting, if there be honour in it, a long-distance and altitude record in Canadian mountaineering.

Simpson told us an interesting tale, portions of which I was able to amplify, regarding the fate of Professor Coleman's folding boat. It seems that this craft, which had been taken to Athabaska Pass in 1893 for the purpose of navigating the Committee Punch Bowl, was utilized on the return journey to carry one of the party down the Saskatchewan from the Kootenay Plains to Edmonton. A canvas boat, presumably the same one, was again taken by Coleman's party in 1907, when travelling from Laggan to Mount Robson. That it never arrived beyond the sources of the Athabaska is indicated by the statement,[49] "As our loads were heavy and some of the horses had sore backs we cached the folding boat and fifty pounds of supplies, enough to take us home from this point, in a thick spruce tree, fastening everything up tight in bags to keep out winged or four-footed marauders. We hoped thus to make better time. This cache we were fated never to see again, and if some later traveller has not lifted it from the crotch among the branches of the old spruce, it may be there still in its waterproof wrappings."

The cache, near Athabaska Glacier, remained untouched for several years. Then along came an outfit and camped beside it. An outfitter, waking suddenly in the night at the scratching of a small animal at the tent door, and with dreams of a grizzly still confusing him, fired his gun point-blank. The porcupine seems to have escaped unscathed, but a gaping hole was blown in the side of the folding boat.

Later in the season Simpson took the boat down to the Saskatchewan Forks, repaired it and used it for several years at the ford. It was finally burned up by a couple of Indians who, for reasons unknown, bore Jim a grudge. Thus ends the strange maritime history of a craft whose lengthiest voyages were made on the back of a pack-horse through high mountain regions!

On July 20th, camp was broken, and in seven hours we had negotiated the "Big Hill," past Panther Fall, and the miles to Graveyard Camp. We could not help walking out on the river-flat that evening for a last look at Mount Saskatchewan. It is such a magnificent peak, the landmark of the entire valley, and it seemed no less glorious now that it was ours.

On the following day we crossed the Saskatchewan ford, camping below Mount Murchison, and in the afternoon enjoyed a much-needed bath in a warm shallow lake behind the tents. The old route was followed up the Mistaya to Wildfowl Lakes and Bow Pass. We had come back from the sources of the North Saskatchewan—it was journey's end.

CHAPTER VIII
ATHABASKA PASS AND THE VOYAGEURS, 1811–1827

(Explorations of the fur-traders, 1811–1827)

"For a long time yet, a few suggestive words grappling with things seen will have the advantage over a long array of precise, no doubt interesting, and even profitable figures. The earth is a stage, and though it may be an advantage, even to the right comprehension of the play, to know its exact configuration, it is always the drama of human endeavor that will be the thing, with a ruling passion expressed by outward action marching perhaps blindly to success or failure, which themselves are often indistinguishable from each other at first."

JOSEPH CONRAD

Mountaineering in the Canadian Alps can truly be said to have had its incidence through events which transpired in the territory now known as Jasper Park.

When I was little; when you were a school-child, geography-books taught that the highest mountains of North America—Mt. Brown and Mt. Hooker—lifted their unsurpassed heights on either side of Athabaska Pass. You can still find these tremendous peaks, preserved in many a modern atlas; they have become a tradition among map-makers. In those school-days, of not so long ago, I had never seen anything higher than a city office-building; but the gargoyles and cornices, seen through the smoke and dust of street-canyons, seemed so impossibly high that the very thought of mountains loftier was incomprehensible. My curiosity was aroused; more often than anyone knew, I would prop up that battered geography on my knees, and wonder at the sky-soaring propensities of those far-away mountains.

Even the light of later years—the knowledge that the supposed elevations are but mythical—has not robbed the old legend of its pristine charm. Best of all, a kind fortune has let me visit the gateway itself, between the basins of the Athabaska and Columbia rivers; and there was nothing of disappointment. It was a journey of expectations exceeded a thousandfold.

But aside from the legendary heights, Athabaska Pass acquired considerable historic interest because of its importance as a trans-Canadian route in the days of the fur-trade.[50] Many descriptions of it are found in the journals of the early *voyageurs*; and its story is a romantic one, furnishing us with a unique record of naïve impressions of mountain travel in the Nineteenth Century—upon people who, save on their one crossing of the Great Divide, never before nor after came in contact with alpine regions. It is not uninteresting, therefore, to see the mental reactions of these wanderers toward great natural phenomena whose magnitude and meaning they could but dimly understand and grasp. The natural result, of course, was an exaggeration of expression; but much of it entertaining and altogether charming.

Athabaska Pass was crossed by white men in 1811, when the party of David Thompson, of the North-West Company, used it as a route to the Pacific slope after hostile Piegan (Peigan) Indians had forbidden them the use of Howse Pass.[51] The route had been found before this, for Alexander Henry[52] speaks of it as a "route by which a party of Nepisangues (Nippisings) and freemen passed a few years ago." It is at least certain that the Pass and the Canoe River region had been visited earlier by both Iroquois and Nippising Indians.

Crossing the pass westward in January 1811, David Thompson[53] writes: "One of my men Du Nord beat a dog to death. He is what we call a 'flash' man, and a showy fellow before the women, but a coward at heart, and would willingly desert if he had courage to go alone; very gluttonous and requires full ten pounds of meat each day. As I am constantly ahead I cannot prevent his dog-flogging and beating. We saw no tracks of animals.

"The snow is full seven feet deep, tho' firm and wet; yet the dogs often sunk into it, but our snow-shoes did not sink more than three inches, and the weather so mild that the snow is dropping from the trees and everything wet. Here the men finished the last of the fresh and half-dried meat, which I find to be eight pounds for each man per day.

"The view now before us was an ascent of deep snow, in all appearances to the height of land between the Atlantic and Pacific Oceans. It was to me a most exhilarating sight, but to my uneducated men a dreadful sight. They had no scientific object in view—their feelings were of the place they were. Our guide Thomas told us, that although we could barely find wood to make a fire, we must now provide wood to pass the following night on the height of the defile we were in, and which we had to follow. My men were the most hardy that could be picked out of a hundred brave, hardy men; but the scene of desolation before us was dreadful, and I knew it. A heavy gale of wind, much more a mountain storm would have buried us beneath it; but, thank God, the weather was fine. We had to cut wood such as it was, and each took a little on his sled; yet such was the despondency of the men, aided by the coward Du Nord, sitting down at every half mile, that when night came we had only wood to make a bottom and on this to lay wherewith to make a small fire—which soon burnt out, and in this exposed situation we passed the rest of a long night without fire. And part of my men had strong feelings of personal insecurity. On our right, about one-third of a mile from us lay an enormous glacier, the eastern face of which, quite steep, about two thousand feet in height, was of a clean fine green color, which I much admired; but whatever the appearance, my opinion was that the whole was not solid ice, but formed from rills of water frozen in their course. Westward of this steep face, we could see the glacier with its patches of snow in a gentle slope for about two miles. Eastward of this glacier and near to us, was a high steep wall of rock. At the foot of this, with a fine south exposure had grown a little forest of pines, of about five hundred yards in length by one hundred yards in breadth. By some avalanche they had all been cut clean off as with a scythe; not one of the trees appeared to be an inch higher than the others. My men were not at their ease, yet when night came they admired the brilliancy of the stars; and as one of them said, he thought he could almost touch them with his hand.

"As usual, when the fire was made, I set off to examine the country before us, and found we had now to descend the west side of the mountains. I returned and found part of my men with a pole of twenty feet in length, boring the snow to find the bottom. I told them that while we had good snow-shoes it was no matter to us whether the snow was ten or one hundred feet deep. On looking down into the hole they had bored, I was surprised to see the color of the sides of a beautiful blue; the surface was of a very light color, but as it descended the color became more deep, and at the lowest point was of a blue, almost black.

"The altitude of this place above the level of the ocean, by the point of boiling water is computed to be eleven thousand feet (Sir George Simpson).

"Many reflections came to my mind: a new world was in a manner before me, and my object was to be at the Pacific Ocean before the month of August. How were we to find provisions, and how many men would remain with me, for they were dispirited? Amidst various thoughts I fell asleep on my bed of snow.

"I sent the men to collect and bring forward the goods left on the way, which they brought except five pounds of ball, which being in a leather bag was carried away by a wolverene."[54]

Gabriel Franchère was a French-Canadian who had enlisted as clerk in the Pacific Fur Company, had rounded the Horn in the *Tonquin*, and largely assisted in the establishment of Astor's post at the mouth of the Columbia. In his journal[55] he recounts the arrival of Thompson's canoes: "A well-dressed man, who appeared to be the commander, was the first to leap ashore, and addressing us without ceremony, said that he was David Thompson, and that he was one of the partners of the North-West Company. We invited him to our quarters, which were at one end of the warehouse, the dwelling-house being not yet completed. After the usual civilities had been extended to our visitor, Mr. Thompson said that he had crossed the continent during the preceding season; but that the desertion of a portion of his men had compelled him to winter at the base of the Rocky Mountains, at the headwaters of the Columbia.

"Mr. Thompson kept a regular journal, and travelled, I thought, more like a geographer than a fur-trader. He was provided with a sextant, chronometer and barometer, and during a week's sojourn which he made at our place, had an opportunity to make several observations."

William Henry followed Thompson across the pass, later in 1811, bringing supplies. In 1812, Thompson himself returned eastward.

At the onset of the War of 1812, with the selling out of the Astoria post to the British, a number of men, unwilling to continue in service, travelled eastward, at various times, crossing the mountains by Athabaska Pass.

Franchère came eastward in 1814: "We quitted Fort George (or Astoria, if you please), the 4th of April 1814, in ten canoes, five of which were of bark and five of cedar-wood, carrying each seven men as crew, and two passengers, in all ninety persons and all well armed.

"We ascended Canoe River to the point where it ceases to be navigable, and encamped in the same place where Mr. Thompson wintered in 1810–11.

"On the 12th of May we began our foot march to the mountains, being now twenty-four in number, rank and file. Fatigue obliged us to camp early. On the 13th we pursued our journey, and entered into the valleys between the mountains, where there lay not less than four or five feet of snow. We were obliged to ford the river ten or a dozen times in the course of the day, sometimes with the water up to our necks. These frequent fordings were rendered necessary by abrupt and steep rocks or bluffs, which it was impossible to get over without plunging into the wood for a great distance. The stream being very swift, and rushing over a bed of stones, one of the men fell and lost a sack containing our last piece of salt pork, which we were preserving as a most precious treasure. The circumstances in which we found ourselves made us regard this as a most unfortunate accident. We encamped that night at the foot of a steep mountain, and sent on Mr. Pillet and the guide, M'Kay, to hasten a supply of provisions to meet us."

Mr. Pillet must have been an interesting character, for Ross Cox has preserved the details of the following amusing incident: "Mr. Pillet (clerk at the Astoria post) fought a duel with Mr. Montour of the Northwest, with pocket pistols, at six paces; both hits—one in the collar of the coat, and the other in the leg of the trousers. Two of their men acted as seconds, and the tailor speedily healed their wounds." Evidently western marksmanship had not yet come into its own!

FORDING BLAEBERRY RIVER BELOW HOWSE PASS

BREAKING CAMP, AMISKWI VALLEY

HOWSE PASS AND NORTH SASKATCHEWAN RIVER

CAMPGROUND AT BOW LAKE

BOW LAKE

PACK-TRAIN FORDING MISTAYA RIVER

UPPER WILDFOWL LAKE, MISTAYA VALLEY

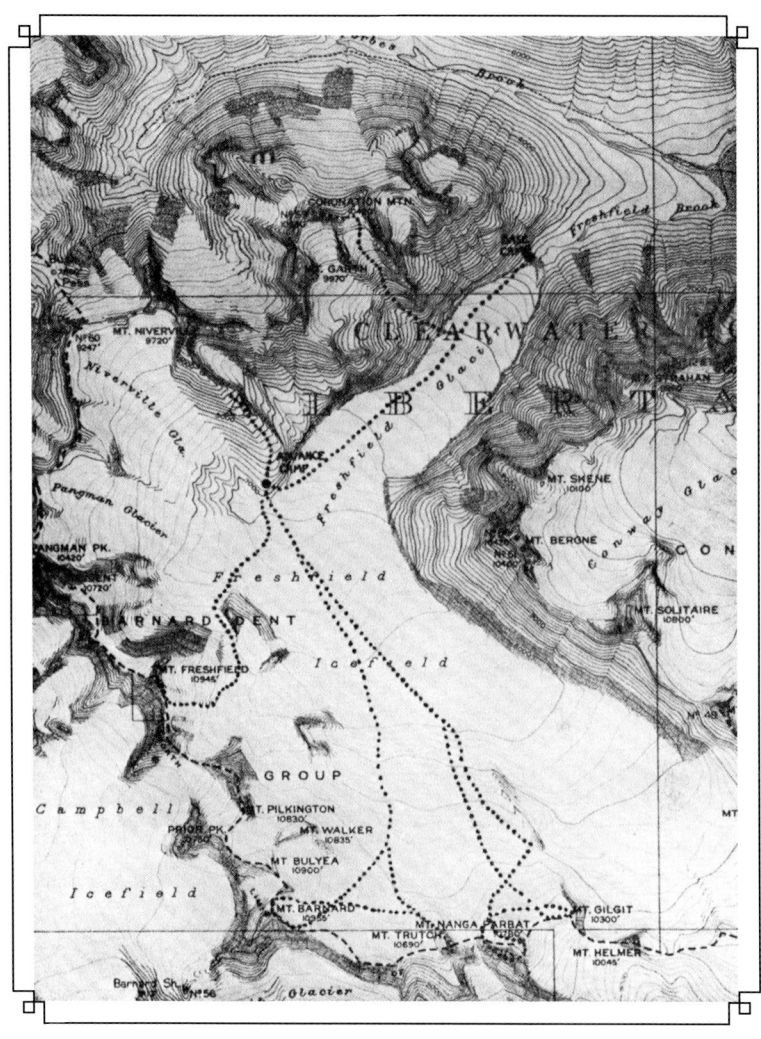

THE FRESHFIELD ICEFIELD

Showing routes travelled. Scale: ½"=1 mile

(Reduced from Interprovincial Boundary Atlas, sheet 18)

APPROACHING CORONATION MT. (10,420 FT.)

TONGUE OF FRESHFIELD GLACIER AND MT. FRESHFIELD (10,945 FT.)

YOUNG ROCKY MOUNTAIN GOAT

Caught near Howse Pass

HEAD BASIN OF FRESHFIELD ICEFIELD

A source of the North Saskatchewan River

THE FRESHFIELD GROUP FROM THE NORTH

HEAD BASIN OF FRESHFIELD ICEFIELD
From the summit of Mt. Freshfield
1. Mt. Whiteaves; 2. Mt. Low; 3. Mt. Barlow; 4. Mt. Cairnes
5. Mt. Gilgit; 6. Mt. Nanga Parbat; 7. Mt. Trutch

MT. WALKER (10,835 FT.) AND MT. PILKINGTON (10,830 FT.)
From the Niverville Meadow

CAMPGROUND ON NIVERVILLE MEADOW (7200 FT.)
1. Mt. Gilgit (10,300 ft.); 2. Mt. Nanga Parbat (10,780 ft.)
3. Mt. Trutch (10,690 ft.)

MT. GILGIT AND MT. NANGA PARBAT
From upper plateau, Freshfield Icefield

MT. TRUTCH AND MT. BARNARD
From Mt. Nanga Parbat

ON THE SUMMIT OF MT. NANGA PARBAT

EDWARD FEUZ ON SUMMIT CREST OF MT. BARNARD

VIEW S.E. FROM SUMMIT OF MT. FRESHFIELD

1. Mt. Trutch; 2. Mt. Walker; 3. Mt. Mummery; 4. Mt. Pilkington
5. Mt. Bulyea; 6. Mt. Barnard

COL LEADING TO BUSH RIVER VALLEY
Between Mts. Pilkington and Freshfield

THE PEAKS OF CHEPHREN, AND HOWSE PEAK
From the Howse–Mistaya angle

THE GREAT FORD, FORKS OF THE SASKATCHEWAN RIVER

NORTH SASKATCHEWAN VALLEY
Looking toward Bow Pass from the slopes of Mt. Coleman

ALEXANDRA GLACIERS AND "TRIDENT COL"
From northern slopes of Mt. Lyell

CASTLEGUARD CAMP WITH WATCHMAN PEAK AND THOMPSON PASS

CAMPGROUND ON CASTLEGUARD MEADOWS

ASCENDING MT. CASTLEGUARD
In background is the head of the Saskatchewan Glacier

NEAR THE TOP OF MT. CASTLEGUARD

"LIKE LONELY SEA-STACKS IN MID-OCEAN"
The Twins, twelve miles across the expanse of the Columbia Icefield

ON THE SLOPES OF NORTH TWIN
Mt. Bryce and the Columbia Glacier basin

RETURNING FROM NORTH TWIN, ACROSS THE
COLUMBIA ICEFIELD TOWARD MT. CASTLEGUARD

MT. SASKATCHEWAN FROM THE SUMMIT OF MT. CASTLEGUARD

EAST FACE OF MT. SASKATCHEWAN (10,964 FT.)

TERRACE VALLEY AND S.W. FACE OF MT. SASKATCHEWAN
Showing route of first ascent

MT. SASKATCHEWAN
From head of Terrace Valley

SUMMIT OF MT. SASKATCHEWAN

THE BEND OF ALEXANDRA RIVER

From the summit of Mt. Saskatchewan

1. Mt. Lyell; 2. Mt. Farbus; 3. Mt. Oppy; 4. Mt. Douai; 5. Mt. Alexandra

MT. COLUMBIA AND COLUMBIA GLACIER BASIN

From slope of North Twin

KAIN AND SIMPSON AT SUMMIT CORNICE OF MT. COLUMBIA

COLUMBIA GLACIER AND MT. COLUMBIA
From the Athabaska Valley

THE TWINS, FROM BASE OF MT. COLUMBIA

APPROACHING MT. COLUMBIA

Three miles distant

VIEW NORTHWARD FROM THE SUMMIT OF MT. COLUMBIA

VIEW WESTWARD FROM MT. COLUMBIA
Mt. King Edward in the foreground

HEAD OF CASTLEGUARD VALLEY
Looking S. to the groups beyond Thompson Pass

THE SASKATCHEWAN GLACIER

MARGINAL LAKELET OF SASKATCHEWAN GLACIER

PACK-TRAIN ON THE ICE BELOW MT. CASTLEGUARD

THE FIRST PASSAGE OF THE SASKATCHEWAN GLACIER WITH HORSES
Mt. Athabaska in the background

SASKATCHEWAN GLACIER AND MT. CASTLEGUARD
From eastern shoulder of Mt. Athabaska. It was down
this glacier that the pack-train was taken

DAVID DOUGLAS (1798–1834)
(From a lithograph in Curtis's *Companion to the Botanical Magazine*)

SIR GEORGE SIMPSON   ALEXANDER ROSS

WAITING TO BE PACKED

MT. EVANS AND MT. KANE

From old Hudson's Bay Co. campground in the Whirlpool Valley. This was the probable site of the Encampement de fusil, some nine miles below Athabaska Pass

MEMBERS OF 1924 EXPEDITION
M.M. Strumia, Conrad Kain, J.M. Thorington, A.J. Ostheimer

CON, JACK, AND DAVE PUT ON A DIAMOND HITCH

SCOTT GLACIER AND MT. HOOKER FROM
CAMPGROUND ON WHIRLPOOL RIVER

From this point first ascents of Mts. Oates and Hooker were accomplished

SCOTT GLACIER AND MT. HOOKER FROM THE WHIRLPOOL VALLEY

HOOKER ICEFIELD FROM SUMMIT OF MT. BROWN
McGillivray's Rock rises over the foreground snow with
Mt. Hooker above and Mt. Serenity to its right

MCGILLIVRAY'S ROCK AND
NORTHERN ENTRANCE TO ATHABASKA PASS

PACK-TRAIN ENTERING ATHABASKA PASS BELOW MT. BROWN

PACK-TRAIN ARRIVING AT THE COMMITTEE
PUNCH BOWL, ATHABASKA PASS

NORTH FACE OF MT. SERENITY (10,573 FT.) FROM MT. OATES

MT. ERMATINGER (10,080 FT.) FROM THE N.

MT. ERMATINGER AND MT. HOOKER FROM MT. OATES

MT. HOOKER AND THE HOOKER ICEFIELD
From the top of the Scott Glacier. Lateral distance
between points 2 and 5 is about one and a half miles
5. Summit; 4. Highest Rocks; 3. West Tower; 2. West Col
(Labelled points correspond with those on companion pictures)

SNOW PRECIPICE OF THE CONTINENTAL DIVIDE S.W. OF MT. HOOKER

LEFT: IN THE SÉRACS OF SCOTT GLACIER
RIGHT: THE WALL BELOW MT. HOOKER

MT. HOOKER FROM THE N.W.

From the summit of Mt. Kane. 6. Mt. Serenity; 5. Summit;
4. Highest Rocks; 3. West Tower; 0. Mt. Bras Croche; 2. West Col

MT. HOOKER FROM THE S.W.

1. Mt. Evans; 2. West Col; 3. West Tower;
4. Highest Rocks; 5. Summit; 6. Mt. Serenity; xx. Bivouacs

MEADOW CREEK APPROACH TO TONQUIN VALLEY
Eremite cirque in background and Surprise Point on the right

THE RAMPARTS FROM AMETHYST LAKES
Surprise Point campground

SIMON PEAK (10,899 FT.) FROM THE S.W.

SIMON PEAK FROM THE HEAD OF GEIKIE CREEK

VALLEY OF SIMON CREEK AND FRASER MASSIF FROM THE S.

MCDONELL AND BENNINGTON PEAKS FROM SURPRISE POINT

MT. RESPLENDENT FROM LYNX MTN.

SUMMIT IN STORM

MT. ROBSON FROM EAST END OF BERG LAKE
12,972 ft., highest peak of the Canadian Rocky Mountains

THE ARÊTE BELOW GREAT ICE-WALL OF MT. ROBSON

SUMMIT ICE-CAP OF MT. ROBSON
Our party traversing to the great couloir

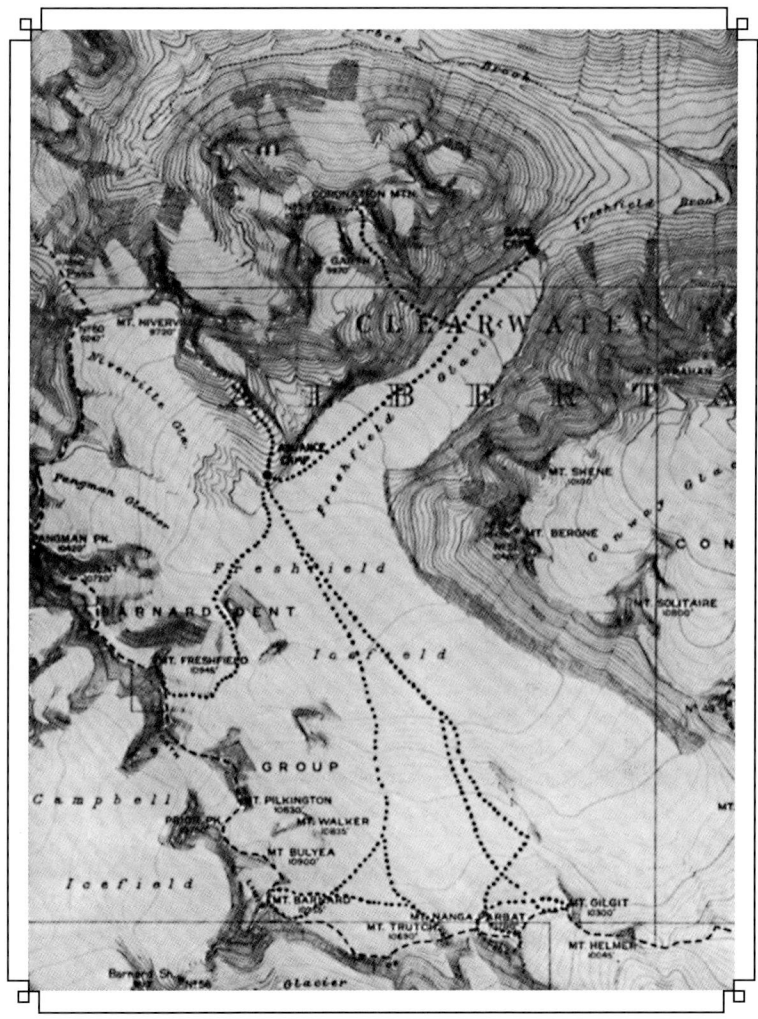

FIG. 3: MAP OF FRESHFIELD GROUP

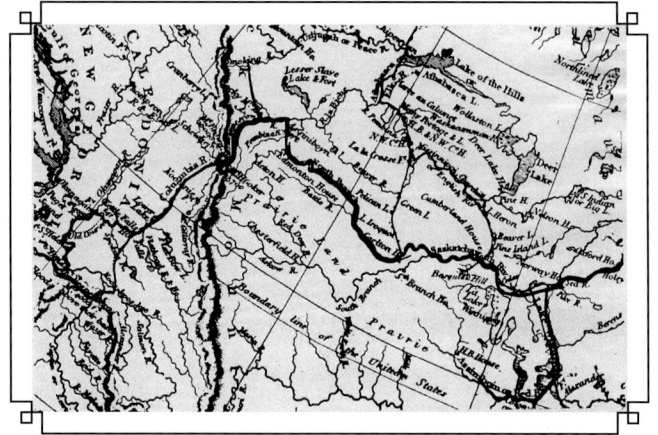

1. Douglas' Map of Athabaska Pass

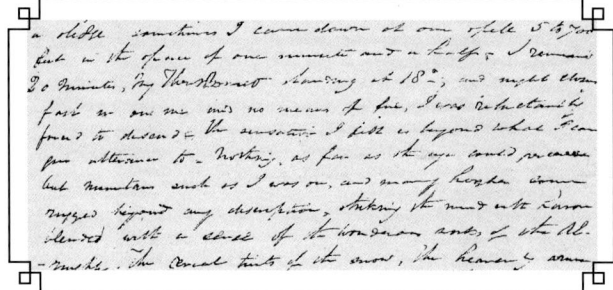

2. Facsimile from Douglas' Longer Journal, 1824–27

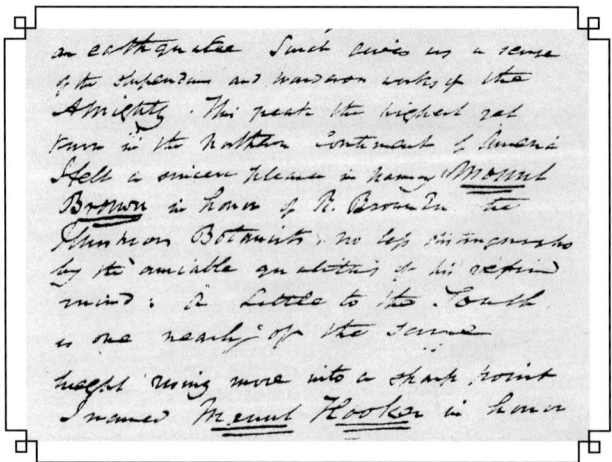

3. Facsimile from Douglas' Shorter Journal, after 1828

LAST RESTING-PLACE OF DAVID DOUGLAS, ISLAND OF HAWAII

The tablet erected to Douglas' memory is on the front wall of Kawaiahao Church, Honolulu. The marble is now much worn, but the inscription is as follows:

Hic jacet

D. DAVID DOUGLAS

Scotiâ, anno 1799, natus;

qui,

indefessus viator,

a Londinensi Regiâ Societate

Horticulturali missus,

in Havaii saltibus

die 12â Julii, A.D. 1834

victima scientiae

interiit.

"Sunt lachrymae rerum et mentem mortalia tangunt."—Virg.

PLATE I

1. General view of tongue from Mt. David

2. The northerly portion of the glacial basin from about 8000 feet. Lateral depression in central distance, with tongue of Niverville Glacier behind Pangman Glacier to the left. Compare plate 4, figure 1.

PLATE 2

1. Gathering basin of Freshfield Glacier looking southeasterly.
Sky-line is Continental Divide
1. Mt. Low, 10,075 ft.; 2. Mt. Barlow, 10,320 ft.;
3. Mt. Nanga Parbat, 10,780 ft.; 4. Mt. Trutch, 10,690 ft.

2. Gathering basin of Freshfield Glacier as seen from promontory below advanced camp. Ice at right slopes down into lateral depression. Compare plate 4, figure 2, which is an approximate continuation.

PLATE 3

1. Surface of the glacier-tongue near advanced camp

2. Mt. Nanga Parbat and Mt. Trutch, showing upper ice plateau; snow line in distance. Compare plate 2, figure 1.

PLATE 4

1. Part of the lateral depression as seen from the main glacier adjacent, looking northwesterly. Note even line of vegetation to which alcove is filled with ice

2. Lateral depression and secondary tongue, looking towards the reservoir of Freshfield Glacier

PLATE 5

2. Ice advancing into the lateral depression, 1922

1. Sérac remaining in lateral depression after last advance of secondary tongue

PLATE 6

Crest of the ice cascade at the southerly corner of the tongue

COLUMBIA ICEFIELD FROM SLOPES OF MT. BRYCE
Showing The Twins (11,675 ft. and 12,085 ft.) and Snow Dome (11,340 ft.)

ON THE SUMMIT OF MT. COLUMBIA
Kain, Thorington, Simpson, and Ladd, 1923

THE ROCKY MOUNTAINS FROM THE COLUMBIA RIVER
Looking N.W. from near the site of Boat Encampment (Reduced from an illustration in *Sketches in North America* by H.J. Warre, London, 1849)

MAP OF TONQUIN VALLEY
AND THE RAMPARTS
Reduced from
Interprovincial Boundary
atlas, sheet 29. Scale
½ inch=1 mile.

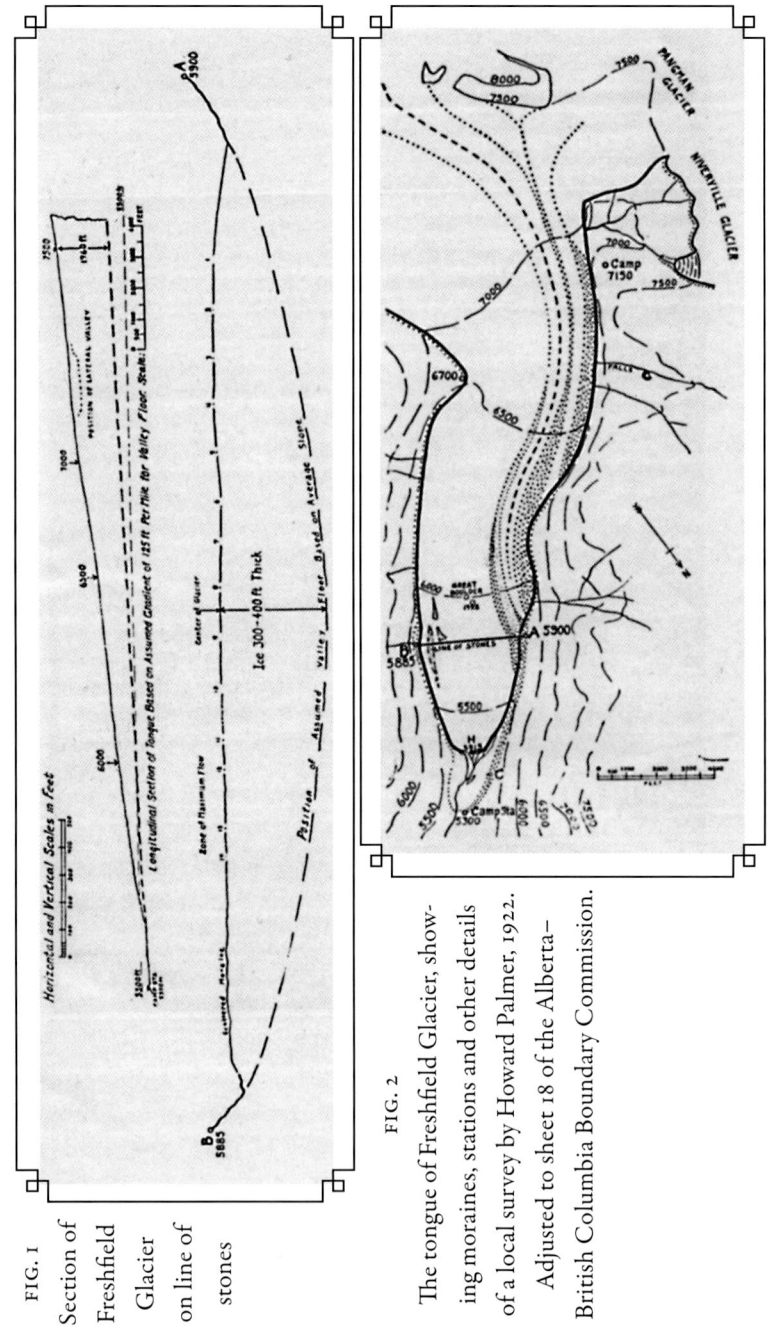

FIG. 1 Section of Freshfield Glacier on line of stones

FIG. 2 The tongue of Freshfield Glacier, showing moraines, stations and other details of a local survey by Howard Palmer, 1922. Adjusted to sheet 18 of the Alberta–British Columbia Boundary Commission.

Franchère continues his narrative: "On the morning of the 14th we began to climb the mountain which lay before us. We were obliged to stop every moment to take breath, so steep was the ascent. Happily it had frozen hard the night before, and the crust of the snow was sufficient to bear us. After two or three hours of incredible exertions and fatigues, we arrived at the *plateau* or summit, and followed the foot-prints of those who had preceded us. This mountain is placed between two others a great deal more elevated, compared with which it is but a hill, and of which, indeed, it is only, as it were, the valley.

"Our march soon became fatiguing, on account of the depth of the snow, which, softened by the rays of the sun, could no longer bear us as in the morning. We were obliged to follow exactly the traces of those who had preceded us, and to plunge our legs up to the knees in the holes they had made, so that it was as if we had put on and taken off, at every step, a very large pair of boots. At last we arrived at a good hard bottom, and a clear space, which our guide said was a little lake frozen over, and here we stopped for the night. This lake, or rather these lakes (for there are two) are situated in the midst of a valley or *cup* of the mountains. On either side were immense glaciers, or ice-bound rocks, on which the rays of the setting sun reflected in the most beautiful prismatic colors. One of these peaks was like a fortress of rock; it rose perpendicularly some fifteen or eighteen hundred feet above the level of the lakes, and had the summit covered with ice. Mr. J. Henry, who first discovered the pass, gave this extraordinary rock the name of M'Gillivray's Rock, in honor of one of the partners of the N.W. Company.

"The lakes themselves are not much over three or four hundred yards in circuit, and not over two hundred yards apart. Canoe River, which, as we have already seen, flows to the west, and falls into the Columbia, takes its rise in one of them; while the other gives birth to one of the branches of the *Athabasca*, which runs first eastward, then northward, and which, after its junction with the *Unjighah*, north of the Lake of the Mountains, takes the name of *Slave* river,[56] as far as the lake of that name, and afterward that of *M'Kenzie* river, until it empties into, or is lost in, the Frozen Ocean."

This is surprisingly accurate geography for 1814, and shows how much Mackenzie and Thompson had advanced the topographical knowledge of the Northwest.

Franchère continues: "Having cut a large pile of wood, and having, by tedious labor for nearly an hour, got through the ice to the clear water of the lake on which we were encamped, we supped frugally on pounded maize, arranged our bivouac, and passed a pretty good night, though it was bitterly cold. The most common wood of the locality was cedar and stunted pine. The heat of our bodies made the snow melt, and by morning the embers had reached the solid ice: the depth from the snow surface was about five feet. On the 15th, we continued our route, and soon began to descend the mountain."

A party whose course was attended with disaster was that of Ross Cox. He had reached Astoria, as clerk on Astor's second ship, the *Beaver*, and came overland, in 1817, with a large company under his charge. Because of illness and accident, seven men were sent back on reaching the mouth of Canoe River. A capsizing canoe carried with it all their provisions, and, with one exception, these unfortunates perished of starvation.

Cox[57] records the journey as follows: "Our baggage and provisions were divided between the nine remaining men, who in consequence of the number we had sent back, were obliged to carry about ninety pounds weight each, besides their own kits, which in such cases are never taken into consideration.

"Canoe River, which here joins the Columbia, is one of its principal sources. In the dry season, it is broad, but very shallow, and near its entrance spreads over several sandy shoals.

"On the morning of the 28th of May, at ten o'clock we set off on foot along the banks of Canoe River, which winds its way through a wide and cheerless valley. We had not proceeded far when we found it impossible, from the great rise of the water, to pass the ordinary fords. It appeared like a lake, and completely set at naught the topographical knowledge of our guide. This obliged us to strike into the woods, our progress through which was extremely fatiguing, and at three p.m. we bivouacked about two miles beyond a long woody point, which stretches some distance across the valley. The weather was cloudy all day, with slight showers, which during the night increased to heavy rain, from which we had no shelter.

"We proceeded on, and about noon, May 30th, encamped within a short distance of the *grande côte*, or principal hill, which we have to ascend in passing from the Columbia. The weather was charming all day.

"Shortly after dawn on the morning of the 31st we commenced the ascent of the first great hill. At its base were cedar and pine trees of enormous magnitude; but, in proportion as we ascended, they decreased in size, and at the summit of the hill their appearance was quite dwarfish. We completed the ascent in about four hours and a half, and did not find it so difficult as we had anticipated. This, however, may be attributed to our having commenced the task early in the morning.

"A short time before we reached the summit, and from thence to the level of the table land, our progress lay through a wilderness of deep snow, which we had to beat down to form a pathway for the loaded men. This work, owing to the holes into which several of the party occasionally fell, was both fatiguing and dangerous.

"At one p.m. we arrived at two small lakes, between which we encamped. They are only a few hundred feet each in circumference, and the distance between them does not exceed twenty-five or thirty feet. They lie on the most level part of the height of land, and are situated between an immense cut of the Rocky Mountains. From them two rivers take their rise, which pursue different courses, and fall into separate oceans; the first winds into the valley which we had lately left, and, after joining the upper part of the Columbia, empties itself into the North Pacific; while the other, called the Rocky Mountain River, a branch of the *Athabaska*, follows first an eastern and then a northern course, until it forms a junction with the *Unjigah*, or Peace River. This falls into Great Slave Lake, the waters of which are ultimately carried by M'Kenzie's River to the Arctic Ocean.

"The country around our encampment presented the wildest and most terrific appearance of desolation that can be well imagined. The sun shining on a range of stupendous glaciers, threw a chilling brightness over the chaotic mass of rocks, ice, and snow, by which we were surrounded. Close to our encampment one gigantic mountain of conical form towered majestically into the clouds far above the others (This is called M'Gillivray's Rock, in honour of the late Mr. William M'Gillivray, a principal director of the Company), while at intervals the interest of the scene was heightened by the rumbling of a descending *avalanche*; which, after being detached from its bed of centuries, increased in bulk in its headlong career downwards, until it burst with a frightful crash, more resembling the explosion of a magazine than the dispersion of a mass of snow."

Then follows that delightful classic paragraph: "One of our roughspun, unsophisticated Canadians, after gazing upwards for some time in silent wonder, exclaimed with much vehemence, 'I'll take my oath, dear friends, that God Almighty never made such a place!'"

In 1825, four years after the merging of the North-West and Hudson's Bay Companies, Alexander Ross, with the young Governor, George Simpson, crossed the pass, eastward bound. Ross[58] gives us an entertaining and graphic picture of the scene:

"Turning round to the east [from Boat Encampment on the Columbia River], the view is abruptly checked by the mountains; not in a continuous range, but heights rising above one another, almost everywhere shrouded in a dark haze, which renders a passage over them extremely doubtful. Yet through the apparently inaccessible barrier the traveller has to make his way.

"The Governor himself, generally at the head, made the first plunge into the river, and was not the last to get out. His smile encouraged others, and his example checked murmuring." Here, in a sentence, is the epitome of leadership!

The narrative continues: "But although we were now on the top of the Grande Côte, or Bell Hill, let not the reader imagine we had reached the highest part of the Rocky Mountains; for we saw heights towering above heights, until their distant summits were lost in the clouds. On the summit of the Grande Côte we found the snow eight feet deep, and there we encamped for the night.

"Leaving now the Grande Côte we advanced on the morning crust at a quick pace, through a broad level valley, thickly wooded with dwarf pines, for about six miles in an easterly direction, when we reached what is called the great height of land. At this place is a small circular basin of water, twenty yards in diameter, dignified with the name of a lake, out of which flow two small creeks. The one on the west side discharges itself into Portage River; that on the east joins the Athabaska River at a place called the Hole."

Then follows an explanation of a historic nomenclature: "This elevated pond is further dignified with the name of the 'Committee's Punch Bowl,' in honour of which his Excellency treated us to a bottle of wine, as we had neither time nor convenience to make a bowl of punch, although a glass of it would have been very acceptable. It is a tribute always paid to this place when a nabob of the fur-trade passes by."

In October 1826, Thomas Drummond, Assistant Naturalist to the Second Franklin Expedition, who had spent the year in the vicinity of Jasper House, made a journey across Athabaska Pass to Boat Encampment, on the Columbia Loop, and return.

He records[59] that "at about fifteen or twenty miles above the commencement of the Portage, we left the main branch of the Red Deer River, and followed a lesser stream that here joins it, winding along its banks, and not infrequently scrambling in the bed of it, until we reached a small lake, and the Height of Land. The lake is not more than two hundred yards in length, and is called the *Committee's Punch Bowl*. Out of its other extremity flows one of the tributary streams of the Columbia.

"On reaching the middle, I took a hearty draught, pleasing myself with the thought that some of the water I had tasted might have flowed either into the Frozen or Pacific Oceans."

He adds, almost in afterthought: "The first glacier I saw, was about twenty miles before reaching the lake; but I visited a very large one at ten miles nearer to the lake." This, as we shall see later, is the splendid icefall of Scott Glacier, a chief source of Whirlpool River.

Drummond reached the Boat Encampment on October 17th, and returned thence with Finan M'Donald to Jasper House, arriving on the 30th.

No man perhaps better exemplifies the fine type of many employed by the Hudson's Bay Company than Edward Ermatinger. The son of Lawrence Edward Ermatinger, Assistant Commissary General, he was born on the Island of Elba, off the west coast of Italy, in February 1797. Something of a genius, he attained fluency in the Latin, Italian, and French languages, and became a proficient musician, playing the flute and the violin—talents which were not unuseful in the later times of lonely winters in the trading posts. Being taken to Canada, he served with the

Hudson's Bay Company from 1818 until 1828, eventually settling in St. Thomas, Ontario, where he became merchant, banker, and postmaster.

In his journal, Ermatinger[60] has recorded three crossings of Athabaska Pass: business-like accounts with but little description of natural surroundings. On the first crossing, in 1827, the botanist David Douglas—of whom more will be said—accompanied him:

"March 20th; fair weather. The Express boat leaves Vancouver [Fort Vancouver, seven miles north of the present city of Portland, Oregon. In 1846 it was the largest Post of the Hudson's Bay Company] at a quarter before six o'clock. A second boat accompanies us as far as the Chûtes to assist in carrying over them, and to strengthen the party. Passengers Messrs. McLoughlin, McLeod, Douglas, Pambrun, Annace, and E. Ermatinger.

"April 28th. Two of our Iroquois who would not have carried snow-shoes from the Boat Encampment, had I not insisted upon their having them, now found them very useful and were glad to put them on. A wolverine hovers about our camp. Mr. Douglas wounds him, but he escapes.

"Monday, 30th. Arrive at the foot of the Grande Côte at eight o'clock. Ascend it for two miles and encamp at eleven a.m. Experienced some difficulty in finding the proper track.

"Tuesday, 1st. Fine weather. Start at half-past four a.m. Snow not less than between four and five feet deep. Continue to ascend the Grande Côte by very short stages for about two miles till we meet the Rocky Hills on the right at eight a.m. when we incline to the left a little and having journeyed I should say between three and four miles, encamp nearly a mile on this side of the height of land at noon. We experienced again much difficulty in finding and keeping our road. In fact we could not ascend fifty yards before the people were wandering in every direction in search of the track. What few marks have been made to point out the way I conceive are concealed by the depth of snow. Kill a partridge.

"Wednesday, 2nd. Fine weather. Resume our journey at three a.m. in order to avail ourselves of the crust on the snow. Course northeast. Travel at a good pace for about seventeen miles and stop at eleven a.m. to breakfast and give the people a rest during the heat of the day."

Leading the York Factory Brigade, westbound, in the autumn of the same year, he writes: "Started at eight a.m. and encamped near the height of land, having passed through some very bad swamps and mires during the day. View of the mountains very grand. The road was never better; we had not the least snow on the way. Apisasis killed a young grizzly bear at the height of land, and one of the men killed a martin on the Big Hill."

In May 1828, Ermatinger was again eastward bound. He tells us there was but little snow on the Big Hill and no necessity for using snow-shoes. "Find little snow till we get half way up the Hill. ...take breakfast on the top of the Hill between 9 and 10— resume at noon and proceed to within 4 miles of the Height of Land and encamp at half past 3 p.m. ...

"Rained and snowed during the whole of last night—day fine but cold. Start at half past 4 a.m. Pass the Height of Land at six. Proceed on deep snow near to Campement de fusil—take breakfast. Afterwards snow diminishes fast."

A journey across Athabaska Pass was, in those days, a serious undertaking; fur-traders could not be expected to keep extensive journals, still less to waste time in admiration of scenic beauty. But what a pity Ermatinger could not have told us a little more about David Douglas and his scramblings at the pass summit!

The young Scots botanist, who came eastward with Ermatinger, in 1827, is remembered because the Douglas fir (*Pseudotsuga douglasii*) bears his name, and because he named mounts Brown and Hooker.

Let us first see what Douglas has to say regarding the pass itself. In his detailed diary,[61] kept while on the trail, he tells us, "In the grey of the morning we resumed our route on snowshoes in the wood about three-quarters of a mile. Entered a second valley, course north-east. Rested after having travelled two and a quarter miles, in the course of which we made seven fordings over the same river that we crossed yesterday. Continued in the same course for the distance of four miles more until reaching the east end, making four fordings more. Here the stream divides into two branches, that on the left flowing from the north, that on the right due east. Took our course in the angle between the two, north-east, entering a thick wood of the same kinds of timber already noticed. *Pinus balsamea* more abundant and of greater size. After passing a half mile in the wood, reached the foot of what is called the *Big Hill,* also thickly wooded. Steep and very fatiguing to ascend, the snow four to six feet deep in the higher spots. The ravines or gullies unmeasurable, and towards noon becoming soft, sinking, ascending two steps and sometimes sliding back three, the snowshoes twisting and throwing the weary traveller down (and I speak as I feel), so feeble that lie I must among the snow, like a broken-down waggon-horse entangled in his harnessing, weltering to rescue myself.

"No water; melted snow, which makes good tea; find no fault with the food, glad of anything. The remainder of the day is spent as follows: On arriving at a camp, one gathers a few dry twigs and makes fire, two or three procuring fuel for the night, and as many more gathering green soft branches of *Pinus balsamea* or *P.canadensis* to sleep on, termed 'flooring the house,' each hanging up his wet clothing to the fire, repairing snowshoes, and arranging his load for the ensuing day, that no time may be lost. In the morning, rise, shake the blanket, tie it on the top, and then try who is to be at the next stage first. Dreamed last night of being in Regent Street, London! Yet far distant. Progress nine miles."

The graphic description continues: "This morning our fire that was kindled on the snow had sunk into a hole six feet deep, making a natural kitchen. Started at daybreak, finding the snow deeper and the trees gradually diminish toward the summit; laborious to ascend. Went frequently off the path in consequence of not seeing the marks on the trees, being covered with the snow. Reached the top at ten, three miles, where we made a short stay to rest. Course north-east. Descended in the same direction and came on the river which we left two days before. Passed in the valley two small level spots clear of wood, and one low point of wood of small trees, where we camped at midday, being unable to proceed further from the deep soft snow. Progress seven miles.

"My ankles and knees pained me so much from exertion that my sleep was short and interrupted. Rose at three a.m. and had fire kindled. Started at a quarter-past four through a gradually rising point of wood which terminated three hundred yards below the highest part of the pass in the valley. An hour's walk took us to one of the head springs of the Columbia, a small lake or basin twenty yards in diameter, circular, which divides its waters, half flowing to the Pacific and half to the hyperborean sea—namely the headwaters of the Athabaska River. A small lake, about 47° of N. latitude, divides its waters between the Columbia and one of the branches of the Missamac, which is singular. This being a half-way house, or stage, I willingly quickened my pace, now descending on the east side. This little river in the course of a few miles assumes a considerable size and is very varied.

"There are two passes, one four miles from its source and one seven, when it finds its way over cascades, confined falls, and cauldrons of fine white and blue limestone and columns of basalt, like the feeders of the Columbia at the deep passes of the mountain; where the torrents descend with furious rapidity it spreads out into a broad channel bounded by the mountains. The descent from the east is much greater than from the west, the mountain more abrupt and equally rugged. Found the snow eight miles below the ridge gradually diminish. The heat increases and the quantity of snow on the east not equal to the west. Passed on the right a very high (perhaps 4000 feet) perpendicular rock with a flat top, and three miles lower down on the same side two higher ones, rising to peaks about a mile apart at the base with a high background which appears two-thirds glacier, and in the valley or bosom of the three, columns and pillars of ice running out in all the ramifications of the Corinthian order."[62]

In a condensed journal, written some time after the actual events, there may be found a further description of the pass. After leaving Boat Encampment, Douglas informs us,[63] "We crossed at the angle between the two streams and commenced our ascent of the 'Big Hill.' The snow being so deep, exceeding six feet, the footpath markings on the trees were hidden, so that some difficulty was experienced in keeping the way; the steep ascent, the deep gullies, and brushwood and fallen timber rendered it laborious. Camped two miles up the hill, having gained in all nine miles.

"We continued our ascent, and at ten had the satisfaction to reach the summit, where we made a short stoppage to rest ourselves, and then descended the eastern side of the Big Hill to a small, round, open piece of ground through which flowed the smaller or east feeder of the Columbia and the same stream we left yesterday at the western base of the Big Hill. Near this point we put up at midday.

"At three o'clock I felt the cold so much, the thermometer stood at only 2° below zero, that I was obliged to rise and enliven the fire and have myself comfortably warmed before starting. Through three hundred yards of gradually rising, open, low, pine wood we passed, and about the same distance of open ground took us to the basin of this mighty river, a circular small lake, twenty yards in diameter, in the centre of the valley, with *a small outlet at the west end—namely, the Columbia;* and *a small outlet at the east end—namely, one of the branches of the Athabasca, which must be considered one of the tributaries of the McKenzie River.* This is not the only fact of two opposite streams flowing from the same lake.

"This, 'The Committee Punchbowl,' is considered the halfway house. We were glad the more laborious and arduous part of the journey was done. The little stream Athabasca, over which we conveniently stepped, soon assumed a considerable size, and was dashed over cascades and formed cauldrons of limestone and basalt seven miles below the pass; like the tributaries of the Columbia on the west side, the Athabasca widens to a narrow lake and has a much greater descent than the Columbia."

In his journals David Douglas describes his ascent of a peak close to Athabaska Pass, and the naming of mounts Brown and Hooker. The over-estimated altitudes, together with the opinions of contemporaneous writers regarding the elevation of the region, require further consideration.

CHAPTER IX
ATHABASKA PASS AND THE VOYAGEURS, 1846–1872

(Later travellers, 1846–1872)

*"Even where all men go, none may have stopped;
what all men see, none may have observed."*

JAMES D. FORBES

The fur-trade was now at its height and, for more than forty years after David Douglas, groups of travellers continued to cross the Continental Divide by way of Athabaska Pass. Few indeed are the individuals who were able or took the trouble to write down their experiences; yet those who did so form a strangely interesting company—a priest, a soldier, an artist, a physician, a surveyor. Remarkable it is that the diverse pursuits of these men should eventually lead them through a common ground; fortunate that their dissimilar viewpoints were for a little while united in the interpretation of the wonders of nature. What matter if the interpretation was often vague and faulty? The wonder of it is that every man who left a written record of his journey—though his outlook in other respects differed completely from that of his fellow-travellers—was spellbound by the natural marvels confronting him.

In April 1846, the Jesuit Father Pierre Jean De Smet—he who first described the geysers of the Yellowstone—*en route* to Oregon Missions, crossed the pass westward. Spending some time in the Athabaska Valley, and being well received by its inhabitants, he informs us[64] that "Lake Jasper, eight miles in length, is situated at the base of the first great mountain chain. The fort of the same name, and the second lake, are twenty miles higher, and in the heart of the mountains. The rivers Violin and Medicine on the southern side, and the Assiniboine on the northern, must be crossed to arrive there, and to reach the height of land at the *du Committees Punch Bowl*, we cross the rivers Maligne, Gens de Colets, Miette and Trou, which we ascended to its source."

The missionary gives a sympathetic description of his leave-taking: "As the time approached at which I was to leave my new children in Christ, they earnestly begged leave to honor me, before my departure, with a little ceremony to prove their attachment, and that their children might always remember him who had first put them in the way of life. Each one discharged his musket in the direction of the highest mountain, a large rock jutting out in the form of a sugar loaf, and with three loud hurrahs gave it my name. This mountain is more than 14,000 feet high, and is covered with perpetual snow. On the 25th of April, I bade farewell to my kind friend Mr. Frazer, and his amiable children, who had treated me with every mark of attention and kindness."

Roche de Smet is still a landmark of Jasper Park, but the visitor of today will not recognize it from the description of the worthy father!

De Smet further describes his route, and the objects which interested him: "We resumed our journey the following day and arrived about nightfall on the banks of the Athabaska, at the spot called the 'Great Crossing.' Here we deviated from the course of that river, and entered the valley de la Fourche du Trou. As we approached the highlands the snow became much deeper. On the 1st of May, we reached the great Bature, which has all the appearance of a lake just drained of its waters. Here we pitched our tent to await the arrival of people from Columbia, who always pass by this route on the way to Canada and York Factory. Not far from the place of our encampment, we found a new object of surprise and admiration. An immense mountain of pure ice, 1500 feet high, enclosed between two enormous rocks. So great is the transparency of this beautiful ice, that we can easily distinguish objects in it to the depth of more than six feet. One would say, by its appearance, that in some sudden and extraordinary swell of the river, immense icebergs had been forced between these rocks, and had there piled themselves on one another, so as to form this magnificent glacier. What gives some color of probability to this conjecture is, that on the other side of the glacier, there is a large lake of considerable elevation.[65] From the base of this gigantic iceberg, the river Trou takes its rise."

All this information De Smet has been communicating in letters to his friends at home: "You have learned that I had arrived at the base of the Great Glacier, the source of the river *du Trou*, which is a tributary of the Athabaska, or Elk River. I will now give your reverence the continuation of my arduous and difficult journey across the main chain of the Rocky Mountains, and down the Columbia, on my return to my dear brethren in Oregon.

"Towards the evening of the 6th of May, we discovered, at the distance of about three miles, the approach of two men in snow shoes, who soon joined us. They proved to be the forerunners of the English Company, which, in the spring of each year, go from Fort Vancouver to York Factory, situated at the mouth of the river Nelson, near the fifty-eighth degree north latitude. In the morning my little train was early ready; we proceeded, and after a march of eight miles we fell in with the gentlemen of the Hudson Bay Company. The time of our reunion was short, but interesting and joyful. The great melting of the snow had already begun, and we were obliged to be on the alert to cross in due time the now swelling rapids and rivers.

"The news between travellers who meet in the mountains is quickly conveyed to one another. The leaders of the company were my old friends Mr. Ermatinger, of the Honorable Hudson Bay Company, and two distinguished officers of the English army, Captains Ward [Warre] and Vavasseur [Vavasour], whom I had the honor of entertaining last year at the Great Kalispel Lake. Capt. Ward is the gentleman who had the kindness to take charge of my letters for the States and for Europe.

"Fifteen Indians of the Kettle-Fall tribe accompanied him. Many of them had scaled the mountains with one hundred and fifty pounds weight upon their backs."

The gentlemen encountered by De Smet are worthy of some notice. In 1845, when there was a possibility of trouble between England and the United States regarding the Oregon boundary, Capt. Henry J. Warre, and Lieut. M. Vavasour, R.E., were sent by the British Government on a secret mission to seek out routes for troops through the Rocky Mountains. Returning, they left Fort Vancouver on March 26, 1846, travelling via Fort Colville to Boat Encampment at the Columbia Loop.

Captain Warre's account of the crossing of Athabaska Pass is brief; but he seems to have been none the less impressed, for he says,[66] "We had for many days been surrounded by magnificent mountains, and had passed through such a beautiful country, that the effect of this grand and solitary scene was partially destroyed by the sublimity of that which had preceded it. The mountains are about 10,000 feet in height, unequalled in any part of Switzerland for the ruggedness of their peaks and beauty of form, capped and dazzling in their white mantle of snow.

"On the fourth day we ascended the 'Grande Côte' to the height of land on which are situated two small lakes, from whence flow two rivers, the waters of which fall into different oceans—the Columbia into the Pacific, and the Athabaska into the Frozen ocean.

"We had scarcely walked ten miles, when the joyful sound of human voices assured us of more immediate relief, and we soon encountered a party of men who had been sent to meet us, with provisions, accompanied by Le Père De Smet, a Jesuit priest from Belgium, and chief of the Roman Catholic missionaries in the Columbia district, who was on his return to that part of Oregon."

Captain Warre was a trained artist: he published his journal, now one of the rarest items in the literature of the Northwest. The plates accompanying the few pages of text are exquisitely done, and present the earliest attempt to illustrate adequately the scenery of the Columbia Valley.

Following De Smet came the wandering artist Paul Kane, to whom Governor George Simpson had granted permission to cross with the Hudson's Bay Express. Kane's purpose was to make portraits and pictures among the various Indian tribes—a work which he carried into effect.

Of his westward crossing, in November 1846, he writes :[67] "We were now close upon the mountains, and it is scarcely possible to conceive the intense force with which the wind howled through a gap formed by the perpendicular rock called 'Miëtte's Rock,' 1500 feet high, on the one side, and a lofty mountain on the other. The former derives its appellation from a French voyageur, who climbed its summit and sat smoking his pipe, with his legs hanging over the fearful abyss.

"Today we attained what is called the Height of Land. There is a small lake at this eminence called the Committee's Punchbowl; this forms the headwaters of the branch of the Columbia River on the west side of the mountains, and of the Athabasca on the east side. It is about three-quarters of a mile in circumference, and is remarkable as giving rise to two such mighty rivers; the waters of the one emptying into the Pacific Ocean, and the other into the Arctic Sea. We encamped on its margin, with difficulty protecting ourselves from the intense cold.

"The lake being frozen over to some depth, we walked across it, and shortly after commenced the descent of the Grande Côte, having been seven days continually ascending. The descent was so steep, that it took us only one day to get down to nearly the same level as that of Jasper's House. The descent was a work of great difficulty on snow shoes, particularly for those carrying loads; their feet frequently slipped from under them, and the loads rolled down the hill. Some of the men, indeed, adopted the mode of rolling such loads as would not be injured down before them. On reaching the bottom, we found eight men waiting, whom M'Gillveray and the guide had sent on to assist us to Boat Encampment, and we all encamped together."

Kane and his party took ten days between Jasper House and Boat Encampment—fast time for loaded men under winter conditions of travel. Just a year later, we find the artist returning homeward over the pass. He took the hardships of the road without grumbling and not without a certain good humour: "We started an hour before daybreak to ascend the stupendous Grande Côte, and soon found the snow becoming deeper at every step. One of our horses fell down a declivity of twenty-five to thirty feet with a heavy load on his back, and, strange to say, neither deranged his load nor hurt himself. We soon had him on the track again as well as ever, except that he certainly looked a little *bothered*. The snow now reached up to the horses' sides as we toiled along, and reached the summit just as the sun sank below the horizon; but we could not stop here, as there was no food for the horses. We were therefore obliged to push on past the Committee's Punch Bowl, a lake I have before described.

"It was intensely cold, as might be supposed, in this elevated region. Although the sun shone during the day with intense brilliancy, my long beard became one solid mass of ice."

What a picture it must have made—that lonely procession, passing the frozen summit lake, in the twilight; the bothered pack-horse (how well-packed he must have been!) led by an artist-adventurer, burdened, in that pre-Gillette era, with his frozen whiskers!

But a more modern day was dawning. The British Government, interested in locating passes and routes suitable for railroads, sent out an Expedition, under Captain John Palliser, which remained in the field during the years 1857–60. Their physician and chief explorer was Dr. Hector, afterward Sir James Hector, a man renowned among the Indians for the cures he made among their people; and well remembered for his long and speedy winter journeys with dog-teams.

In February 1859, Dr. Hector was at Jasper House contemplating a visit to Athabaska Pass. He mentions[68] that Jasper House "is a small post of the Hudson's Bay Company which had been abandoned for some years, but was this winter again occupied and placed under the charge of Mr. Moberly, who received us most kindly.

"Jasper House is beautifully situated on an open plain, about six miles in extent, within the first range of the mountains. As the valley makes a bend above and below, it appears to be completely encircled by mountains, which rise from 4000 to 5000 feet, with bold craggy outlines; the little group of buildings which form the 'fort' have been constructed, in keeping with their picturesque situation, after the Swiss style, with overhanging roofs and trellised porticos. The dwelling-house and two stores form three sides of a square, and these, with a little detached hut, form the whole of this remote establishment. The general direction of the valley of the Athabasca through the mountains seems to be from south to north, with a very little easting. Four miles below the fort the Athabasca receives a large tributary from the W.N.W., which is known either as the Assiniboine or the Snake Indian River. Opposite to the fort, from the opposite direction, comes Rocky River, and these two streams, with the Athabasca, define four great mountain masses. Thus, on the east side of the main river there is the Roche Miette, which, although really some miles distant, seems to overhang the fort. Higher up the valley is Roche Jacque, and on the west side of the valley, and opposite to these two, we have the Roche de Smet and Roche Ronde. These names were given long ago to the mountains, at a time when a great number travelled by this route across the mountains."

Dr. Hector always enjoyed a mountain-scramble, for a few days later he notes, "I started with Moberly to ascend the Roche Miette, and as we had to follow down the valley for some miles and cross the river, we took horses with us for so far. I now saw where we had forded the river the other night in the dark, and it certainly looked an ugly place, and if we had only seen where we were going, we might have hesitated to attempt it. Having ridden about six miles from the fort, we left our horses, and commenced the ascent of the mountain, carrying with us a small pair of snow shoes, with which to cross any bad places we might come to; but as we found the snow was everywhere hard, with a glassy surface that supported our weight, we soon left them behind. Indeed it was only at intervals that we required to cross patches of snow, for we followed a ridge or *'crate,'* as they call it, from which it had been swept by the violent wind of the last few days. After a long and steep climb, we reached a sharp peak far above any vegetation, and which, as measured by the aneroid, is 3500 feet above the valley. The great cubical block which forms the top of this mountain, still towered above us for 2000 feet, and is quite inaccessible from this side at least, and is said to have been only once ascended from the south side by a hunter named Miette, after whom it was named."

On February 10th Dr. Hector started up the Athabaska, in company with Moberly, the guide Tekarra, and a Canadian named Arkand. On the following day they reached a point opposite to Miette's House where there was once a trading post, at the point where the track branches up the Caledonian Valley to Fraser River, from that which leads to Boat Encampment and the Columbia.

Dr. Hector was now on the present site of Jasper, describing it as follows: "The valley of the Athabasca, above Miette's House, is very wide, and is bounded to the east by a long mountain composed of the earthy shales, with only a few detached masses of the more massive strata capping them. We now descended to the south, and passed the *Campement des roches,* where we found many signs of former travellers, and among others our friend Hardisty's[69] name, written on a tree last summer as he returned from the boat encampment, where he had been sent to meet Mr. Dallas. We then reached the *Prairie des vaches,* where we encamped, intending to take our horses no further, as beyond this point there is little or no pasture at any season, but especially in winter."

No further progress was made, because "Tekarra's foot is so much inflamed with his hunting exertions, that he will not be able to guide us up the valley to the Committee's Punch Bowl, so I changed my plan and followed up the main stream of the Athabasca instead. At noon we reached the mouth of Whirlpool River, which is the stream that descends from the Committee's Punch Bowl, and I found the latitude 52° 46' 54". Leaving the rest to follow up the Athabasca, I ascended a mountain opposite to the valley of Whirlpool River, and had a fine view up it towards the boat encampment. Having been directed by Tekarra, I easily recognized Mount Brown and Mount Hooker, which are much like the mountains towards the source of the North Saskatchewan. They seemed distant thirty miles to the south by west. At nightfall we encamped where high rocky banks began to hem in the river.

"After following up the river for ten miles we found it became quite a mountain torrent, hemmed in by lofty and rugged mountains, two of which, that were very prominent, I named after my friends Mr. Christie[70] of Edmonton, and Moberly."

Then came the later, final exploring for the railroads. During the summer of 1872, Walter Moberly, having been ordered to discontinue his survey for the Canadian Pacific Railroad through Howse Pass, came northward across Athabasca Pass.

On the Columbia River he writes,[71] "We ran many rapids and portaged others, then came to a lake which I named 'Kinbaskit,' much to the old chief's delight."

Moberly did not go all the way to Boat Encampment, but says that on August 27th "...we resumed our journey, and cross[ed] a high ridge, from which the view was magnificent, particularly of the Selkirk Mountains, where we could see hundreds of snow-capped peaks. We waded the [Wood] River many times, and camped at the foot of Mount Brown, opposite the old camping ground of the H.B. Company.

"We now began the steep ascent by the old H.B. Company's trail to reach the depression between mounts Brown and Hooker—the 'Athabasca Pass'—gaining an elevated valley, with grassy glades and groves of firs. Where the walking was fair we made good headway, and camped a short distance north of the celebrated 'Committee's Punch-Bowl.' Following along, and gradually ascending Mount Brown, we saw a grizzly bear above us, and shot a ptarmigan, and then coming on a well-beaten cariboo trail, reached the top of a ridge with a high conical peak immediately on our right, and a mass of hard perpetual snow on the north side of the ridge, down which we went with difficulty, seeing the fresh tracks of four cariboo. There was a fine view from the top of this ridge, the mountains to the north forming a magnificent amphitheatre, some five miles in width, and the innumerable torrents dashing down the rocks, with the white foam like silver spray, the thick groves of dark firs, the grassy glades and many small lakes, or ponds, rendering it enchanting."[72]

"From what I saw of it, my impression is that there is a pass through from the Canoe to the Whirlpool River, which at some future day may be utilised, but I cannot be quite certain of the pass, as my examination was very limited, and therefore imperfect. The stream I followed is the true source of the Fraser River, and I had thus been within a comparatively short space of time at the source of the two large rivers of the Pacific Coast, the Columbia and the Fraser."

Moberly later returned to Kinbasket Lake and assisted in getting the remainder of his outfit to the site of Henry House, where they wintered. His description[73] indicates the difficulties under which the early survey parties labored: "On the evening of the 1st of October the trail was passable though not finished, as a good deal of corduroying was needed, to the foot of Mount Hooker, a distance of about twenty miles from the Columbia, and nearly all the pack animals on the way between the Boat Encampment and the above point. On the 2nd I started back for party T, from the foot of the mountain, taking Messrs. Green and Hall a part of the way up Mount Hooker to show them where to open the trail and get the supplies to. My endeavor now was to get the supplies all to the height of land, the ascent to which in one place is at an angle of elevation of about seventy-five degrees, so that should I not be enabled to pack them all the way to the Athabasca depot before stopped by the snow, they would be over the height of land, and there would be a descending grade along the Whirlpool and Athabasca rivers over which to convey them on dog sleighs."

Thus we have followed the stories of the *voyageurs* over a period of sixty years, forming a historic tradition excelled in by no other area of the Canadian Alps. The narratives are many, scarcely two in exact agreement as to detail, exaggerated as were the tales of the early European alpine wanderers: yet all possessing a certain fascination in the evident appeal of natural phenomena to men unaccustomed to mountain travel, but nevertheless impressed by the strange wonders of a higher level.

Athabaska Pass was one of the first trans-continental gateways of North America—the first through which came any large number of white people. Through it passed pioneers to whom, in a measure, we owe the foundation of civilization on the North American continent. Fortunate are we that something of their story has been preserved. How utterly strange that their difficult "Height of Land" should become an alpine playground of today!

CHAPTER X
NINETEENTH CENTURY SPECULATION IN REGARD TO ALTITUDE AT ATHABASKA PASS

"The adventure and sport of exploration are but a fleeting record compared with contributions to knowledge, for they are incidents on the way and not the goal of exploratory research."

ISAIAH BOWMAN

Dr. Hector, of the Palliser Expedition, has summed up the traffic across the Athabaska Pass, writing: "As late as 1853 there was communication at two seasons by this post [Jasper House] with the Columbia district. In March, when the snow had acquired a crust, the express, with letters and accounts, started from Edmonton by the route I had just followed, and continued on to the boat encampment, to which place, by the time they arrived, owing to the earlier spring on the west side of the mountain, the brigade of boats had ascended from Vancouver. The mail from the western department was then exchanged, and taken back to Edmonton, and thence to Norway House, along with the Jasper House furs.

"The second time of communication was in the autumn, after

the Saskatchewan brigade returned to Edmonton in the beginning of September, upon which the officers and men bound for the western department, taking with them the subsidy of otter skins that the Company annually paid the Russian Government for the rent of the N.W. coast, crossed the portage to Fort Assiniboine, then ascended the Athabasca in boats to Jasper House with pack-horses, reached the boat encampment, and then descended the Columbia to Vancouver, where they arrived generally about the 1st of November. The journey from York Factory or Hudson's Bay to the Pacific coast by this route generally occupied three and a half months, and involved an amount of hardship and toil that cannot be appreciated by those who have not seen boat travelling in these territories."

Nearly every individual who has left a descriptive record of the Athabaska Pass region, seems to have indulged in speculation as to the altitude of the nearby mountains. Thus we find David Thompson stating:[74] "To ascertain the height of the Rocky Mountains above the level of the Ocean had long occupied my attention, but without any satisfaction to myself. At the greatest elevation of the passage across the Mountains by the Athabasca River, the point by boiling water gave 11,000 feet, and the peaks of the Mountains are full 7000 feet above this passage, and the general height may be fairly taken at 18,000 feet above the Pacific Ocean."

James Renwick, professor of chemistry and physics at Columbia College, communicated, in 1836, the following information to Washington Irving:[75] "In conversation with Simon M'Gillivray, Esq., a partner of the Northwest company, he stated to me his impression, that the mountains in the vicinity of the route pursued by the traders of that company were nearly as high as the Himalayas. He had himself crossed by this route, seen the snowy summits of the peaks and experienced a degree of cold which required a spirit thermometer to indicate it. His authority for the estimate of the heights was a gentleman who had been employed for several years as surveyor of that company. This conversation occurred about sixteen years hence.

"A year or two afterwards, I had the pleasure of dining, at Major Delafield's, with Mr. Thompson, the gentleman referred to by Mr. M'Gillivray. I inquired of him in relation to the circumstances mentioned by Mr. M'Gillivray, and he stated that, by joint means of the barometric and trigonometric measurement, he had ascertained the height of one of the peaks to be about twenty-five thousand feet, and there were others of nearly the same height in the vicinity."

It may be calculated from this, that Thompson made his statement to Renwick about 1822; and, if the material be reliable, it would indicate that Thompson was responsible for the exaggerated altitudes. At least this dating of his statement precedes the crossing of Athabaska Pass by either Sir George Simpson or David Douglas.

While it has been supposed that Thompson later obtained certain of his figures for altitude from Sir George Simpson, there was another gentleman named Simpson, who may have been equally responsible for the erroneous figures. Thomas Drummond, Assistant Naturalist to the Second Franklin Expedition, makes the following statement in his journal:[76] "The kindness of Lieut. Simpson, R.N., who was at this time employed in surveying the country, gave me the opportunity of ascertaining the latitude of the commencement and termination of the Rocky Mountains Portage. The height of one of the mountains, taken from the commencement of the Portage, Lieut. Simpson reckons at 5900 feet above its apparent base, and he thinks that the altitude of the Rocky Mountains may be stated at about 16,000 feet above the level of the sea."

In none of the literature consulted is there the slightest evidence that David Thompson and Sir George Simpson ever met.

David Douglas, however, became acquainted with Sir George, at Norway House, in 1827.

Franchère,[77] more conservative, comes nearer the truth: "The geographer Pinkerton is assuredly mistaken, when he gives these mountains an elevation of but three thousand feet above the level of the sea; from my own observations I would not hesitate to give them six thousand; we attained, in crossing them, an elevation probably of fifteen hundred feet above the valleys, and were not, perhaps, nearer than half way of their total height, while the valleys themselves must be considerably elevated above the level of the Pacific, considering the prodigious number of rapids and falls which are met with in the Columbia, from the first falls to Canoe river.

"Be that as it may, if these mountains yield to the Andes in elevation and extent, they very much surpass in both respects the Appalachian chain, regarded until recently as the principal mountains of North America; they give rise, accordingly, to an infinity of streams, and to the greatest rivers of the continent."

Ross Cox[78] goes to the other extreme: "The height of the Rocky Mountains varies considerably. The table land which we crossed I should take to be about 11,000 feet above the level of the sea. From the immense number of rapids we had to pass in ascending the Columbia, and its precipitous bed above the lakes, I consider that at their base the mountains cannot be much under 8000 feet above the level of the Pacific; and from the valley of Canoe River to the level part of the heights of land cannot be less than 3000 feet, but the actual altitude of their highest summits must be much greater. They are covered with eternal ice and snow, and will probably be for ever inaccessible to man."

Thus we see that by the time David Douglas crossed the pass, in 1827, there was already a well-established tradition as to the exalted heights supposed to flank the Height of Land. Douglas saw the mountains under the snow conditions preceding spring, and this may also have added to his perplexity. Too much blame, therefore, must not be placed upon Douglas as the originator of the over-estimated figures of altitude, and we had best be content to retain Douglas' accounts of his doings as a charming historic story, and not inquire too earnestly into the facts of the case.

Douglas wrote two journals—a lengthy one, on the trail; and a shorter, done apparently after his return to England. From the shorter journal[79] we quote: "After breakfast, about one o'clock, being well refreshed, I set out with the view of ascending what appeared to be the highest peak on the north or left-hand side. The height from its apparent base exceeds 6000 feet, 17000 feet above the level of the sea.

"After passing over the lower ridge of about 200 feet, by far the most difficult and fatiguing part, on snow-shoes, there was a crust on the snow, over which I walked with the greatest ease. A few mosses and lichens, *Andreae* and *Jungermanniae*, were seen. At the elevation of 4800 feet vegetation no longer exists—not so much as a lichen of any kind to be seen, 1200 feet of eternal ice. The view from the summit is of that cast too awful to afford pleasure—nothing as far as the eye can reach in every direction but mountains towering above each other, rugged beyond all description; the dazzling reflection from the snow, the heavenly arena of the solid glacier, and the rainbow-like tints of its shattered fragments, together with the enormous icicles suspended from the perpendicular rocks; the majestic but terrible avalanche hurtling down from the southerly exposed rocks producing a crash, and groans through the distant valleys, only equalled by an earthquake. Such gives us a sense of the stupendous and wondrous works of the Almighty. This peak, the highest yet known in the northern continent of America, I felt a sincere pleasure in naming MOUNT BROWN, in honour of R. Brown, Esq.,[80] the illustrious botanist, no less distinguished by the amiable qualities of his refined mind. A little to the south is one nearly of the same height, rising more into a sharp point, which I named MOUNT HOOKER, in honour of my early patron the enlightened and learned Professor of Botany in the University of Glasgow, Dr. Hooker,[81] to whose kindness I, in a great measure, owe my success hitherto in life, and I feel exceedingly glad of an opportunity of recording a simple but sincere token of my kindest regard for him and respect for his profound talents. I was not on this mountain."

In the lengthy diary[82] the account is simpler, and more accurate: "After breakfast at one o'clock, being as I conceive on the highest part of the route, I became desirous of ascending one of the peaks, and accordingly I set out alone on snowshoes to that on the left hand or west side, being to all appearance the highest. The labour of ascending the lower part, which is covered with pines, is great beyond description, sinking on many occasions to the middle. Half-way up vegetation ceases entirely, not so much as a vestige of moss or lichen on the stones. Here I found it less laborious as I walked on the hard crust. One-third from the summit it becomes a mountain of pure ice, sealed far over by Nature's hand as a momentous work of Nature's God. The height from its base may be about 5500 feet: timber, 2750 feet; a few mosses and lichen, 500 more; 1000 feet of perpetual snow; the remainder, towards the top 1250, as I have said, glacier with a thin covering of snow on it. The ascent took me five hours; descending only one and a quarter. Places where the descent was gradual, I tied my shoes together, making them carry me in turn as a sledge. Sometimes I came down at one spell 500 to 700 feet in the space of one minute and a half. I remained twenty minutes, my thermometer standing at 18°; night closing fast in on me, and no means of fire, I was reluctantly forced to descend. The sensation I felt is beyond what I can give utterance to. Nothing as far as the eye could perceive, but mountains such as I was on, and many higher, some rugged beyond any description, striking the mind with horror blended with a sense of the wondrous works of the Almighty. The aerial tints of the snow, the heavenly azure of the solid glaciers, the rainbow-like hues of their thin broken fragments, the huge mossy icicles hanging from the perpendicular rocks with the snow sliding from the steep southern rocks with amazing velocity, producing a crash and grumbling like the shock of an earthquake, the echo of which resounding in the valley for several minutes."

Good description this, for a non-mountaineer; exaggerated, of course, but containing no mention of naming the peaks or over-estimation of their altitude as does the short journal. As will be shown (see Appendix G), the latter, embellished at a later time, was not composed in the field but in England and had the names and altitudes added upon information received from outside sources.

Letters from Douglas to William Hooker show that Douglas superintended the map which appeared in Volume I of *Flora Boreali Americana*. Dated 1829, it is the first map on which mounts Brown and Hooker appear, and indicates them as flanking *either side* of the pass. Drummond's route is marked in red, Parry's in blue, and Douglas' in green.

In the *Companion to the Botanical Magazine*,[83] in which Douglas' journal is transcribed, the copyist has made changes: "Being well rested by one o'clock, I set out with the view of ascending what seemed to be the highest peak on the North. Its height does not appear to be less than 16,000 or 17,000 feet above the level of the sea. After passing over the lower ridge, I came to about 1200 feet of by far the most difficult and fatiguing walking I ever experienced, and the utmost care was required to tread safely over the crust of snow."

Thus there have been preserved several versions of what Douglas did. As we shall see later, no one of them accurately fits in with the existing topography of the pass, although the long diary, of the trail, quite probably represents the actual facts as Douglas recalled them.

Archibald McDonald, companion of Sir George Simpson in 1828, kept a journal of their canoe voyage across the continent, and their crossing through Peace River Pass. In notes added by Malcolm McLeod, editor of this journal, we find the following reference:[84] "The 'Big Athabasca,' or Athabasca River proper, draws from the glaciers of Mount Brown, the highest Peak (16,600 feet) of the Rocky Mountains, and also from a much lower height called the *Miette*, not far from the Leather or Yellowhead Pass. I have seen, but remember not, the glaciers that feed this noble river, having passed and repassed them in very early life and once with 'thirty feet' of snow after mid April, under foot in the pass (Athabasca Pass), the highway, then, of the Hudson's Bay Company, to the Columbia."

De Smet, the priest, is most emphatic of all in his statement:[85] "Upper Athabasca is, unquestionably, the most elevated part of North America. All its mountains are prodigious, and their rocky and snow-capt summits seem to lose themselves in the clouds. At this season, immense masses of snow often become loosened and roll down the mountains' sides with a terrific noise, that resounds throughout these quiet solitudes like distant thunder—so irresistible is the velocity of their descent, that they frequently carry with them enormous fragments of rock, and force a passage through the dense forests which cover the base of the mountain. At each hour, the noise of ten avalanches descending at once, breaks upon the ear; on every side we see them precipitated with frightful rapidity.

"From these mountains, the majestic river of the north, the upper branch of the Sascatshawin, the two great forks of the McKenzie, the Athabasca and Peace rivers, the Columbia, and Frazer at the west, derive the greater part of their waters."

Dr. Hector, somewhere in doubt, although more accurate

than his predecessors, is influenced by them; for he remarks,[86] "I am inclined to think that none of the Rocky Mountains rise above 13,000 or 13,500 feet, and that my estimate of the height of Mount Murchison, which I made last year, is too great."

Thus we have recorded the varying opinions of travellers, eye-witnesses, regarding the mountain heights of the upper Columbia Valley and of the Athabaska Pass area. Let us now turn our attention to the actual facts of the topography as known at the present time.

CHAPTER XI
THE MOUNTAINS OF THE WHIRLPOOL

(The Ascents of Mounts Kane and Brown)

"Geography is an art as well as a science. And in parenthesis I may say that I doubt whether any science is complete which has not art behind it. We shall never be able fully to know and understand the Earth or to describe what we see if we use our intellectual and reasoning powers alone. If we are to attain to a complete knowledge of the Earth, and if we are to describe what we learn about it in an adequate manner so that others may participate in our knowledge, then we must use our hearts as well as our heads. We must be artists as well as meticulous classifiers, cataloguers and reasoners.

"And, therefore, I hold that if the function of Geography is to know the Earth and to describe the Earth, then the objection that the description of its Natural Beauty is outside the scope of Geography is not a valid objection. The picture and the poem are as legitimate a part of Geography as the map."

SIR FRANCIS YOUNGHUSBAND

Twenty years ago, with an objective group of peaks several hundred miles distant by trail, a journey to a remote district was not to be lightly undertaken. The early days of mountaineering in the Canadian Rockies began when there was as yet no railroad through Yellowstone Pass. Consequently, most expeditions, at that time—even when bound for the Far North—started from points on the Canadian Pacific Railroad, Banff or Lake Louise.

A.P. Coleman[87] and his companions are responsible for the early enthusiasm, resulting in the repeated searches for the mysterious high peaks of Athabaska Pass. In 1888, they attempted to enter the region by way of the Columbia Loop, and actually reached Kinbasket Lake before abandoning the enterprise. In 1892, a second attempt, by way of North Saskatchewan and Athabaska headwaters, led them to Fortress Lake—which but for the absence of mounts Hooker and Brown, and the discrepancy in the size of the lake, might have been the Committee Punch Bowl.

In 1893, a third expedition, led by Coleman, successfully reached the Athabaska Pass. The highest mountain on the western side of the pass was ascended, and was considered to be the peak which Douglas climbed. They also ascended M'Gillivray's Rock, the point where Mount Hooker is indicated on the Palliser map, but noted that "a much higher, finer peak rises a few miles east of the Punch Bowl, with fields of snow and a large glacier, and was estimated at about eleven thousand feet." Because of the small size of the Committee Punch Bowl, a folding canvas boat, intended for use on the lake, remained in its pack-cover.

None of the other early expeditions actually reached Athabaska Pass, although the search for the high peaks was by no means given up. Wilcox and Barrett in 1896 reached Fortress Lake. Wilcox triangulated the massive glacier-bearing peak to the west—the present Mount Serenity—at 10,573 feet.

Habel,[88] the German explorer, in 1901, spent several days near the lake and mentions Serenity as "a very prominent snowy mountain, visible nearly from top to bottom, in shape similar to Mont Blanc."

Collie, who came out from England first in 1897, became interested in the Brown–Hooker problem. In those days, knowledge of the topography was so imperfect that it was thought that the North Fork of the Saskatchewan had its source in the neighbourhood of Athabaska Pass. Collie had seen high peaks in the north, from the slopes of Mount Freshfield, and, in 1898, visited many of them by way of the North Saskatchewan. The Athabaska Pass was not reached, but the climbers had their reward in the discovery of the huge Columbia Icefield.

Following the visit of Coleman, the next attempt at mountaineering from the pass was made, in 1913, by Messrs. Howard and Mumm,[89] of the Alpine Club, accompanied by the guide Moritz Inderbinen. On the way in from Jasper, minor summits were attained; but in the immediate vicinity of Athabaska Pass the weather became so unfavourable that little could be done. Mumm and Inderbinen ascended Mount Brown and later visited the great glacier—the present Scott Glacier—at the source of Whirlpool River.

The first ascent of importance in the Whirlpool Group was that of Mount Serenity, made from Fortress Lake, in 1920, by Messrs. Carpe, Palmer and Harris. The route to the summit, by way of the Serenity Glacier and the southern arête, required ten hours from a camp at the glacier-tongue.

In 1920, the Interprovincial Survey visited the Athabaska Pass and established the present nomenclature. A large number of stations were occupied, including Mount Brown, McGillivray Ridge (Mount Brown E.), Alnus and Divergence peaks.

The Survey Commission[90] published the following conclusions in regard to the Hooker–Brown problem:

"*Mt. Brown.* The mountain ascended by Douglas and named Mt. Brown by him is the one rising directly on the west side of the pass summit, the altitude being 9156 feet, 3405 feet above the pass.

"*Mt. Hooker.* The location is not so clear. Douglas writes in his journal, (1) 'A little more to the south is one nearly the same height, rising more into a sharp point which I named Mt. Hooker.' (2) 'I set out with a view of ascending what appeared to be the highest peak on the north or left-hand side.' Against these statements is the fact that the direction of the valley at the summit of the pass is practically north and south and consequently Douglas' 'north or left-hand side' would truly be 'west, or left-hand, side;' so also with reference to Mt. Hooker, 'a little to the south is one nearly the same height' would truly be 'a little to the east is one nearly the same height.' Douglas' idea of his direction seems to have been as inaccurate as his idea of altitude. On a bearing 18° north of east lies a peak, rising into a sharp point, which is distant approximately six miles from the summit of Mt. Brown and which has an altitude of 10,782 feet, or 1626 feet more than that of Mt. Brown. It seems more likely that this is the mountain Douglas refers to as Hooker. (This is the mountain seen by Coleman and Stewart, and estimated at 11,000 feet.)

"From the vicinity of Fortress Lake this mountain peak stands up in a sharp white cone. It is not conceivable that the long, evenly crested ridge (i.e., McGillivray's Rock) rising directly above the Punch Bowl from Athabaska Pass summit has anything to do with the question. It was, therefore, recommended to the Geographic Board that the 10,782 foot peak about six miles easterly from Mt. Brown be confirmed as Mt. Hooker, which has been done." Thus rests the question officially.

For a moment let us consider the modern topography of the mountains south of Jasper. The Whirlpool Group occupies the rough triangle enclosed between the Whirlpool and Athabaska rivers on west and east, and by Fortress Lake and Wood River on the south. It includes the portion of the Continental Divide between Fortress and Athabaska passes, an air-line distance of twenty miles, and its continuation to Whirlpool Pass. The airline distance between Athabaska and Whirlpool passes is eight miles.

The northern tip of the group, in the angle of the Whirlpool–Athabaska junction, although visible and but a day's trail-riding from Jasper, has yet to be mapped. In this angle is a striking peak, known by local name as "Whirlpool Mountain," south of which, with its upper crags visible from Jasper above the eastern shoulder of Mount Edith Cavell, is Mount Fryatt (11,026 feet), one of the outstanding mountains of the Park. Other peaks east of the Divide, included in the mapped area, are Lapensée (10,190 feet), and Belanger (10,200 feet), just south of Fryatt; while farther east, Mount Christie (10,160 feet), and Brussels Peak (10,370 feet), culminate a subgroup toward the Athabaska. Only a few miles north of Fortress Mountain, Catacombs Mountain, attaining 10,800 feet, is the chief peak in the southeastern section.

From Fortress Pass (4388 feet), and Fortress Mountain (9908 feet), the Divide westward includes no peaks of importance as far as the head of Alnus Creek. At the western end of Fortress Lake, Alnus Valley enters Wood River at an acute angle from the northwest. At the head of Alnus Creek, low passes lead over to Divergence Creek, a Whirlpool tributary, and form a major trench extending through the Whirlpool Group.

It is chiefly with the area west of Alnus and Divergence valleys that mountaineering interests have been concerned, as this portion of the group contains important peaks and many of the finest scenic features.

At the head of Alnus Creek, on the Divide, is Divergence Peak (9275 feet), whence the watershed swings sharply southward, crossing the summits of Alnus (9673 feet), Ross Cox (9840 feet), Scott (10,826 feet), Oates (10,220 feet), and Ermatinger (10,080 feet). The watershed now swings abruptly westward, crossing

Mount Hooker (10,782 feet), and, dropping across McGillivray Ridge, descends to Athabaska Pass.

This division of the group, it will be seen, lies between terminal sources of Whirlpool and Wood rivers. On the British Columbia side of the Divide, Mount Serenity (10,573 feet), connected by spurs with the main watershed between mounts Ermatinger and Hooker, fills in the sharp angle formed by Alnus Creek with Wood River.

On the Alberta side of the watershed, Mount Evans (10,460 feet), and Mount Kane (10,000 feet), rising above the valley of the Whirlpool, form supporting buttresses for the immense basin of the Hooker Icefield, discharging through the icefalls of Kane and Scott glaciers as a chief source of Whirlpool River.

The Hooker Icefield is spread across onto the British Columbia side of the watershed and includes perhaps another ten square miles: a total of from twenty to twenty-five square miles. Nearly a dozen small ice-tongues pour down their streams southward into the gorge of Wood River, between Serenity Creek and Athabaska Pass. North of, and partially walled in by, Mount Serenity, the South and North Alnus glaciers—of the alpine, winding type—descend from the slopes of Ermatinger, Oates, and Scott, to form sources of Alnus Creek.

Between Mount Hooker's eastern wall and the point south of Ermatinger where the western arête of Serenity joins the watershed, there is a conspicuous pass, of relatively flat snow, about 8700 feet in elevation, leading across the Continental Divide. Bear and cariboo appear to make use of it as an occasional route from the Whirlpool to Wood River, and we noticed tracks, high on the snow, on several occasions.

The air-line distance between Divergence Peak at the head of Alnus Creek, and the Committee Punch Bowl on Athabaska Pass, is twelve miles. On the Pass summit (5736 feet), are the Punch Bowl and two other adjacent lakelets, giving rise to terminal sources of the Whirlpool River, on the east, and Wood River, through Pacific Creek, on the west.

The Continental Divide continues from the Pass, rising westward to the summit of Mount Brown (9156 feet), thence turning northward and dropping to the icy lakes at the head of Robert Creek, and to Canoe Pass (6772 feet), connecting Whirlpool River with a branch of Canoe River. Crossing Mallard Mountain (9330 feet), the Divide reaches Whirlpool Pass (5936 feet), linking the Middle Whirlpool with the Mazama Creek branch of Canoe River. It will thus be seen that there are no peaks of importance immediately west of Athabaska Pass and the Whirlpool; the Divide is relatively low and can be crossed at several points. The feature of interest is the large area of glacier and snowfield on the southwest side of Mount Brown, extending into the angle between Wood and Canoe rivers. The Continental Divide bends considerably in rounding the head of Whirlpool River, consequently the air-line distance between Divergence Peak and Whirlpool Pass is only about eight miles, practically equal to the distance between Athabaska and Whirlpool passes.

The author's expedition, in 1924, was the third to reach the Athabaska Pass for purely mountaineering purposes. Fortunate were we in coming to a place so little known—new peaks were everywhere at hand. Within a short space of time we were able to make the first ascent of Mount Hooker and other peaks of the vicinity, and to explore the intricacies of the Kane and Hooker icefields, as well as a portion of the vast topography of the mountains of the Whirlpool.

From the Canadian National Railroad, with fourteen horses furnished by the well-known outfitter Donald Phillips, our party, including Mr. Alfred J. Ostheimer and Dr. Max Strumia of Philadelphia, myself, and the guide Conrad Kain, left Jasper on June 26th, bound for Athabaska Pass. In charge of the horses came David Washington Moberly, a Cree breed, grand-nephew of Walter Moberly who years before served as locating engineer for the Canadian Pacific. Our cook, Jack MacMillan, had assisted his father in building the first trails to Emerald Lake, and had worked for the pioneer Tom Wilson in the old days.

By road leading from The Lodge, across the Miette bridge, toward the snows of Mount Edith Cavell, we started up the Athabaska Valley, a broad trail bringing us to the mouth of Whirlpool River, the stream which we were to follow to its southern sources. Here was the location of the old ford—la Grande traverse—by which the *voyageurs* crossed to the Prairie de la Vache, or Buffalo Prairie, on their way to Jasper House.

Past the snow-powdered crags of Kerkeslin, through a broad valley, there are glimpses of distant peaks on the Sunwapta and Chaba; while looming in the Athabaska–Whirlpool angle, companion to many another dark tower, the precipices and pinnacles of the Whirlpool Mountain, grim and repellent, hide the towering mass of Fryatt, loftiest of the Whirlpool Group.

Through a small lumber camp, where railroad ties are cut and floated down to Jasper, we passed and camped by the Whirlpool, quiet pools nearby reflecting Needle Peak, guardian of the entrance to Simon Creek—the old "North Whirlpool." Across the river, sunset colouring of the range blends with the dull, glowing embers of our campfire: soft wind-music in the jack-pine tops; rush of the river; distant bells tinkling—first days on the trail are well remembered.

The second elevation in the central area of Jasper Park,[91] Mount Fryatt, has long been recognized by climbers as a mountain difficult to approach. Situated back from the river, with heavily wooded slopes, a formidable looking peak it is; rising so much above its neighboring valleys that mountaineers have left it severely alone. The Interprovincial Survey had photographed it from the southwest, from the head of Alnus Creek, revealing the presence of three attractive lakes and high meadows at the sources of Divergence Creek, the Whirlpool tributary immediately west of Mount Fryatt.

On June 27th we crossed the Whirlpool by a lumber-camp bridge, and attempted to take our horses up the creek west of Whirlpool Mountain to a low pass leading over to the head of Divergence Creek, where it seemed possible that we might establish a high camp. We were unsuccessful in our effort. After several hours in the dense timber, we gained an elevation of less than 6000 feet, where canyons and cut-banks make the creek bed almost impossible for horses. It would have been necessary to spend one or two days cutting trail through the high timbered shoulder on the west bank of the stream in order to reach the desired upper levels.

While we were investigating the route, several restless packhorses succeeded in dislodging one of their fellows over a low rock ledge, the horse turning a complete somersault and landing head downward in the water. It required quick and skillful work on the part of the guides to cut the pack ropes and prevent the struggling animal from drowning. As usual, more damage was done to the packs than to the horse; but the delay assisted our decision not to proceed farther.[92] So we recrossed the Whirlpool and camped on a terrace, by an old cabin not far from the mouth of Simon Creek.

Passing by the cook-house of the lumbermen, we were just too late to witness a lively incident. The cook, preparing lunch, had heard some scratching noises on the roof of the house. Thinking it was a squirrel, he did not pay much attention to it, but, happening to look up suddenly through the little skylight above, found himself looking squarely into the face of a large black bear. Both were immensely startled, the bear being much the more frightened of the two. The cook threw a frying-pan full of hot grease straight up in the air; bruin made an unceremonious dive over the eaves and galloped off amid a shower of kettles and dishes. We arrived in time to help the cook gather up his scattered utensils, and to confirm his story by examining the muddy paw-marks on the cabin roof.

When we returned along this trail, more than a week later, we found that a sudden rise of water had carried away the bridge over the river. So future visitors, approaching Mount Fryatt from this direction, will cross a difficult ford. From our camping place, evidently a very old one, we could see far sunlit peaks—Scott, Hooker, Evans, Kane—toward the head of Whirlpool River. How thrilling is the anticipation aroused by the first distant view of an unexplored group!

Morning came, brilliant after a night of heavy showers. In two hours we had forded Simon Creek, happily without wetting any packs. Then over parallel timbered ridges, with intervening muskeg and shallow reedy ponds, emerging on river-flats opposite the ribbed cliffs of Mount Scott, with new snow melting and sparkling. Then into the timber again, arcaded groves of cottonwood, with the Middle Whirlpool coming down in no apparent bed of its own, but spreading about the gnarled tree-roots, and the pack-train splashing through. It was as if one wandered in a splendid irrigated garden; a garden of primeval trees, grey-green in their veils of hanging moss, with tops so interlaced that only here and there might shafting sunlight penetrate the forest shadows.

As we neared the timbered point which is the campground, the magnificent ridges of Mount Hooker, with walls of twisted strata above the Scott icefall, slowly revealed their grandeur. Near our tents was an old roofless log-cabin, of spacious dimensions, with hand-forged nails in its crumbling walls.[93] There are huge stumps in the clearing, so rotted that a touch will topple them over. We picked up bits of hand-made boxes with marks of the Hudson's Bay Company still legible. Not far away, on a bit of cliff, four goats looked down in silent astonishment at our caravan's arrival. In the evening, white-tailed deer passed close to the campfire on their way to the river: graceful and unafraid they moved along the gravel-bars, from one silvery pool to another, and disappeared at last in the sun-glint along the edge of the bush.

The Scott Glacier will be much visited in days to come because of the tremendous spectacular icefalls in which it plunges down to the valley level, to spread in a broad flat tongue toward the wooded morainal fans far below timber-line. We passed close below it on our next day's travel and were to know it better within a short time. The upper névé spreads below the northern wall of Mount Hooker, and one must journey far in the Canadian Rockies to find ice-scenery which can compare with the wild splendour of this view. The western margin of the glacier is flanked by the symmetrical rock peak of Mount Evans, contrasting with the sheer snowy wall of Mount Kane just beyond, resembling the southern portion of the Victoria ridge above Lake Louise. From the col between Evans and Kane a slender precipitous icefall hangs in apparent defiance of the laws of gravity, pale-blue with a tinge of green, and its tiny stream ending in an airy waterfall that sprays to a rock-bowl close to the trail.

Rounding the shoulder of Mount Kane, trail leads through evergreen timber and thickets of pussy-willow, and patches of spring snow. Crowded clusters of anemones and avalanche-lilies press up through the melting margins. In the shadow of McGillivray's Rock, with the snows of Mount Brown ahead, we enter on the Athabaska Pass.

The valley broadens above the gorge at the foot of Kane, snow becomes deeper, entirely covering the trail; pack-horses, floundering at first, gradually gain confidence in their footing. A gaunt cariboo stalks up and over a nearby ridge, moving so slowly. How surprising, to reach the summit lakes on the pass and stop by the central one—the Committee Punch Bowl! A skim of ice lay on the water, too cold for bathing; and, unlike Coleman, we had not brought a canvas boat. But one of us can at least be credited with having swum a horse across the Great Divide! Here Thompson and Douglas had come; here Ross and Simpson had drunk their wine; here had passed De Smet and Kane, and all the rest... .

The lakes are desolate, lonely tarns, and in winter may be entirely covered. Of course there are no lofty mountains on either side, and one is almost at a loss to pick out Mount Brown, for on the western side of the pass are several summits all about equal in height and resembling each other in outline. It is all so plain in Douglas' journal; a visit to the pass is the really confusing thing. A traveller of today, writing on the spot, could never describe the pass and its peaks in Douglas' words—the journal and the lay of the land simply do not agree.

On account of the snow, we placed camp among the trees on Pacific Creek about a mile below the pass summit, with a group of serrated splintered peaks in view down the valley of Wood River.

Hoping to reach Mount Hooker, on June 30th we left camp at 5.20 a.m. Following the north margin of the glacier-tongue coming from the shoulder of McGillivray's Rock and the Kane Icefield, in two hours we had reached the upper snows. But on crossing to a higher ridge of the Divide, at 9300 feet, we found ourselves cut off from Mount Hooker's southern wall by an impassable snow precipice, overhung with cornices and dropping to the broken Wood River glaciers of the Hooker Icefield. The arête connecting with Hooker rises into an intervening peak which would have to be traversed and forms a route impossibly long for a single day. So realizing that we were defeated, we followed our ridge northward and tramped the long stretches of snow to the Kane–Evans col, which we reached over a small schrund and up some slabby chimneys. We were now at the head of the hanging glacier which is so striking in appearance when seen from the

Whirlpool, and upward over snow and ledge made our way to the top of Mount Kane. It was a few minutes after two o'clock when we arrived.

A little to the southeast there is a break in the curiously banded rock-wall separating the Kane Glacier and Hooker Icefield, affording a possible approach to Mount Hooker; but from Athabaska Pass it will be a very long journey. Beyond the north face of Hooker the view extends to far-away Athabaska sources, with Mount Alberta, The Twins, and Mount Columbia, stupendous even through the distances.

The Wood River Group is seen from an unusual angle and presents a fine array of glacial cirques on the northwest, by which the flat upper snows of Bras Croche might be reached and other peaks explored. Yet one hesitates to recommend a visit by way of Athabaska Pass and the low, timbered reaches of Wood River.

The northern snows of Mount Kane, so steep they are, seem to overhang the Whirlpool. It was the first summit from which all four of the 12,000 foot peaks of the Rockies are visible that any of us had attained. Far beyond the Rampart Group and southern Fraser sources, our gaze was held by Mount Robson. Towering nearly two thousand feet above its highest neighbours, its elevation emphasized by low surrounding valleys, one is yet attracted more by the mountain's isolation than by its appearance of height. No great group masks its precipices. From our viewpoint the peak is a steep-angled pyramid, slightly blunted in the summit ice-cap, a streaming glacier continuous with the névé in a vertical rise of nearly 4000 feet, and the southeastern shoulder, conspicuous from the Grand Forks Valley, so foreshortened as to be almost unrecognizable.

The west is a chaos of unravelled topography: the northern peaks of the Columbia Loop, the Fraser–Canoe divide, the Gold Range, the Cariboos and far peaks of the Fraser Valley. Long familiarity with the main chain of the Canadian Rockies cannot dull the overwhelming sense of hopeless awe aroused by the extent of those unnamed western peaks.

It is not easy or profitable to describe precisely the Kane traverse. Suffice it to say that the arête west of the summit affords a delightful climb of several hours, with work which does not lack in excitement. The snow-ridges encountered are quite narrow, with airy drops to the Whirlpool Valley; the arête possesses a blunt central tower, with opportunities for interesting hand-and-friction traverses on the southern slabs. A last curling ladder of snow leads to scree slopes, and broken rock descending to the glacier. We walked home across the Kane field, in the lengthening shadow of McGillivray's Rock, and the evening glow on the ranges beyond Wood River. At precisely 8.20 p.m., Jack was requested to cook an enormous supper for four!

On the following day we wandered up Mount Brown, past ice-glazed lakelets on benches of snow, like gigantic steps, above the Committee Punch Bowl. Then following the eastern margin of the Brown Icefield, we took what climbing we could find—the rope was unnecessary—and were soon walking up the long shale ridge to the top. The ascent took five hours, and we arrived at a quarter before three; the time was slow, but it was a blistering day and we were a lazy lot. Still it makes one doubtful whether David Douglas, under winter conditions and with limited time due to a late start, could have reached this particular summit.

The Brown Icefield drains to Canoe River and to Wood River; the peaks on its western margin, all unnamed, are attractive and should preferably be reached from a camp at the head of Jeffrey Creek. The unnamed pass through the Divide, immediately north of Mount Brown, deserves a visit. Three lakes, icy and varying in hue, form the sources of Robert Creek and drain to Canoe River. The Wood River and Columbia groups are practically in line, Alberta and The Twins visible, but Columbia hidden by square-topped Bras Croche. Two hours passed; cameras clicked busily, pipes were smoked; we snoozed in the sunlight. The view delighted us—we could not think of it as being "too awful to afford pleasure." In another two hours we had glissaded merrily back to the campfire, tracking in over the lower snow-patches just before seven o'clock.

CHAPTER XII
CLIMBS FROM THE SCOTT GLACIER

(The Ascents of Mounts Oates and Hooker)

"Starving men are early risers."

GABRIEL FRANCHÈRE

"They were awakened by the severity of the cold, and there was no walking to procure themselves warmth: the day was never so long in coming, and the night seemed never to have an end. They set out again at day-break, as benumbed as Marmotts, and it was some time before they could recover the use of their limbs."

BOURRIT

Feeling that we had made a satisfactory reconnaissance of the Athabaska Pass and its surroundings, we returned down the Whirlpool, on July 2nd, and camped near the Scott Glacier, beside a shallow lake in the wooded moraine. It was a day of travel when Nature seemed pleased to show us her valley inhabitants—the soaring eagle that guards the rock of McGillivray; a lonely startled duck skittering across the Punch Bowl; marmots playing and boxing in sunny snow-patches beside the balsam trees. Flowers everywhere: columbine and heather; Dave, our

Indian, riding ahead with a bright bouquet nodding from his hat.

A night of thunder-storms; the morning of July 3rd clearing slowly after a threatening dawn. Such an electrical display and a pounding of thunder there had been—crashing and reverberating. During the flashes, white ghostly figures could be seen scurrying about, making the canvas secure. Now and then one would hear a muffled clanking on the gravel, indicating that the interior of a tent had been vacated by axes which might serve as impromptu lightning-rods. We believe this to be not entirely superstition; on the ridge of Mount Brown many pitted slabs of shale were found, with square-cut holes where metallic crystals had been cleanly destroyed by electrical agencies.

We made a late start, at half-past nine, expecting only to prospect the Scott icefall for a route to the upper basin. Our camp in the Whirlpool Valley was quite low (4500 feet), and it was on this account that we had first investigated the higher level of Athabaska Pass. We now had our tents within a quarter-mile of the ice, and soon passed the huge isolated boulders of the terminal débris and were on the flat tongue. The nearly level ice can be traversed for about a mile, and the eastern moraine, below Mount Scott, brings one almost to 7000 feet before it becomes necessary to rope and take to the ice again.

The glacier plunges down from the Hooker névé, at an elevation of 8000 feet, through the portal between mounts Scott and Evans, with a width of nearly a mile. The fall is extremely broken, with gigantic séracs on the verge of tumbling. A fragmentary medial moraine is formed through the erosion of a buttress, partially exposed in the middle of the icefall, at which level there is a lessening of the ice slope before the final drop to the bulbous tongue.

From our roping place, one ascends another thousand feet before reaching the Hooker Icefield in the extensive basin between Evans, Hooker, Ermatinger, Oates, and Scott. This entails a good deal of step-cutting and some careful icemanship; it was half-past one before we were through. The basin is more than three miles across, and from cols in its bounding ridges—the eastern and southern are on the Continental Divide—other icefalls, all badly shattered, pour in until the field presents a wild scene of unsupported pinnacles and broken séracs over an extended area. A.L. Mumm, who, with the guide Inderbinen, visited the lower reaches of the glacier in 1913, wrote of it [see note 89], "We were in the centre of an immense battlemented cirque, and straight ahead of us, in particular, stood out against the sky the most menacing array of towers and pinnacles I have ever seen." There is very little in other Canadian icefields with which to compare it: one thinks rather of the northern glaciers of Mont Blanc as they come down from the Grand Plateau, but the Hooker Icefield gives an impression of greater breadth and breakage.

Turning eastward and rounding the cliffs of Mount Scott, our way lay across a flat of snow, toward a tumultuous waterfall, a broad gully of shale bringing us quickly to an upper snow plateau between mounts Scott, Oates, and Ermatinger. It was a quarter past two.

Mount Ermatinger is a mountain of inspiring beauty: a long, knife-edged arête, rising from the Hooker Icefield in a jagged crest of uptilted rock strata, continuing into the north face and merging with a sheer, fluted wall of shining, green ice. The ice-wall is nearly a thousand feet high, broad and unbroken; in our combined experience we could think of but few so glorious. More than anything else it suggested the oncoming mass of a curling sea-wave, about to break and with the sunlight in its crest. Had time and weather permitted it would have been ours within a few days, the difficulties being easily avoidable. We passed it by with regret, envying those who will first stand on its lovely heights.

We had still the opportunity of making a climb and it was

necessary to decide upon the most accessible peak. We had been heading for what seemed to be the highest of the group, believing it to be Mount Scott. The peak adjoining Ermatinger on the north we took to be Mount Oates; but on closer examination of the ground we saw that this is a lower, unnamed summit—which will give someone an enjoyably strenuous climb—and that the peak we were approaching was really Mount Oates itself. We climbed to a little col overlooking the South Alnus Glacier and followed up the ever steepening shale and rock to the summit (10,220 feet). On the last thousand feet the rope was discarded.

Not far away, and only six hundred feet above us, were the shale-tops of Mount Scott, with a lengthy talus slope of moderate angle running down to the snow plateau. We had been told that the mountain would afford good rock-work, but from this side it looks monotonously easy. Our own peak was immensely preferable. The only way to climb Scott, with pleasure, will be by its western wall.

Although it was 5.45 p.m., we settled down to enjoy our surroundings. Below us, on the north, there was a profound drop to the North Alnus Glacier, while down Alnus Creek the waters of Fortress Lake were completely in view. Alberta, The Twins, and Columbia limit the southeastern horizon, and one might trace the Divide around the head of the Chaba icefields, across Fortress Pass, up to the acute angle at Divergence Peak; and back again to the conquered peak where some of us—not all—were hard at work cairn-building. Thence southward goes the watershed, around the Hooker basin and the subsiding ridges, shimmering in the saffron light of evening, that carry it to Athabaska Pass. And beyond Mount Ermatinger—we were always looking back—the majestic northern walls of Serenity, its lower slopes in the long shadows that fill the valley of Fortress Lake and the head of Wood River.

The return was a race with daylight. It took us only an hour to return to the top of the séracs (7.15 p.m.), and two hours more to go down through the intricate labyrinth. We were soon off the upper ice, and, thanking all natural forces for the long twilight of northland July, made camp at half-past ten, just as darkness became annoying. We are convinced that, in most instances, approaching darkness is tantalizing in inverse ratio to the distance from the frying-pan! On the upper snows it doesn't matter so much; in the last uncertain scrambling in the moraine and glacial brook it brings out profanity.

July 4th was a day of rest in camp. The national holiday was celebrated with spasmodic efforts at bathing and laundry, and in the futile attempts to construct steam-bombs out of jam tins. Conrad was the object of much photographic activity; all the horses of the pack-train followed him into the pond—we had been out from Jasper for more than a week and there was a lot of salt on his hide!

Next day, July 5th, an ascent was begun which eventually took more time than we had expected. In fact it turned out to be something of an endurance record for a Canadian climb—a record that we have since been told we are quite welcome to. We started for Mount Hooker at a quarter before five, taking forty-five minutes to the ice and an equal time to the rocks at the foot of the west wall of the glacier. In selecting the wall, below Mount Evans, it had been hoped to establish a quicker approach to the upper snows than had been found in the ice route to Oates. Further, the rocks offered a more direct route to the mountain. It proved not to be so short.

Two twenty-foot chimneys were followed by ascending ledges and slabs, and consumed an hour. We traversed southward and upward across a slanting watercourse and crossed below a large waterfall in the center of the wall. By re-entering this gully it seemed possible to ascend directly by broken ledges. We had barely started when a whizzing, and Conrad's cry of "Stonefalls!"

made us take to what cover was available. It was the beginning of a raking fire in which we were all struck, but luckily without damage. Conrad, calmly saying "Gentlemen, we must move a little to one side," relieved the tension; we quickly got out of range, in time to avoid a heavy bombardment of larger boulders that came banging down over our intended path and would surely have done for us had we persisted. We realized afterward that in Conrad's cool leadership, in emergency, we had seen one of the finest things produced by mountaineering art.

So, selecting a new way, we went on; the ground became increasingly difficult; in one narrow chimney of thirty-five feet the axes and sacks had to be roped up, and the last man, looking up at a wrong moment, got the returning coils full in the face and rather to the detriment of a treasured incisor. Above the chimney was a low bulge of exposed cliff and the two formed a little section on which an hour was spent. Easier ledges brought us up to the glacier and we saw that the ice route would after all have been decidedly preferable.

It was eleven o'clock, and we halted twenty minutes for second breakfast. Mount Hooker was now in front of us, across an extent of threatening séracs, with northern cliffs surmounted by a twisted, corniced arête that makes direct ascent impracticable. The eastern end of the mountain swoops down in a fearful ice-bulge that seems to overhang, and, even from Mount Oates we had not seen a plausible way up. And so we chose the western col, knowing it might give us a long fight; yet we had seen this side from the Kane Icefield and had found nothing better.

Crossing, not without some windings through the crevasses, we reached a poorly bridged schrund, and thence cut forty-five ice-steps to the col. We were at 9300 feet; the delay was an unexpected one, and it had taken us from 1.45 until 2.30 p.m. to cross the schrund and reach the saddle. The sharp buttress and tower rising from the col to the west arête were avoided by traversing and ascending ledges on the south face, above the glaciers draining to Wood River. Steepening pitches of no great difficulty, close to the margin of a broad snow-gully, brought us to the mountain's crest below the rocky tower near the junction of the middle and western thirds of the summit arête. It was at this point that I was taking advantage of some awkward attitudes on the jutting rock, to take a picture of those ahead of me. But the handling of the rope requires first attention, and in caring for this a coil touched the open camera. Over it went, rolling a few feet on the shale and dropping out of sight. It must have fallen nearly two hundred feet before striking; we looked over the edge and finally located it. Conrad eventually recovered the splintered box, and beyond our wildest expectations the lens, shutter, and bellows were intact. The roll-film had not been thrown out, and, although the picture last exposed was ruined, the film eventually produced ten perfect negatives out of twelve exposures. All which is recorded as evidencing that miracles still occur!

The top of the tower is shaly, but we avoided it entirely and maintained our altitude by crossing a broad snow-shoulder extending southward. Here was a really bad schrund, with flat, thin bridges, and a cornice lip—all which we treated with marked respect and crossed cautiously on all fours. We adopted the slow motions of the breast-stroke to this particular situation, in a way that would have delighted a swimming-instructor.

We now gained height on the main arête, for the first time able to gaze over the northern wall. We pushed on rapidly, the heavy, compact snow-crust requiring superficial cutting, and pulled through some small chimneys to the highest rocks at half-past seven. From below, we had thought that these last rock-towers might be the highest point, but, arriving, it was plain that the snow-crest beyond culminated in two wave-like points, with the eastern the higher. After making a tiny cairn and leaving a record, we followed the cornice base to the steep snow of the highest point. It was eight o'clock, and more than fifteen hours had elapsed since we left camp. Had David Douglas been with us he might well have thought his estimate of height was not so far wrong! We anchored, and each, separately, had a look over the cornice down the north wall to the icefield. Smoke had just begun to come in from a distant forest-fire in the direction of Canoe River; we gazed back along the line of dripping, curling cornices into a red sun—it was as if one were living in the atmosphere of an early lithograph of "The Alps," so gaudy it was. Our more rational interest, however, during the few minutes on the actual summit (10,782 feet), lay in the fact that we appeared to overtop Mount Scott. We later confirmed this from Mount Fraser, in the Rampart Group, and are almost convinced that Hooker is the loftiest peak of the group.[94] We would not, however, be understood as placing our eyesight in competition with the work of the Interprovincial Survey; so for the present Mount Scott must remain supreme, at least so far as elevation is concerned.

It was becoming late, and there was quite evidently insufficient time for us to get off the mountain and return by the way we had come. We had no desire to return down the rock-wall in the dark, nor, for that matter, at any time. So we started down a long snow-shoulder, direct from the peak and descending westward of the snow-flats which form an irregular pass between Hooker and Serenity. As we walked down, close to the edge, about sixty feet of cornice split off and sank silently, its impact far below producing echoing crashes. We came to the southern extremity of the shoulder without seeing any way down until the terminal buttress was reached. Following down the margin of a broad couloir for a little way without trouble, another six hundred feet of ledges would have taken us to the glacier.

We stopped for a moment to look at the sunset: the base of the Wood River massif half hidden in violent mist; the sky tinged with the faint green of arctic twilight, with a tracery of smoke wisps, grey and red; Clemenceau's pyramid lifted into the heavens, with no apparent foundation, a floating thing, serene, above Bras Croche, with the pearl-pink colorings of an oriental mosque.

Perhaps we were hypnotized; the weather was fine, the view entrancing; we had come down to the respectable level of 9600 feet, and it was too late to get home. We planned a night on the rocks. What more natural than when we saw a perfectly fine cave close at hand, we should make for it? It was roomy and dry, with doorway rather larger than one would have selected for a permanent habitation; but altogether not to be sniffed at. There was a trickle of water only a few feet away, so we consumed most of our remaining provisions and thought little of it.

We spread our things about, crawled near to each other, and for a while slept quite comfortably. And then the trouble began. About midnight there were flashes of lightning and a rumbling of thunder. Rain fell, soon turning to snow. A wind came up, gusty and carrying snow into the cave. We were fairly well protected and kept dry. We got up at four o'clock, with the first signs of daylight, peering out to find a dense fog which obscured everything more than fifty feet away. There was a light covering of snow on the ground and the sleet continued.

Roping, we started downward, thinking to reach the glacier, round eastward to the pass and get over to the Scott icefall. We got down to the glacier margin without much difficulty, although progress was slow and care was required where the rocks had become icy. The fog was most deceptive and we had trouble in distinguishing height and pitch of quite simple bits of cliff; judgment was frequently at fault.

And here we stopped. We had map and compass and knew our direction; but the Wood River slope of the Hooker Icefield is so fearfully put together with different levels of sérac and twisted, insinuated buttress, that we simply could not tell, in the fog, just where the Hooker–Serenity pass might lie. There were several chances of going astray and wandering over farther on the Wood River side; which, away from our base of supplies, might be disastrous. We stamped around in the snow for two hours and attempted to reach the pass by keeping close to the southern buttresses of Mount Hooker. The fog, contrary to expectation, did not break, and the snow kept coming down. We were making very little headway, so at ten o'clock, finding a protected corner, walled in on three sides and roofed over by a gigantic slab, we decided to wait out the storm rather than waste energy in fruitless efforts. The wet snow had soaked us; our food was gone except for some bits of chocolate and cheese; we had but a little extra clothing, and no means of making fire. We were at 9300 feet and the snow kept on throughout the day. We arranged things as well as possible, flooring the cavern with flat slabs, blocking the open side with boulders and filling the chinks with snow. Fog hid everything but near objects. We were wet and cold, beginning to get hungry. All suffered more or less with intermittent cramps in the thigh and abdominal muscles.

There was a good deal of shivering, that was hard to conceal, done that night; and quite a bit of gastric burning, not so evident, but none the less painful—luckily we could get water in the cave. We had no way of keeping out the fine blown snow, although we sacrificed the warmth of one rucksack to stop the largest hole in the wall.

Morning came, a cheerless dawn, but we had been watching for it. The snow seemed to be lessening; the fog ebbed and billowed. Just before four o'clock, the snow ceased; the fog wavered and lifted, so that as we looked out we could see the ground below us and the way to the pass. We were a stiff lot, but Conrad made a leap for his boots that startled us. It is hard work putting on half-frozen shoes, and our guide was first out, pushing over the snow-crusted boulders in the doorway in his hurry.

Miserably uncomfortable as we were, it was impossible not to think of Samson and the pillars of the Temple!

Conrad went ahead to break trail; the ground was not difficult, once the way was seen, and the rest of us roped and followed. For a few minutes, as we zigzagged down to the glacier, we could see the lower slopes of Bras Croche, of Ghost Mountain, across Wood River, and Chisel Peak on Fortress Lake. It was only a few hundred feet down to the ice and, as we slowly followed Conrad's track, the fog closed down gradually. We found Conrad returning with the good news that he had found the pass and had been nearly to it. He roped with us and we proceeded as fast as we were able. It began to snow and blow harder than ever; but we were sure of ourselves. Our faces and clothing became coated with ice, and hands were cramped through holding a frozen rope. For an instant we saw a dark stretch of open water in the lakelet on the pass summit, and everything was hidden again. The wind blew with great violence, making balance on level ground an uncertain affair; our tracks were not very straight, but the slope began to be downward, and we knew we had come across into territory that was familiar. Through rifts in the mist we recognized the cliffs of Ermatinger and the eastern ice-bulge of Hooker, and came at last out of the storm to the main icefall.

The séracs were all snow-covered; but we would have tackled worse things to get off the mountain. Conrad's never failing craft brought us down in good order to the unroping place, and we followed the route used for Mount Oates, down the eastern moraine and the glacier-tongue. Camp was reached shortly after eleven o'clock. It was July 7th, and we had been out a little more than fifty-four hours.

Things had been happening at camp. High on the ice, above the place where we unroped on descending, we noticed tracks of a man. Dave had become worried when we did not appear on the second day, and had gone up in an unsuccessful effort to find us. When we arrived at camp we found that he had left at 2.30 a.m. to ride to Jasper for help. Jack was in camp, mighty glad to see us, and immediately got us a meal—several perhaps, all in a row—which we devoured, and then turned in. Jack was sent off with instructions to ride as fast as possible and turn back any search-party. We learned later that Dave had ridden the forty-five miles from Scott Glacier to Jasper in nine hours, secured new horses and, with Phillips, had sent out a party, including Mr. Val A. Fynn, A.C., with the Oberland guides Alfred Streich and Hans Kohler. If one were in real danger, it would be impossible to conceive of a more efficient lives-saving unit.[95]

By fast riding, Jack turned back the search-party at the Whirlpool tie-camp; and before noon next day he and Dave had come back to us. They needed sleep and their horses were used up. The climbing party, after a few hours, recovered sufficiently to do camp work in the absence of Jack and Dave; and the impression remains that none of us missed a meal.

By the campfire that evening, Conrad remarked that Mount Hooker was the most interesting mountain he had climbed in recent years, and that the summit arête reminded him of Mount Cook, in New Zealand. There are few Canadian peaks that he finds worthy of such praise.

Mount Hooker, we believe, teaches two lessons: first, that it rarely pays to wander over broken glacier or snowfield in fog; second, that a party in good condition can wait out a storm of considerable duration. Of the two things, clothing is more important than food. One night out at the 9000-foot level is plenty; the second is bound to be unpleasant. On Canadian peaks, however, one is rarely in a position where timber-line cannot be reached. The storm in which we were caught was of unusual duration; it continued for a total time of four days, snowing constantly at higher levels. We were lucky to get out when we did;

but we would have come through eventually, no matter what the weather.

To show that our climbing party did not return in a hopeless condition, it may be added that the only damage done was in the shape of superficial frostbite of the hands, acquired on the third day out, as the result of holding with wet mittens on a hard-frozen rope. On July 9th, with only one day of rest, our time in the area being up, the entire outfit made the twenty miles to the Whirlpool tie-camp, and on the following afternoon was in Jasper.

We were *en route* to the Rampart Group and had hoped to find a pass through the valley of Simon Creek over to Tonquin Valley. Because of the amount of spring snow this was not possible; but on July 11th, we rode from Jasper, by the Miette and Meadow Creek trails, to Tonquin Hill. Camp at the southern end of Amethyst Lakes was reached during the following morning and Surprise Point was climbed later in the day. On July 13th—eight days after the start for Mount Hooker—we ascended the Fraser Glacier to the Erebus–Fraser col; crossed to Simon Glacier, the head of the "North Whirlpool"; made the first ascent of Simon Peak (10,899 feet), the high unclimbed summit of Mount Fraser and the loftiest of the Rampart Group, and then traversed McDonell Peak (10,776 feet), back to camp. This is no program for an exhausted climbing party! A week later we were climbing in the Robson Group. But that is another story.

The ascent of Mount Hooker was the fulfilment of a great desire. To see and to climb Mount Brown and Mount Hooker will perhaps not be thought of as a remarkable alpine ambition. They are probably not the peaks Douglas named; in fact we remain in ignorance as to precisely where he went, what he did, and what he named during his few hours at Athabaska Pass. The Interprovincial Survey has unquestionably done the best thing possible in perpetuating these classic names by applying them to a lovely peak on either side of the pass. But the ambition to stand upon them is a deeper thing than it appears; for the naming of peaks by Douglas, and the over-estimation of altitude—no matter how strange and ludicrous the mistake may seem; no matter who was at fault in figuring—these things first led men in search of great Canadian heights. They came from the far corners of the earth, following pioneer trails, seeking beauty. And none there was who returned insensitive to the glory of that mountain vastness.

So we turned back from Athabaska Pass, on the Whirlpool trail toward the site of Jasper House, feeling that we too had come under the spell of this overland route of the long ago, and, on Mount Hooker at least, had shared a little in its adventure.

CHAPTER XIII
THE RAMPARTS AND MOUNT FRASER

(The Ascent of Simon Peak)

"Lo! Evening comes on its wings of darkness. Oh my soul bow down and tame your voice of mutiny into the hush of evensong. On the banks of the dark a million lights are lit—those stars, for the worship of Him through His silence; leaning on the wall of the end of the day, make your peace with the Endless."

RABINDRANATH TAGORE

The Indians believed that Jasper Park was the lurking-place of prehistoric monsters. David Thompson knew of this superstition, as he mentions,[96] "Continuing our journey in the afternoon we came on the track of a large animal, the snow about six inches deep on the ice; I measured it; four large toes each of four inches in length to each a short claw; the ball of the foot sunk three inches lower than the toes, the hinder part of the foot did not mark well, the length fourteen inches, by eight inches in breadth, walking from north to south, and having passed about six hours. We were in no humour to follow him: the Men and Indians would have it to be a young mammoth and I held it to be the track of a large old grizled Bear; yet the shortness of the nails, the ball of the foot, and its great size was not that of a Bear, otherwise that of a very large old Bear, his claws worn away; this the Indians would not allow."

We ourselves never came in contact with this unclassified beast, although we had looked for it throughout our journey to the mountains of the Whirlpool. We came to the conclusion that it was a dragon, dwelling in Ostheimer's interior—his appetite indicated clearly that he was feeding something beside himself. But then he may have thought similar things about us; canned peaches were our special weakness.

It was when we arrived in Tonquin Valley that we really located the solution of the mystery—The Ramparts. When one sees that range, curving in sinuous, unbroken length, with spaced peaks like vertebral spines age-old and worn, it takes but little imagination to think of it as the dorsal skeleton of some gigantic creature of ages past. It is the glacier dragon of the Middle Ages turned to stone. In reality it forms a part of the backbone of a continent for it is situated on the main Divide; best of all, it is easily accessible.

Visitors to Jasper Park are invariably advised to visit Tonquin Valley. Much has been written of its spectacular scenery—its unique combination of lake, precipice, and ice—which presents itself with a singular beauty almost unequalled in alpine regions of North America. From high peaks of the Whirlpool we had glimpsed its towers and glaciers in the north, and had looked into misty, forested valleys at Fraser headwaters. We knew that Simon Peak, the highest elevation of Mount Fraser and the loftiest summit of the Divide between Fortress Lake and Yellowhead Pass, had yet to be climbed. And so we went.

The Athabaska[97] is an important river even to its very sources. It was not far from Jasper House that David Douglas, in the spring of 1827, met the philosophical old guide Jacques Cardinal,[98] who, observing that he had no spirit to offer, turned toward the river and said, "This is my barrel and it is always running."

The Athabaska flows from two important passes of the Divide: Athabaska itself and Yellowhead. The Athabaska Pass we already knew, and a portion of the Yellowhead route was to be followed on our way over the Meadow Creek trail to Tonquin.

The pass of Yellowhead, in the old days, was the gateway to the settlements of New Caledonia, as British Columbia was then known. It assumed importance a few years after the lower reaches of its great western river had been explored by Simon Fraser, John Stuart, and Jules Quesnel, in 1808. The fur traffic through the pass had become so extensive that, about 1820, the pass was commonly known as Leather Pass. Then came the gold rushes to the Cariboo, in 1861 and 1862, when the pass was used by crowds of adventurers on their way to the North Thompson River. Among the earliest travellers who came through Yellowhead, bound for the North Thompson and Kamloops, were Viscount Milton and Doctor Cheadle, in the summer of 1863. Accompanied by the wandering eccentric Eugene O'Beirne—the mysterious Mr. O'B.—and a one-armed Assiniboine guide with his courageous squaw, these gentlemen were the first to describe Mount Robson, and, indeed, much of the Yellowhead region. Their book, *The North-West Passage by Land*, among many interesting things, contains their dramatic discovery of the Headless Indian, who no doubt perished on the way to Cariboo.

The story[99] and its sequel are worth retelling: "The corpse was in a sitting posture, with the legs crossed, and the arms clasped over the knees, bending forward over the ashes of a miserable fire of small sticks. The ghastly figure was headless, and the cervical vertebrae projected dry and bare; the skin, brown and shrivelled, stretched like parchment tightly over the bony framework, so that the ribs showed through distinctly prominent; the cavity of the chest and abdomen was filled with the exuviae of chrysales, and the arms and legs resembled those of a mummy. The clothes, consisting of woollen shirt and leggings, with a tattered blanket, still hung round the shrunken form." Nine years later, in 1872, several hundred yards up the bank of the river, the head was found by members of the T. Party, Canadian Pacific Survey. They buried the head with the body; but it was exhumed later in the year by Dr. Moren of Sandford Fleming's Pacific Expedition. The skull, placed in the Canadian Pacific offices in Ottawa, was destroyed by fire in 1873.

Poor old Shuswap cranium; what a wandering career it had! But since we ourselves were starting out on the Yellowhead trail, it is scarcely to be wondered at that our own heads were filled with thoughts of these strange events that transpired within the memory of our fathers.

Jasper was our starting-point for Tonquin Valley; and, on the morning of July 11th, the day immediately following our return from Athabaska Pass, we headed the pack-train westward into Miette Valley toward Yellowhead. An Iroquois hunter was this Tête Jaune, whose original Câche was not at the station of the Canadian National now bearing the name, but at the mouth of the Grand Fork of the Fraser. And there he hid the furs he obtained on the western slope before bringing them to Fraser. On the day of the starting, furs would have been useless as skis; we were riding in our shirt-sleeves and the sun beat down unmercifully. Worst of all, when we wanted a drink we had to scramble down the steep bank to the river. Still we were in no danger of having a recurrence of the sad misfortune which befell Sandford Fleming:[100] "The Chief's bag got a crush against a rock, and his flask, that held a drop of brandy carefully preserved for the next plum-pudding, was broken. It was hard, but on an expedition like this the most serious losses are taken calmly and soon forgotten." We should have been less philosophical; but now, sagging low in our saddles, with dust of the trail rising in a golden cloud and obscuring all but the heads and the packs of horses behind us—with water close at hand, we were just too lazy to climb down and get it. As this was our third consecutive day of long riding, we felt our lethargy was excusable.

We had looked backward to Mount Edith Cavell—"La montagne de la grande traverse"—southward and closing the Athabaska Valley, with a face "so white with snow that it looked like a sheet suspended from the heavens." It was hidden as we crossed an old trestle above the sparkling Miette and the horses plodded on beyond. We eventually came near to Geikie station where begins the trail up Meadow Creek, cut out by the park rangers in 1922. A beautifully engineered affair, it rises first in breathlessly steep zigzags and curves for a thousand feet above the Miette to an upper forested level that swings into the side-hill beyond a canyon in the creek bottom. Snow peaks are seen across the valley, a brilliant little group centered about Mount Majestic; we gazed upon them first from the base of Roche Noir as the horses splashed through a stream near the mouth of Crescent Creek. A few minutes later we climbed again to higher slopes where the trail leaves the darkness of mossy nooks and giant trees, and emerges in thinning timber to willow meadows near Tonquin Hill. From camp beside a gurgling brook we gazed out to the northern outposts of The Ramparts—Bastion, Turret, and Geikie—fantastic wedges and pinnacles, tinged with the metallic glow of light through the western passes.

That night we were entertained by the amusing story which Conrad had to tell of a mountaineering parson with whom he had travelled. It seems that the parson was much worried about the future salvation of our guide's soul, and tried to convert him to the fold. He said one day, "Conrad, when you have been in a tight place on the mountains, has the Angel of the Lord never stood by you and told you to be unafraid?" Con, who is an amiable, open-minded philosopher, replied that no such angelic visitation had ever occurred, but that he was ever hoping for such a miracle. The parson earnestly advised him to pray for it, adding,

"I am sure that there are mountains in the after-world. I have always desired to make the ascent of the Matterhorn, a feat which my financial condition has prevented. The after-world is, therefore, made up for different degrees of attainment. If I live my life righteously, I shall perhaps find my Matterhorn in the world to come. You, remaining unbeliever, will surely pass eternity on a prairie."

The doom sounded harsh to Conrad. A few days later, on the trail, a straying horse snagged a pack and fell bodily into the creek. Much to the surprise of Conrad, the parson burst into expressions of profanity that are seldom associated with the clergy. Con wheeled his horse and rode back. "Shake hands, parson," he called, "sometimes I think you are almost a man. I don't know for sure how far down in dot after-world *you* come; but chust be yourself, and maybe yet we climb dot Matterhorn together!"

This bit of alpine humour may relieve a few paragraphs of topographical explanation, which will make clearer what follows. The Rampart Group forms the chief mountain uplift of the Continental Divide between Athabaska and Yellowhead passes. Its western slopes are drained by the head of Fraser River and its tributary creeks, Geikie and Tonquin. On the east, Simon Creek, Astoria River, Maccarib and Meadow creeks flow into the Athabaska system.

Following the Divide northward from Whirlpool Pass (5936 feet), the first peaks of any importance form the western wall of the basin in which a number of glaciers converge, like wheel-spokes, at the head of Simon Creek—the "North Whirlpool." These peaks are Whitecrow (9288 feet), Blackrock (9580 feet), Mastodon (9800 feet), and Scarp (9900 feet). All are attractive rocky summits, with long radiating ridges and interconnected snowfields. Just east of the Divide, Needle Peak (9668 feet), requires special mention because it will no doubt afford some very interesting and spectacular work for ambitious climbers of the future. It is a slender flake of rock, with broad base flanking the mouth of Simon Creek; the best approach is by way of Whirlpool River in two long days from Jasper.

At the head of Simon Creek the Divide rises to Mount Fraser, the culminating elevation of the group, and over its three peaks[101]—Simon (10,899 feet), McDonell (10,776 feet), and Bennington (10,726 feet)—to the rampart-wall of aiguilles beyond.

The Fraser Glacier, on the southeast side of the Fraser massif, occupies a pass between the head of Astoria River and the "North Whirlpool," Simon and Mastodon glaciers forming the chief sources of Simon Creek, although a tongue from the Fraser Glacier also enters its headwater. The main drainage from the Fraser Glacier, however, is into Astoria River.

Southeastward from the Fraser névé there extends an interesting and unvisited group of peaks bounding the Eremite Glacier cirque. These peaks are Outpost (9449 feet), Erebus (10,234 feet), Eremite (9500 feet), Alcove (9219 feet), and Angle, (9547 feet), all of them lying in Alberta, within easy climbing distance from Surprise Point and Amethyst Lakes.

From Mount Fraser the Divide circles over the sheer wall of The Ramparts—Paragon (9800 feet), Dungeon (10,000 feet), Redoubt (10,200 feet), and Bastion (9812 feet)—dropping abruptly to Tonquin Pass (6393 feet), the crest of the range then swinging westward into British Columbia and supporting the precipitous trio: Turret (10,200 feet), Geikie (10,854 feet), and Barbican (10,100 feet).

The headwaters of Astoria River are derived in part from Chrome Lake, into which flow rushing streams from the Eremite and Fraser glaciers; but a somewhat larger creek rises in the Amethyst Lakes, two lovely bodies of water closely connected with one another and lying close below the stupendous east wall of The Ramparts.

Moat Lake is finely situated in the eastern hollow of Tonquin Pass and sends a stream to join with a northern outflow from Amethyst Lakes; and, in an expanse of willow-covered, marshy ground, drains both to Meadow and Maccarib creeks.

In the western cirque of The Ramparts, glaciers streaming from Mount Fraser drain to Geikie Creek. Scarp and Casemate glaciers slope off abruptly to Icefall Lake; while the long, winding Bennington Glacier is separated from them by the jagged rock arête extending northwest from Simon Peak and supporting the dark towers of Casemate (10,160 feet) and Postern (9720 feet).

In the central part of Jasper Park, just west of the Whirlpool–Athabaska junction, Mount Edith Cavell (11,033 feet), had been climbed by Messrs. Gilmour and Holway in 1915. In the same year a portion of the Park was surveyed by Bridgland, but no station except Surprise Point was made in the Rampart–Fraser range. No climbing party left a record on this portion of the Continental Divide until 1919, when Messrs. Carpe, Chapman, and Palmer, from campground at the southern end of Amethyst Lakes, made first ascents of McDonell and Paragon. They were the first to see Simon Peak and the Bennington Glacier at close range and to appreciate their grandeur and importance. Mr. Carpe, at that time, obtained an altitude of 10,900 feet for Simon Peak and the party recognized it as the main apex of the massif. It was not then thought of as a part of Mount Fraser because the Bridgland map had applied the name "Mount Fraser" specifically to the east peak. The use of "Mount Fraser" to cover the whole massif—Simon, McDonell, Bennington—is a recent development, and has been incorporated with the maps of the Interprovincial Survey. Members of the latter survey, in 1921, occupied many high points as stations, including Beacon (9795 feet), Whitecrow (9288 feet), and Rufus (9053 feet), and connected the triangulation with the earlier Bridgland survey of the central area of the Park.

In the fourth volume of *Modern Painters*, John Ruskin expressed his doubts as to whether we live in a world just in its prime or in the ruins of former Paradise. One realizes instinctively in the valley of Tonquin that the carving of its great rock spires is still in the formative stage. The work is still going on; the mountains are but roughly hewn out, with an impressionistic technique as fantastic as it is fanciful. The great slopes of sharp chips and ragged blocks indicate plainly that Nature has but shaped out the plan; there is as yet nothing of the soft smoothness of finished work.

It was a gay day, bright with sunshine, when we rode the trail toward Amethyst Lakes. The surveyors who christened The Ramparts thought of it as a castellated range and bestowed upon the peaks the mediaeval names suggested by their counterparts—Turret, Bastion, Redoubt, Dungeon, Postern, and Casemate. But the crest is so sinuous and angulated that, as we looked toward it from across the valley floor, we felt that the analogy to the spiny remains of a petrified dinosaur or some similar creature was an equally good one. Certainly there were never any man-built castles in Jasper Park; but did we not know from the Indian stories that it had always been the abode of dragons?

In the valley of Maccarib Creek, on a sloping alp-land, is a tiny cabin. Freshly painted with a bright red roof, it serves as the palatial home of Ranger Goodair—that is, when he is at home. We had met him on the Whirlpool River, where he had been of service to us in helping cut trail during our attempt to reach the head of Divergence Creek and the base of Mount Fryatt. A quiet, pleasant man, he had had the usual interesting career of those whom one runs across in the far places. Studying medicine in London, he enlisted and went to Africa during the Boer War, remaining afterward in the South African diamond fields, wandering as a prospector to strange corners of the earth, and at last finding a life in the Canadian wilderness that pleased and held him. We could quite understand it, and not without a touch of envy.

We followed the trail through flowering meadows—heather and paintbrush—on the shore of Amethyst Lakes; broad sheets of translucent blue reflecting the steep buttresses and crescentic hanging glaciers of Redoubt and Dungeon. There is one conspicuous horizontal snowy ledge, mid-high in the wall and continuous with scarcely a break save where icy gullies cut through at right angles from the high notches in the jagged crest-line. In a little while camp was pitched in the trees near the southern margin of the lakes, and we eagerly awaited Jack's announcement that luncheon was served. I dare not tell you what we would have for breakfast or dinner, but lunch in those days might include pork-and-beans, fried potatoes, buffalo pemmican, salmon, bannock with jam, and dried fruit. There was no serving of courses, everything was on one's plate at once, and nothing ever left over.

Surprise Point is an amusing little pinnacle that rises above the camping place to a height of 7873 feet. It looks so easy, but is really quite a scramble if one tries it in moccasins and with each hand encumbered by a camera. Strumia and I climbed up during the afternoon, in something less than two hours, although we made frequent stops to photograph some queer little rickety towers of the ridge, that looked for all the world as if a giant's child had been playing at building blocks and had finally disjointed his construction with a push. There is not much room on the summit, but we found a ledge where snow was melting and a place where we could stretch out for a snooze on the warm rocks. We stayed there for more than three hours in rapt absorption of the lovely overlook on peak, meadow, and winding stream. Tonquin Valley is wide and almost filled by the glistening stretches of the two Amethyst Lakes, whose waters are connected only by a narrow channel between two little wooded peninsulas. The lakes are larger than many we had seen, and with their flat, meadowed shores it is almost as if a bit of the prairie had been transported and placed there to contrast with The Ramparts' wall. It was all spread below us like a map, and only when the westward sun threw a dark serrated silhouette of the range down upon the water did we tear ourselves away and race down to the campfire.

Simon Peak, although it is the culminating height in the group, is most retiring and quite invisible from campground at Surprise Point. Next morning, July 13th, we left at half-past five with the idea of finding and climbing it if we could. An old game trail was followed through the dense forest to the ancient moraine and the stream which comes from the Fraser Glacier. We entered a shadowed glen where the bed of the creek is somewhat wider and the waters spread into limpid pools that perfectly reflect the symmetrical outlines of Bennington, towering above a line of stately pines. Unfortunately the ground is marshy and forms a breeding place for mosquitoes, which followed us in clouds until the breeze from the ice drove them away.

Hurrying up some rising grassy slopes we were soon among the enormous morainal blocks below the glacier, and in a few minutes had rounded a tiny blue marginal lake to the ice itself. Past a corner of Outpost the circle of little peaks bounding Eremite Glacier presented themselves in snowy line. Eastward we looked down upon the curious yellow brilliancy of Chrome Lake, and into the Astoria Valley where Mount Edith Cavell raises a shaly, snowless gable to a sharp point wholly unlike the great white face one sees from Jasper. The Fraser tongue is almost unbroken and we rapidly gained height on long slopes of snow and moraine. A little to the south rises Erebus, in a series of steep cliffs and receding ridges in step-like formation that would make direct attack a difficult procedure. Foreshortening makes the peak seem very sheer, but toward Simon Creek, southwesterly, it breaks down into an easy gradient of shaly strata.

We had heard that Simon Peak possessed a formidable

ice-crest, and for that reason it had seemed best to reconnoitre a little in order to spy out a satisfactory route. In two hours and a half from camp we reached the nearly level snow-plateau on the Erebus–Fraser saddle and could look over to the radiating glaciers at the head of the "North Whirlpool." It was quite unnecessary to make use of climbing-rope and I went on ahead to a higher slope whence I could photograph the rest of the party on a wind-blown snowy ridge below, with Mount Erebus for a background. Distantly in the south, the Scott Group and the mountains near Athabaska Pass were visible through a thin veil of forest-fire smoke. We stopped for a few minutes and then crossed two small snow basins to the head of Simon Glacier. We sat down for lunch in the shadow of a curious little tower, perhaps forty feet high and looking for all the world like a "pill-box" of wartime days. It was a blunt needle with steep walls which nearly aroused us into an attempt to climb it. Food, however, proved more enticing.

The actual peak of Simon was still hidden, but we could now see that it would be possible to get onto the glacier, cross to its head and ascend steep slopes toward the col between our objective and McDonell Peak. This plan was duly followed out and we were soon a considerable distance up the snow. Due care was necessary in avoiding the base of a small icefall which enters the snowfield at the edge of our proposed route, and locks of blue ice imbedded far out on the snow gave indication that little avalanches sometimes came down. We crossed a deep schrund below a rocky wall, over a bridge that was narrow and steep, and then mounted steadily over down-tilting strata where water cascaded down and filled our sleeves if we were not careful in our choice of hand-holds. There was a gully in the margin of the icefall where a careful watch was made to avoid the flakes of shale which frequently scaled down and sailed over a rocky bench to lower snows.

It was soon possible to cross above the top of the fall and take to the rocks, after which we made good time to the ridge above. For the first time we now saw Simon Peak, a little to the north, icy, and with superb frozen cornices overhanging the gorge of Bennington Glacier. The rope became a real necessity; Conrad cut steps along the southern slope where the ice fragment swished down and vanished. There were patches of quite hard ice, slowing our progress, and more than a hundred steps were made to the first snow point of the final crest. Beyond us lay a higher cornice, and then a short level of rocks and shale forming the summit; it was just half-past one when we arrived and took off the rope. The difficulties had been less than we expected.

It was a pleasurable surprise to find a rock outcrop on the very highest point of our mountain, and we sat down in a comfortable spot to have lunch. It was not the best of days for a distant view, as smoke hid many of the far peaks that we had hoped to see. Most spectacular, however, was the gorge of Bennington Glacier. Formed by the snows that lie in the northern cirque of Mount Fraser's three peaks, it winds sinuously below the barren west wall of The Ramparts and disappears around the corner of Casemate—the lowest portion of visible ice being more than four thousand feet below our viewpoint. The glacier is more than three miles long and gives rise to Geikie Creek flowing to Fraser River; the long northern arête of Simon Peak walls the ice on the west and plunges down in snow-powdered precipices and broken ridges that support the gigantic towers of Casemate and Postern. Beyond the muddy waters of Icefall Lake are two smaller pools of a clear, transparent blue, and on the meadows across Geikie Creek we discovered the tents of Messrs. Fynn, Geddes and Wates, who were carrying out a mountaineering campaign in the vicinity.

Above their camping-place rises Mount Geikie; a tremendous

grim wall it is, seared and fissured by ice-filled couloirs, and surmounted by two fine towers sprinkled with new snow. We thought that the rocks would be scarcely dry enough for climbing, and were pleasantly surprised to learn that a successful ascent was achieved only a few days later.[102] During our little stay on the highest point of Mount Fraser we gazed at Geikie's fascinating crags and could scarcely believe that our summit was by a few feet the loftier.

It was now quite plain that nothing of difficulty intervened between Simon and McDonell Peak; so rather than retrace our roundabout route, we built a cairn, walked back in the ice-steps, and traversed McDonell.[103] We were just one hour between summits, Strumia leading up the ridge on steep crags where every hold was firm and belays for the rope were found wherever required. We had some thought of going on and adding the unclimbed Bennington Peak to our bag; but it looked long and not too interesting; storm clouds were blowing over and we decided to go on down. Besides it was half-past three and Ostheimer, as usual, was beginning to think of supper.

Long slopes of scree and shale lean down to the Fraser Glacier; we took off the rope and were soon far below. Peals of thunder were heard in the north, and a shower of rain swept by as we left the ice. At five o'clock we were once more among the mosquitoes—Con heard them buzzing nearly half a mile away and put a turn of the rope about his ice-axe lest they carry it off—and spent a miserable hour fighting them in the woods below our camp. On arrival we found Jack and Dave stretched on the grass, looking through the binoculars toward the Astoria meadows. What they at first had thought was a grizzly turned out to be a cariboo; and on watching we counted no less than twenty-five of them feeding and slowly moving across the grassy slopes. As we turned toward the fire, drawn by the appetizing odors from Jack's cookery, the clouds were breaking above The Ramparts and a broad shaft of golden light formed a bright pattern on the Eremite Glacier.

Early in the morning we broke camp and returned to Moat Lake, a ride of some three hours. The sky was overcast and the spires of The Ramparts were all hidden in trailing mist. Our tents were set up near the little ponds on the summit of Tonquin Pass, with a frontal view of the cliffs of Bastion and Turret. During the afternoon Conrad and Strumia went over to examine the northern wall of Geikie, but were able to see little of the upper portion because of low clouds that swirled about without lifting. Below the Turret pinnacle is a narrow gully with a broad, funnel-shaped top which collects the stones that come rattling and banging down night and day. Dave told me that the Indians for generations had known of this place of "mountain thunder." Sunset glow cast crimson and purple lights on the buttresses of Geikie and Barbican, with sulphur light suffusing the transparent mists through which the higher ridges were occasionally revealed.

Although the next day came with a grey dawn, Conrad and Strumia went out for a climb on Bastion. Dave rode off to explore a pass leading toward Yellowhead. Jack and I watched the mountaineers cut over a steep slope of snow high up and disappear into the hollow beyond. A lazy afternoon was spent in photographing groups of the pack-horses and their reflections in calm pools near Tonquin Pass. The climbers were back in time for supper, having reached a lofty notch through which they looked down upon Bennington Glacier. The final wedge, like a huge stone spade, had been out of the question under such weather conditions and with the limited time at their disposal; the path was hidden in fog and there was nothing to do but come down. As they neared camp they came upon a huge old antlered cariboo within a range of twenty feet; they held still, but the great beast scented them and moved off snorting and pawing the ground.

It was our last night in camp with the outfit, and as usual the weather showed signs of immediate clearing. My conviction is that Conrad is the reincarnation of Scheherazade, with several hundred extra yarns thrown in. Would that we had the wit to reproduce his own inimitable style! At all events he was in great form that evening, and treated us to tales of startling adventure: snake-collecting in Egypt, sheep-herding in Australia, gold-washing in the Northwest, wanderings in the South Seas, hunting in the Siberian Altai. The most beautiful place in the world, he believes, is the island of Madeira; there he would like to spend a little of his old age before retiring to a cottage in the Tyrol. And the most interesting place of all is New Zealand. Among the many strange things which befell him there, none had a more amusing sequel than his experiment in spiritualism:

During a long climbing tour in the New Zealand Alps, Conrad had a mystical lady under his guidance who often attempted to communicate with spirits of the departed. Her guide appearing interested, she imparted much information, and after his return to Canada sent him a considerable amount of literature on the subject. So one night, Con told us, he attempted to mesmerize himself into a trance. Placing a lighted candle on the foot of the bed, he lay down and gazed steadily at the flame. He was on the point of arriving at that exalted state when his spirit would be free of its body, when his big toes suddenly received a horrible scorching from hot candle-grease. The candle fell over and bedding blazed up. With a fearful yell he made a dive for a bucket of water, extinguished the conflagration, but ruined the floor and almost drowned his wife in the room below! We were almost hysterical with mirth before the end of the story and narrowly escaped rolling into our own fire.

Gradually recovering our equanimity we noticed that from behind Maccarib and Oldhorn, beyond the little lakes, a full moon had come up to light the shadowy walls of The Ramparts. Pinnacle after pinnacle caught up a gleaming moonbeam as if hidden sprites were racing along the ridges and touching them with torches into a silver glow. Slowly rose the moon; not in solemn grandeur, but rather with full face smiling as if in sympathy with our merriment. A wind from the Tonquin Pass was gently moving the pine-tops; there was a tinkling of bells as our horses wandered across the meadows.

CHAPTER XIV
IN THE SHADOW OF MOUNT ROBSON

"No game was ever worth a rap
For a rational man to play,
Into which no accident, no mishap
Could possibly find a way."

EVEREST EXPEDITION, 1924

It was during my first season of real mountaineering in the Northwest that I saw Mount Robson. Our climbing had been in widely separated regions that summer—in the Rockies, along the Canadian Pacific; in the Selkirk Range. We had tramped through the Cascades, voyaged up the coast in a tiny steamer to the islands of southeastern Alaska, and had camped by the glaciers that come down to Taku and Atlin. It was late in the fall when we started eastward from Prince Rupert, on the Grand Trunk road; there was a delightful crispness in the clear September air, sharpening the outlines of jagged little peaks of the Coast Range that lifted above the dim violet of distant, forested slopes, and the nearer brilliance of yellowed birch and poplar banking the Skeena River.

And then, for a day, our train had followed the canyon of the Fraser, past the hilly mining country near Prince George; and, at evening, we were on the bend near Tête Jaune, with the glorious massif of Robson towering afar. Clouds were gathering, and the vision was soon gone; but we had one splendid moment when the mountain's crest was golden, above a mist-wreathed base.

Of course I had read about the mountain before. It was first described by Lord Milton and Dr. Cheadle, early travellers through the North Thompson Valley, in their book *The North-West Passage by Land*. "On every side," we are told,[104] "the snowy heads of mighty hills crowded round, whilst, immediately behind us, a giant among giants, and immeasurably supreme, rose Robson's Peak. This magnificent mountain is of conical form, glacier-clothed, and rugged. When we first caught sight of it, a shroud of mist partially enveloped the summit, but this presently rolled away, and we saw its upper portion dimmed by a necklace of light feathery clouds, beyond which its pointed apex of ice, glittering in the morning sun, shot up far into the blue heaven above, to a height of probably 10,000 or 15,000 feet. It was a glorious sight, and one which the Shuswaps of The Cache assured us had rarely been seen by human eyes, the summit being generally hidden by clouds."

The very origin of the mountain's name is lost in the past;[105] but the Indians had their own names for it, long before the arrival of white men. A.R.C. Selwyn,[106] Director of the Geological Survey of Canada, as early as 1871, reported that the Indians told him their name for the mountain signified "The lines in the rocks." As Dr. Dawson, in a paper presented before the Royal Society of Canada in 1891, informs us,[107] "The Kamloops Indians affirm, that the very highest mountain they know is on the north side of the valley at the Tête Jaune Câche, about ten miles from the valley. This is named *Yuh-hai-haś-kun*, from the appearance of a spiral road running up it. No one has ever been known to reach the top, though a former chief of Tsuk-tsuk-kwãlk, on the North Thompson was near the top once while hunting goat. When he realized how high he was he became frightened and returned." The Cree Indians call Robson simply "The Big Mountain," but this seems to be a modernism; old men, with whom I have talked, say that their tribe never had a special name for the peak.

Mount Robson is the highest summit in the Rockies of Canada; but, like many a lesser peak, its height has diminished with recent measurements. The first triangulation, that of McEvoy, resulted in a figure of 13,700 feet; but the more recent determination of the Interprovincial Boundary Commission has brought this down to 12,972 feet. Thus an old illusion is shattered, and no peak of the Rockies of Canada attains thirteen thousand feet.

Dark was the night when the train pulled through Yellowhead Pass and down to Jasper. This was in the days before hotels, and one obtained lodging in rooms above the grocery-store; or, if the vacation was an extended one, in the "tent city" on Lake Beauvert, where the attractive Lodge of the Canadian National is now situated. The Grand Trunk was then running a through train to Prince Rupert only on alternate days; so in order to go back next day for a better view of Mount Robson—as I had decided to do—it was necessary to get permission to ride on the freight. There was less trouble about it at that time than there is now, and I know of no more delightful way of seeing the mountains—I refer of course to the railway zone—than from the caboose of a slow-moving "side-door pullman." If the engineer happened to be very good-natured, you rode up front on the cow-catcher; with every opportunity for photographs, and, perhaps, if there was a delay in waiting for an express to pass, the chance to go fishing with the train-crew.

Roadbeds of the mountain area, recently constructed, were not yet equal to the rolling-stock which passed over them. We started off early in the morning, up the valley of the sun-flecked Miette, and on through Yellowhead Pass. Standing on the rear platform, looking across at the heights of Mount Fitzwilliam,[108] we were startled by a crashing and grinding. Jumping off, we saw that a spread rail and a buckled truck had wrecked the whole train ahead, and that several huge loads of groceries had spilled down the embankment of the Fraser River, with more than one car slanted out on a precarious angle and threatening to follow.

So the engineer wired for a wrecking crew, and the trainmen got out their fishing-tackle. We were only half way to Robson, and I walked back along the tracks to Lucerne to await another train that was due on the Canadian Northern road. I have never regretted this pleasant stroll; there was no reason for hurrying—a small boy informed me that my train would be four hours late—and the time was passed on the lake shore, where ducks were swimming and the placid water mirrored the peaks of Yellowhead.

It was again dark when we started westward. In a few minutes, across the Fraser, we could see the fires lit by the train crew to assist them in clearing the wreck of our freight. The night was calm and clear, and a red, waning moon rose over the hilltops as we neared Moose Lake and the Rainbow Range. I had no very accurate idea as to the exact location of Mount Robson, or just how one would set about getting near to it. We had seen it from Tête Jaune, and realized that the mountain lay north of the Fraser; but of the trails through the intervening valleys and forests we knew nothing. Still I knew that I could again see it from the railroad, and under better weather conditions; I thought it might be possible to find a way across the river. I was quite determined to go as close as possible to that loftiest of mountains.

It is a strange and interesting little adventure to look back upon. I knew practically nothing of the ways of the trail; I had no equipment save a camera and a rucksack filled with provisions; it was late in the month of September. The train slowed down to let me off by the box-car filled with hay, which then served as Robson Station. It was midnight; I was alone, and a cold wind blowing from the west and the rising moon were my sole companions when the train had passed around a bend and out of sight. I could not see that much was to be gained in waiting for morning to come; it was almost impossible to restrain my eagerness for a sight of the mountain. And so I started off along the tracks in the semi-darkness. Youth does such things.

And suddenly the vision appeared! Mist and vapour play strange tricks with one's judgment of size and distance—moonlight affects it to perhaps an even greater degree. I had walked several hundred yards along the tracks, and then I stopped, scarcely believing what I saw. There it was: Robson, "the mountain of the spiral road," seeming to touch the very heavens, flooded with soft light and gleaming like molten silver. The light of the moon seemed to become tangible, as if one were swimming in a luminescent haze that altered and exaggerated refraction. I had seen higher peaks before, and have since stood on the summits of many, but nothing has ever equalled the impression of stupendous height that Robson gave on that starlit night of years ago. It seemed to me then as if I were gazing up to the throne of some Divinity; although maturer years have somewhat tempered this idea to the thought that there is merely a feminine quality in some mountains which makes them best seen at night.

But certainly that did not enter my head at the time. I sat down on a trestle and dangled my legs over the side, and looked and looked. But contemplation of the sublime cannot maintain the body at an even temperature on a freezing night. I got up and moved slowly along, rubbing my eyes and still half afraid they were deceiving me. And then a piece of luck: a bobbing twinkling light along the rails ahead. It was carried by Bert Wilkins, an outfitter then working for Donald Phillips, who had come out looking for me. I had met him for a moment when the train came through a few days before and had told him that I would try to come back. He still had some horses down in the Grand Forks and in a few minutes we had arranged for a pack-train trip to Robson Pass. I was glad at the thought of having company who knew the way.

The keeper of a section-house put us up for the night, and next morning we went down for the horses. There was then no bridge over the Fraser; but a logjam, long since departed, afforded a place of crossing. We rounded up the cayuses, and finished a tremendous breakfast of bear meat, potatoes and steaming coffee. On the preceding day Bert had shot a large black bear on a nearby berry-slide, and the hide was now nailed up on the door of the shack. A "homesteader," whose section is in the angle of the Grand Forks, came over and joined us as cook. We were off shortly after seven o'clock, three riders and two pack-horses, not long after the first sunbeams reached us across the high hills bordering the Fraser. One crosses the old freight road and, entering the woods, leaves civilization behind.

The trail is unforgettable in its beauty, with spruce and cedar trees straight and perfect above a carpet of berries, fern-brakes, and devil's club; tropically luxuriant. The stream descends in cascades and rapids, with the southern cliffs of Robson almost above one's head. Far behind, in the direction of Tête Jaune, rises the multicolored ridge of Mica Mountain in the Cariboos. We are soon in Robson's shadow and the top is no longer in sight. Turning a corner we come out on the shore of Kinney Lake, with the slopes of Little Grizzly and the pinnacle of Whitehorn far above. Just now there is not a cloud to relieve the deep blue of the sky, nor a ripple on the lake to disturb the images of tall trees and soaring peaks. Some day there will be a hotel here and perhaps a funicular; how much the worse!

Rounding the northern shore of the lake, through the trees along the water's edge, we cross the expansive delta of glacial silt at its western end and take up the trail again in the Valley of a

Thousand Falls. There is a beautiful glacier and a rock spire at the valley head, and if not quite a thousand falls come streaming down from the cliffs on either side, the number is at all events most satisfactory and surpassed only by the beauty of their unbroken height. We cross through rushing streams, and slowly climb up the thousand feet or more of zigzag trail, cleverly engineered with wooden trestles, to the upper levels where the roar of Emperor Falls is heard—dissonant to our vocal efforts in urging the horses along.

Across the deep valley-trench, Whitehorn is magnificent with its icy arête and hanging glaciers, above a black precipice streaked with threadlike, silvery waterfalls. Beyond the misty rainbows formed in the cauldron of Emperor Falls, above tier on tier of horizontal strata and cliff-belts, rises Mount Robson, steep and snowless, into an enormous wedge. Skirting a burned-over, level area, and emerging from the woods, we reach the marshy flats at the western end of Berg Lake, with distant views to Robson Pass. The north side of Robson is sheer, but snow again appears. The little basin at the foot of the snowy Helmet gives rise to the five thousand feet of icefall known as the Blue, or Tumbling Glacier. There are few places in the world where lake scenery can equal this prospect; as we ride along, bits of the ice-front break off with a crash and the fragments add to the number of floating bergs already sparkling in the dark-blue water.

Just east of Tumbling Glacier is the rocky promontory of Rearguard, with the tongue of the Robson Glacier protruding beyond. The eastern end of the lake, Robson Pass, is the end of our day's ride. Stiff and tired, we slip down from our sweating ponies, fatigue somewhat lessened by thoughts of a square meal soon to be ours. The outfit was very sporty and had packed along a portable stove, on which bear steak and potatoes were soon sizzling and sending up delectable odours that distracted one's attention from the business of putting up tents. It was bitterly cold when the sun went down, but we moved close to the fire, while Bert regaled us with tales of sheep-hunting in the north country.

When I crawled out of my blankets in the morning there was a film of ice on the nearby brook. The northern face of Robson was clear and tinged with a rosy pink; and promising noises from the cook-fly suggested a successful day ahead. Breakfast over, we set out to explore the lower reaches of Robson Glacier. Clambering over the morainal débris and up the tongue to the glacial surface, we made our way over the parallel ridges of ice which run in the longitudinal direction of the glacier. The tongue splits on Robson Pass, a Pacific–Arctic watershed, some of the water flowing to Berg Lake and reaching the Fraser, while another brook runs northward to Lake Adolphus and Smoky River—a Mackenzie headwater. The glacier originates in the high saddle and extensive névé fields between Robson and Mount Resplendent, an extensive area of sérac and crevasse running eastward to the base of a curious buttress, resembling a candle-snuffer and known as the Extinguisher, whence the level and unbroken glacier runs northward for more than three miles to the pass. To the west, just seen along the cliffs of Rearguard, Whitehorn lifts to a needle-point; northward, the view is closed by Mount Mumm and peaks near Moose Pass that border the valley of the Smoky.

During the afternoon we sauntered over to Lake Adolphus and took a nap on the mossy banks. There were superb views of the dazzling cone of Resplendent, and the glacier; but Robson itself was hidden by the cliffs of Rearguard. Day ended in glorious sunset, with afterglow on the snowy peaks. Even the cook could not draw us into the tent until the last bit of gold and purple colouring had merged into the green and dull grey of nightfall.

We made an early start on the down-trail next morning and were back at the corral in the Grand Forks by eleven o'clock. I spent a couple of hours fishing in the Fraser and landed several small trout for lunch, rather opportune, for by this time there was not much left of the bear steaks. It was the off day for train service, so we decided on a hunting trip in the cabins at the mouth of Grand Forks, and successfully bagged a choice assortment of pack-rats that had grown sleek and fat from their forays on our provisions. On the day following, we packed several fifty-pound sacks of potatoes from the homestead's garden to the railroad, and had still energy enough to ride horses over to the old freight-road where we shot three coyote that we had noticed in the edge of the grass. It was a tame sport, but the fur was in good condition and the hides were soon tacked up beside the bearskin.

In the evening we rode bareback for a little way along the Fraser trail, driving the other horses ahead toward Jasper.

It was not for a number of years—the Great War had come and gone—that we could come back again to Robson; not until the summer of 1924. In that season we were completing our exploration of the Continental Divide, northward from Lake Louise; we had been to Athabaska Pass and to the peaks of Tonquin and on to Yellowhead. It was a July day, the 17th and cloudy to be exact, when Conrad Kain, Alfred Ostheimer, and I unloaded our packs before a crowd of curious tourists at Robson Station.

This time we had come to climb; there would be more of hard work and less of sentiment than on my first visit. But how changed things were! Cabins had sprung up like mushrooms; there was a broad trail, almost a road, leading to a well-engineered bridge spanning the Fraser canyon; permanent camps on the summit of Robson Pass made it unnecessary to use horses or even carry provisions. It was getting altogether too civilized! We put our packs on our backs and started off, arriving in due course at Kinney Lake. There we met the Oberland guides employed by the Canadian National, Hans Kohler and Alfred Streich. They had been of the party that came looking for us on Mount Hooker, and were now making themselves acquainted with the Robson district prior to the camp of the Alpine Club of Canada.

We had a pleasant walk together, next morning, when we all went up to the cabins at Robson Pass. We had not yet seen the top of Mount Robson, weather seemed to be getting worse instead of better, and we were quite ready to believe the Indians' statement that it was, after all, rarely beheld by human eyes. Fog hung in the valley, blowing in from the Fraser; then, in a change of wind, coming back again from the Smoky. The mountain rises so much above its immediate surroundings—scarcely a peak nearby approaches within two thousand feet of its elevation—that, by its very isolation, it becomes a storm centre. I thought longingly of the cloudless September days in another year.

Enforced inactivity was making us jumpy; so, on July 20th, although it was cloudy and a high wind blowing, we all decided that something must be done. It occurred to us to try Resplendent (11,240 feet), and go up as far as we could. So we started out at half-past six, and made our way to the glacier, wandering up to the séracs and through a portion of them, killing time in the hope that the wind would die down. It seemed amusing to try the rocks of the north arête, the crest of which had been but twice followed throughout. We roped below a little schrund, as well-guided a party as has ever tackled a Canadian mountain. Ostheimer, with Kohler and Streich, made one rope; while Conrad and I followed behind, showing wisdom therein, as we could use them for a wind-break while they cut the steps. Streich had quite a job of it; it was terribly cold, and the slopes below the rocks were steep and hard. However, in an hour we were in the lee of a rocky pinnacle and enjoying a second breakfast of bread and sardines. Conrad and I then went ahead and found some quite delightful climbing in a short stretch of chimneys and slanting slabs, where handholds were few and body-friction alone kept one from swinging sideways on the rope. At one o'clock we were on the upper snow-level below the peak; everything was enveloped in swirls of mist, but the wind had lessened in force and we could occasionally see for a short distance ahead. Resplendent is not an easy mountain on which to lose the way, and though there was no view to be had, Conrad led us through the fog to the steep-corniced summit in another ninety minutes. There was still enough of a gale so that the last portion had to be done carefully; Streich cut up to the cornice, while the rest of us crouched down in the driving snow and anchored. Each of us had a look over the edge, and then we beat a retreat to the western snow-col at the head of Robson Glacier.

The fog-level had risen to 10,000 feet, and under the edge of its grey blanket we looked far out across the sunlit Fraser Valley to the borders of the Cariboos and peaks beyond. Still no sign of a real break in the weather. As we descended with long glissades into the main basin, the Bess Group was visible in the north. There was just one momentary glimpse of Robson's peak, rising like a sword-point, vanishing again in the veil of billowing cloud. We were back in camp, with good appetites, just twelve hours after our start, feeling that we had accomplished something even under unfavorable conditions.

Camp was being put up for the annual activities of the Alpine Club of Canada, and the first hikers arrived next afternoon. On the 22nd, although the clouds hung low, a large party on three ropes ascended Lynx Mountain (10,471 feet), an attractive peak of the Robson cirque, commanding a widespread view of the Robson and Coleman glaciers and of Resplendent Valley. One ascends snow-slopes, with a few steps to be cut, nearly to the southwestern saddle whence a broad highway of rising shale leads to the summit. It took six hours to reach the highest point, and but half that time for returning, with many a boisterous glissade in the softening snow carrying us almost to the glacier. Resplendent and Robson appeared several times; never quite clear, but moist and shadowy in the mist. Down Resplendent Valley we could see the slender needle known as the "Finger of Kain," and far to the south, momentarily of course, we thought we could discern the jagged outlines of the Rampart Group.

Professor Coleman may be considered the first to approach Mount Robson with the idea of climbing it. As early as 1907, he and his companions had come over the Saskatchewan and Athabaska trails from Laggan, and had reached the head of Grand Forks Valley. They returned in the year following, going in from Edmonton and gaining Robson Pass by way of Moose River and the Smoky. After several attempts in bad weather, a final climb from the glacier broke down at 11,000 feet.

In August 1909, Rev. G.B. Kinney and Donald Phillips attained the summit crest by way of the northwest arête and western face. It was a fine, sporting effort and deserves the credit of a first ascent. Later in the summer a party of distinguished British mountaineers—Messrs. Amery, Hastings, and Mumm, under the guidance of Moritz Inderbinen—had a further try at the eastern face, but desisted after a narrow escape from an avalanche. The very highest point was not attained until A.H. MacCarthy and W.W. Foster, with Conrad Kain, reached it during the summer of 1913. Their route was also by the dangerous eastern slope, but descent was made in a southwesterly direction, with a night out, to Kinney Lake.

Writing for the *Alpine Journal*, Conrad said of the southwestern ridge, "There is no doubt that this ridge will be the future route to ascend to the summit of Mt. Robson. But the climb cannot be done from Lake Kinney in one day. It will be necessary to build a hut at the head of the Lake Kinney Valley. The snow conditions on the highest peaks in the Canadian Rockies can never be compared with those in the Alps, as there are more avalanches in the Rockies on account of the dryness of the atmosphere, which leaves the snow powdery and unpacked. And so I may say that Mt. Robson will always be a risky climb, even on the easiest side, on account of avalanches."

In an article for the *Canadian Alpine Journal* Conrad was no less emphatic, writing, "In all my mountaineering in various countries, I have climbed only a few mountains that were hemmed in with more difficulties. Mt. Robson is one of the most dangerous expeditions I have made. The dangers consist in snow and ice, stone avalanches, and treacherous weather."

During the ten years since, Conrad no doubt modified this opinion of the mountain; but his view in regard to the length of the climb was unchanged. He had so carefully prospected the southwestern slopes of the mountain that the real climbing difficulties were reduced to a minimum; but the danger from falling ice could never be ignored. And so, although we had come to the very foot of the all-highest, I had very little idea of doing more than look up at it from lesser height. But the wretched weather had most of the time effectually prevented even that much. Under the direction of Phillips, a high camp (at about 6500 feet) had been placed near the last trees in the gully above Kinney Lake; we had seen the white speck of a tent, high on the green point, when we had come by the lake a number of days before. We were rather pleased to be chosen to make an attempt with the first official party from the main camp; as a matter of fact, our vacation time was drawing near a close and the trial must be made now or postponed for a long while.

And so, on July 23rd, with Messrs. Geddes, Moffat, and Pollard, Ostheimer and I—all members of the Alpine Club of Canada—packed down to Kinney Lake. Conrad, of course, led the way, adding considerably to our remarks about the unpromising weather. As this would prevent serious climbing on the morrow we decided to spend the night at the lake rather than go up to the higher level.

Mount Robson may be considered as a gigantic wedge, rising—although structurally the lowest point of a syncline—in buttressed heights to the summit ice-cap, ten-thousand feet above the Grand Forks Valley. On its northern slopes, exposed for only seven thousand feet, it presents a spectacle of snow and ice; but the western and southern slopes, above timber-line, are comparatively bare and rocky. It was this southern aspect that we had beheld from the mountains of the Whirlpool, during our journey to Athabaska Pass, when we marveled at the lonely isolation of the great peak. From that point of view, the precipitous southeastern shoulder had been so foreshortened as to be almost indistinguishable; but now, from the shore of Kinney Lake, the lower cliffs and couloirs, with their lines of horizontal strata, attracted our attention.

Next day it took five hours to mount the steep trail through the woods to the climbing-camp. Conrad had the heaviest pack of all—only slightly smaller than himself—and was forced to "build a fence" of willow-twigs in order to accommodate a pail and several loaves of bread on top. The afternoon was spent in camp-work: chopping wood, carrying water, and in constructing a well in the nearby gully.

Above the cliffs, a little to the north of our tents, we could see rolling clouds which hid the crest of Robson, but which lifted enough to show us the green séracs of a lower icefall, from which two crashing avalanches came down just before we started supper. Sitting on the limb of an ancient, storm-gnarled tree, one felt that it would be quite possible to throw a stone into the grey waters of Kinney Lake, three thousand feet below. The lake was now in shadow, but the sun, breaking through the upper levels, flooded Whitehorn with a luminous red-gold light. To the southwest we could see across the bordering hills of Fraser River, almost to the head of Canoe and North Thompson rivers, and beyond to the Cariboos, whose winding central glaciers were steeped in lavender, and heliotrope—last pale colours of evening.

During the night the clouds rolled back, and we started out at four o'clock on the finest of clear mornings. In two hours we had climbed over long slopes of shale and scree to the limits of vegetation, in the top of a small cirque near the lower icefalls. These icefalls, two in number and separated by a narrow partition of cliff, owe their formation to a reconsolidation in the avalanche ice that breaks off from the summit cap. Walled in on one side by the southeastern shoulder it is forced, for the most part, into the couloirs bounding the head of Kinney Lake Valley.

Early in the morning, it was quite safe to cross close below these falls; we were quickly through the short distance, floored with shattered blocks, without a sign of anything giving way above. Then up and up the crest of a long, rocky ridge, where the sun met us, to a flat ledge with a trickle of water that met the requirements of a breakfasting place. On such a level, Conrad told us, a hut should be constructed. It would necessitate the carrying up of fuel, since timber-line is more than a thousand feet below, but it would immensely facilitate the ascent.

We sat there, eating bread and jam, a little below the first snow, and looked across to the shoulder. Above the icefalls, under which we had recently crossed, is a level of hardened snow swept by tracks of immense avalanches that had come from the great furrowed ice-cap that sparkled above us. The cap itself, from the western crest of the mountain to the top of the southeastern shoulder, is guarded by a veritable barrier of ice, some hundred feet high. This is the real danger of the southwestern route: one must work up through this upper fall, not often feasible, or traverse under it, or a portion of it, toward the western arête.

We were soon on the snow; Conrad, Ostheimer and I on one rope, striking up a sharp snow-crest that connects the rock ridge from the southwest with the base of the ice-cap. We stopped to reconnoitre, while the other rope came up. In the ice-cliff there was a choice between a frozen chimney, nearby, blue and steep, which Conrad pronounced hazardous for the leading man, and a lateral traverse on horizontal, snow-covered ledges, below the séracs, to a break that seemed to afford access to higher slopes. The traverse seemed the only course; but it looked nasty. It meant an exposed crossing through the head of the great southwest couloir, so conspicuous from the Grand Forks Valley. It was past the noon hour, the ice was in the full light of a hot sun for the first time in a fortnight; and the summit of the mountain, although less than two thousand feet above us, showed us plainly enough that to go on meant a night bivouac. Not very much more than two weeks before we had had two long nights of shivering in the caves of Mount Hooker, and Ostheimer and I were not keen for an immediate repetition of that mode of existence.

Just then there was an ominous cracking, and Conrad shouted: "It's coming down," and we all ducked under the nearest ledge. Fortunately only a few small cakes fell, and these not near us. Still it does not take a very big piece to put one *hors de combat*, and the business might not yet be done with. I made up my mind that the amateurs on our rope must turn back. Everyone has his own standard about what is to be done under such circumstances—mine is that there is plenty of good mountaineering to be done without knowingly placing oneself in an exposed position, requiring time for its passage, where ice or rock *may* come down. I sometimes subject this to a very liberal interpretation; but on this day, toward the end of a long and successful season, I was not willing to take a chance on the good behaviour of those ice-pinnacles.

The others felt differently about it and inclined to go on. Conrad said, "Gentlemen, it is risky. I am willing to go on if you wish." So we decided that Conrad should rope with them and continue, while Ostheimer and I on the rope remaining should descend the ridge below, and continue to the high camp. So we parted, wishing each other the best of luck.

The four were immediately lost to sight behind a hummock of snow, while we descended in the steps cut on the way up. We were near the level of Whitehorn, with a widespread view across the Fraser Valley. It seemed to us worth while to ascend the little rock-point which forms the very apex of a buttress just south of the main couloir. From near Kinney Lake it seems to rise as a sharp spire; but from below one does not see the snow that extends behind and toward the ice-cap. We built a little cairn, and sat down to watch the climbers' progress. All at once there was a grinding crash in the direction of the couloir, and some large blocks of ice came tumbling down. The men were still out of sight, but that shower of pieces must have been uncommonly close to them. They were untouched, however, and a little later we saw them gain the ice-cap through the break in the séracs. Still later, as we descended, we saw them high up on the snow, half hidden at times by veils of mist.

We had come down nearly to the lower icefalls; we stopped to finish off some sardines and coffee, seating ourselves on a broad ledge that seemed almost to overhang Kinney Lake. Then something made us turn our gaze to the lower ice. There was not a sound, but as we looked the entire front of pinnacles began to move. Slowly the green wall tottered and sank, splintering laterally and sweeping the path through which we had come in the early morning. Then came the crashes. We sat as if petrified until the last echoes died away. Conrad heard the noise, on top of Mount Robson. He told me, afterward, that they spent the night near where we had been sitting and thought that the avalanche had caught us. But no such misfortune overtook us, and before dark we were in the blankets beside the campfire.

Conrad and his successful party came in at four o'clock next morning, all rather tired—a night on the rocks is never restful. I got up, did what I could to help get breakfast ready, and then packed down-trail to Kinney Lake, eventually making Robson Pass in time for a belated lunch. The last pull was a hard one. And so, after more than a thousand miles of trail-riding through the

Canadian Alps, with success on many high peaks, in more than one long season, I have not conquered Robson—yet.

It is not fair to the mountain to say that conditions are always such as have been described. Later on, within only a couple of weeks, in 1924, a total of twenty people had reached the summit without mishap. Perhaps after a few days of sunlight the ice conditions were better. But to my mind there is always a potential menace in those westerly-exposed séracs. If enough parties try it, there will at some time be an accident from avalanche.[109] I have not yet forgotten what Conrad wrote after the first ascent, in 1913, "I do not know whether my *Herren* contemplated with a keen alpine eye the dangers to which we were exposed."

Mountaineering includes a philosophy too optimistic for one ever to dwell on defeat; there is always happiness in having tried with good comrades. Perhaps it were best that I should never attain that height; I might think the less of it.[110] For, to me at least, it would be nothing short of sacrilege to stand on the very summit of the majestic mountain that, when little more than a boy, I went hunting for—and found—in the pale splendour of northern moonlight.

CHAPTER XV
TRAIL'S END

"These splendid limbs—
Life lent you them; you did not make nor choose them;
  but yours the right to use them
  right royally for a span.
When the light dims,
When their day wanes, and all the stars are beckoning,
  see you return them proudly for the reckoning,
  to prove you lived a man."
— GEOFFREY WINTHROP YOUNG

And so we come to the End of the Trail. What, after all, has it amounted to—this riding in the wilderness, this mad scrambling on inaccessible crags? If you ask us, "Of what use?" perhaps we shall only smile and remain silent, answering not at all. If your curiosity be aroused, perhaps you will go and see for yourself—and find the answer we might have given. That for a little moment we have transcended ourselves; and, upon a mountain top, looking off across the vastness of a glorious earth, have felt ourselves apart from the sham and pettiness of daily life, and have come a little nearer to the Unfathomable Presence.

It seems to me as if the *Striving for a Goal* were the outstanding virtue of mountaineering. Life, and Youth in particular, are uncertain in their offerings of success. Most of us have ideals, of course, but the opportunity for attaining them is often remote, and the desired ends float away into the realm of impossibility. How different it is with the climber! He has a peak to scale, and with it the enjoyment of all the splendour of the mountain world—and in a day, usually in less time, he sets foot on the desired height with all the joy that comes from the completion of a self-appointed task.

One should visit the Canadian Northland with eye and mind alert to the beauty of Nature's handicraft: the artistry in all of it; from the broad sculpturing of crag and chasm to the delicate perfection of a tiny flower.

The things we treasure—the memories of peak and sunlit icefield; of forgotten trails; of haunting melodies of the homeland, piped on a harmonica, in the glow of northern campfires—where indeed can one discover these in the musty pages of a geography? No map of a river valley can visualize a Canadian forest, with laden horses swinging along in line; no plaster relief can ever make one understand the moods of mountains, half hidden in cloud or towering in the many-hued glory of early morning. What atlas can picture Singing Youth, on horseback, crossing a sparkling ford to flower-decked meadows, with distant mountain spires dim blue in the noon haze? These trails are not for everyone, but for those who go there will result such memories "as dreams are made on," and the reward is great enough.

Pack-trains of yesterday: "Slim," the horse that always had to be packed twice; "Fanny," who carried the dishpan and the ice- axes; "Gunboat," who carried me; "Beauty," the white, belled steed that Conrad rode and who bucked on occasion; "Hammerhead," "Briden," and all the rest—I wonder if they remember the boys who rode them so gaily, cinched them so tightly after a night's feeding of green grass, and drove them with such strange language? I think it unlikely; their minds—and with all their eccentricities, I still believe those cayuses have minds—are doubtless more attuned to the present and the future than to any thoughts of the past. Their dreams, quite likely, are of lush pastures where the grass is never bitter, and of shady paths where flies and the diamond-hitch are things unknown. We, remembering, are ourselves forgotten.

Back-trails of tomorrow—God willing, there will be some who come after us, finding in the light of new campfires, built on hearth-stones that were once ours, that Peace we know. We who have travelled the long, lone trails of the Northland, know that Peace-of-the-hills is an Angel whose blessing is only obtained by wrestling.

> *"What if I live no more those kingly days?*
>   *their night sleeps with me still.*
> *I dream my feet upon the starry ways;*
>   *my heart rests in the hill.*
> *I may not grudge the little left undone;*
> *I hold the heights, I keep the dreams I won."*

APPENDIX A

SUMMARY OF ASCENTS, BETWEEN KICKING HORSE AND ROBSON PASSES, ACCOMPLISHED BY THE AUTHOR'S EXPEDITIONS, 1922–24

(Names of Swiss Guides are in italics.)

Mt. Robson	12,972 feet.	July 25, 1924. Ascent to point *ca.* 11,000 feet on S.W. shoulder. A.J. Ostheimer, J.M. Thorington.
Mt. Columbia	12,294 feet.	July 14, 1923. Second ascent. W.S. Ladd, J. Simpson, J.M. Thorington, *C. Kain*.
North Twin	12,085 feet.	July 10, 1923. First ascent. W.S. Ladd, J.M. Thorington, *C. Kain*.
Mt. Athabaska	11,452 feet.	July 19, 1923. Third ascent. W.S. Ladd, J.M. Thorington, *C. Kain*.
Mt. Resplendent	11,240 feet.	July 20, 1924. Traverse via N.N.W. arête. J.M. Thorington, *C. Kain;*

		A.J. Ostheimer, *H. Kohler, A. Streich.*
Mt. Saskatchewan	10,964 feet.	July 12, 1923. First ascent. W.S. Ladd, J.M. Thorington, *C. Kain.*
Mt. Barnard	10,955 feet.	July 14, 1922. First ascent. H. Palmer, J.M. Thorington, *E. Feuz.*
Mt. Freshfield	10,945 feet.	July 18, 1922. Fourth ascent. H. Palmer, J.M. Thorington, *E. Feuz.*
Simon Pk.	10,899 feet.	July 13, 1924. First ascent. A.J. Ostheimer, M. Strumia, J.M. Thorington, *C. Kain.*
Mt. Hooker	10,782 feet.	July 5, 1924. First ascent. A.J. Ostheimer, M. Strumia, J.M. Thorington, *C. Kain.*
Mt. Nanga Parbat	10,780 feet.	July 16, 1922. First ascent. H. Palmer, J.M. Thorington, *E. Feuz.*
McDonell Pk.	10,776 feet.	July 13, 1924. First traverse. A.J. Ostheimer, M. Strumia, J.M. Thorington, *C. Kain.*
Mt. Trutch	10,690 feet.	July 14, 1922. First ascent. H. Palmer, J.M. Thorington, *E. Feuz.*
Lynx Mt.	10,471 feet.	July 22, 1924. Miss M. Gold, A.J. Ostheimer,

		J.M. Thorington, with party of Alpine Club of Canada guided by *H. Kohler, A. Streich.*
Coronation Mt.	10,420 feet.	July 20, 1922. First ascent from Freshfield Glacier. J.M. Thorington, *E. Feuz.*
Mt. Gordon	10,336 feet.	July 24, 1923. W.S. Ladd, J.M. Thorington, *C. Kain.*
Mt. Gilgit	10,300 feet.	July 16, 1922. First ascent. H. Palmer, J.M. Thorington, *E. Feuz.*
Mt. Oates	10,220 feet.	July 3, 1924. First ascent. A.J. Ostheimer, M. Strumia, J.M. Thorington, *C. Kain.*
Mt. Castleguard	10,096 feet.	July 6, 1923. First traverse. T. Frayne, U. LaCasse, W.S. Ladd, J. Simpson, J.M. Thorington, *C. Kain.*
Mt. Kane	10,000 feet.	June 30, 1924. First ascent. A.J. Ostheimer, M. Strumia, J.M. Thorington, *C. Kain.*
Terrace Mt.	9570 feet.	July 9, 1923. First ascent. J.M. Thorington, *C. Kain.*
Mt. Brown	9156 feet.	July 1, 1924. A.J. Ostheimer, M. Strumia, J.M. Thorington, *C. Kain.*

APPENDIX B

SUMMARIZED ITINERARY OF EXPEDITIONS

I. EXPEDITION OF 1922

July 6	Field to camp on Amiskwi River.
July 7	Amiskwi (Baker) Pass. Ascent of Ensign Station.
July 8	Blaeberry River crossed.
July 9	Howse Pass. Visit to Conway Glacier.
July 10	Freshfield Glacier Camp.
July 11	Niverville Meadow Camp.
July 12	Mt. Niverville to 8500 feet. Return to Base Camp.
July 13	Survey work, Freshfield Glacier.
July 14	Ascents of Mt. Barnard and Mt. Trutch.
July 15	In camp.
July 16	Ascents of Mt. Nanga Parbat and Mt. Gilgit.
July 17	In camp.
July 18	Ascent of Mt. Freshfield. Return to Base Camp.
July 19	Survey work, Freshfield Glacier.

July 20	Ascent of Coronation Mt.
July 21	Howse River Camp.
July 22	Pyramid Camp.
July 23	Bow Lake.
July 24	Hector Slide.
July 25	Lake Louise.

II. EXPEDITION OF 1923

June 27	Lake Louise to Hector Slide.
June 28	Bow Lake.
June 29	Via Bow Pass to Upper Wildfowl Lake.
June 30	Saskatchewan Forks crossed.
July 1	Graveyard Camp. Ascent to Pinto Pass. Mt. Coleman to 7500 feet.
July 2	Last Grass Camp, head of Alexandra River. Visit to tongue of East Alexandra Glacier.
July 3	East and West Alexandra glaciers visited.
July 4	East Alexandra Glacier ascended to north basin of Mt. Lyell.
July 5	Castleguard Camp. Head of Saskatchewan Glacier visited.
July 6	Traverse of Mt. Castleguard, with crossing of portion of Columbia Icefield.
July 7	Emergency camp taken to Castleguard shoulder.

July 8	Visit to head of Castelets Creek.
July 9	Ascents of Terrace Mt.
July 10–11	Crossing of Columbia Icefield and ascent of North Twin.
July 12	Ascent of Mt. Saskatchewan.
July 13	In camp.
July 14	Ascent of Mt. Columbia.
July 15	In camp.
July 16	Castleguard Pass and descent of Saskatchewan Glacier with horses.
July 17	Saskatchewan Pass to Sunwapta.
July 18	Visit to Athabaska Glacier.
July 19	Ascent of Mt. Athabaska.
July 20	Graveyard Camp.
July 21	Saskatchewan Forks crossed. Murchison Camp.
July 22	Upper Wildfowl Lake.
July 23	Bow Pass. Visit to Peyto Glacier. Bow Lake.
July 24	Wapta Icefield. Traverse of Mt. Gordon, via Vulture Col. Descent to Balfour Pass, Yoho Glacier and Takakkaw Camp.
July 25	Lake Louise.

III. EXPEDITION OF 1924

June 26	Jasper to Whirlpool tie-camp.

June 27	Attempt to reach base of Mt. Fryatt. Camp three miles below mouth of Simon Creek.
June 28	Camp at junction of Scott Glacier stream with Whirlpool River.
June 29	Athabaska Pass. Ascent of Mt. Brown to 8500 feet.
June 30	Via Kane Glacier, ascent of Unnamed Point of Continental Divide, 9100 feet, S.W. of Mt. Hooker. Traverse of Mt. Kane.
July 1	Ascent of Mt. Brown.
July 2	Scott Glacier Camp.
July 3	Ascent of Mt. Oates.
July 4	In camp.
July 5–7	Ascent of Mt. Hooker.
July 8	In camp.
July 9	Whirlpool tie-camp.
July 10	Jasper.
July 11	Via Miette River and Meadow Creek to Tonquin Hill Camp.
July 12	Via Amethyst Lakes to Surprise Point Camp. Ascent of Surprise Point.
July 13	Ascent of Simon Peak. Traverse of McDonell Peak.
July 14	Moat Lake Camp.
July 15	Attempt on Bastion Peak.
July 16	Jasper.

July 17	Kinney Lake.
July 18	Berg Lake, Robson Pass.
July 19	In camp.
July 20	Ascent of Mt. Resplendent.
July 21	Ascent of Unnamed Point, 10,000 feet, E. of Mt. Resplendent.
July 22	Ascent of Lynx Mt.
July 23	Kinney Lake.
July 24	Climbing Camp, 6500 feet, Mt. Robson.
July 25	Mt. Robson to base of summit icefall.
July 26	Robson Pass.
July 27	Jasper.

APPENDIX C

A LIST OF SOME OF THE LOFTIEST TRIANGULATED PEAKS OF THE ROCKY MOUNTAINS OF CANADA, ARRANGED IN ORDER OF HEIGHT, TO WHICH ARE ADDED THE YEAR AND THE NAMES OF THOSE WHO TOOK PART IN THE FIRST ASCENT

(The names of amateurs are given alphabetically, irrespective of leadership. Names of Swiss Guides are in italics.)

Mt. Robson	12,972 ft.	[1909	G.B. Kinney, D. Phillips.]
		1913	W.W. Foster, A.H. MacCarthy, *C. Kain.*
Mt. Columbia	12,294 ft.	1902	J. Outram, *C. Kaufmann.*
North Twin	12,085 ft.	1923	W.S. Ladd, J.M. Thorington, *C. Kain.*
Mt. Clemenceau	12,001 ft.	1923	D.B. Durand, W.H. Harris, H.S. Hall, W.D. Harris, H.B. deVilliers-Schwab.
Mt. Forbes	11,902 ft.	1902	J.N. Collie, J. Outram, H.E.M. Stutfield, G.M. Weed, H. Woolley, *C. Kaufmann, H. Kaufmann.*
Mt. Alberta	11,874 ft.	1925	Y. Maki and five companions, *H. Führer, H. Kohler, Weber.*

Mt. Assiniboine	11,870 ft.	1901	J. Outram, *C. Bohren, C. Häsler.*
Mt. Goodsir (S.)	11,675 ft.	1903	C.E. Fay, H.C. Parker, *C. Häsler, C. Kaufmann.*
South Twin	11,675 ft.	1924	F. Field, O. Field, L. Harris, *J. Biner, E. Feuz Jr.*
Mt. Temple	11,626 ft.	1894	S.E.S. Allen, L. Frissell, W.D. Wilcox.
Mt. Goodsir (N.)	11,555 ft.	1909	J.P. Forde, P.D. McTavish, *E. Feuz Sr.*
Mt. Bryce	11,507 ft.	1902	J. Outram, *C. Kaufmann.*
Mt. Kitchener	11,500 ft.		Unclimbed
Mt. Lyell (5 pks.)	11,370 ft.		Unclimbed
	11,495 ft.	1902	J. Outram, *C. Kaufmann*
	11,495 ft.		Unclimbed
	11,260 ft.		Unclimbed
	11,180 ft.		Unclimbed
Mt. Athabaska	11,452 ft.	1898	J.N. Collie, H. Woolley.
Mt. Hungabee	11,447 ft.	1903	H.C. Parker, *C. Kaufmann, H. Kaufmann.*
Mt. King Edward	11,400 ft.	1924	J.W.A. Hickson, H. Palmer, *C. Kain.*
Mt. Victoria (S.)	11,355 ft.	1897	J.N. Collie, C.E. Fay, A. Michael, *P. Sarbach.*
Snow Dome	11,340 ft.	1898	J.N. Collie, H.E.M. Stutfield, H. Woolley.
Mt. Stutfield	11,320 ft.		Unclimbed

APPENDIX D

THE FRESHFIELD GLACIER, CANADIAN ROCKIES[111]
BY HOWARD PALMER

(Smithsonian Miscellaneous Collections, Vol. 76, No. 11)
To the student of the phenomena of active glaciers the Canadian Rockies offer an advantageous and almost untouched field. Three of the most accessible ice tongues along the Canadian Pacific Railway have been made the subject of detailed investigation, but on the remoter and larger ice systems almost no work has yet been done. During recent years, the Alberta–British Columbia Boundary Survey has produced a series of admirable contour maps (scale 1 : 62500) which delineate the Continental Divide, together with its adjacent mountains and glaciers. Thus there is now available to the glacialist an excellent groundwork for the prosecution of his particular researches.

Of the newly mapped glaciers, the Freshfield is the most attractive. Size, ease of access, and majesty of scenery all commend it. Lying in a direct line 40 miles northwest of Lake Louise, five days of comfortable travelling will take one to its tongue. The trail distance is about 65 miles, all the way through wild mountain valleys with peaks, glaciers, torrents and lakes in plenty to beguile the march. A good camp ground is to be had not far from the tongue and there is ample feed for the horses.

The Freshfield massif is a well-defined group of peaks about 12 miles square situated in a semicircular loop of the Continental Divide between tributaries of the North Saskatchewan and Columbia rivers. Its drainage is principally to the former. It is separated from the Yoho–Waputik group on the southeast by Howse Pass (5010 feet) of historic fame, and from the Forbes–Lyell group on the north by Bush Pass (7860 feet). There are 25 peaks in the group surpassing 10,000 feet in elevation, Mt. Barnard (10,955 feet) being the loftiest. Eleven of them exceed 10,500 feet.

The Freshfield Glacier and tributaries occupy an elliptical basin in the midst of the group, nine miles long from southeast to northwest, and four miles wide. Around the periphery the peaks stand in line, forming a retaining wall which almost completely incloses it. The ice discharges through a gorge-like valley to the northeast in a single tongue three-quarters of a mile wide and three miles long, buttressed on both sides by mountain masses over 10,000 feet high. Excepting this valley, there is no real break below 9000 feet in the entire sweep of the rim. The area of the ice and névé in the Freshfield system proper is approximately 22 square miles, but adjacent connected, or nearly connected, glaciers on the outer slopes of the basin bring the total area of ice in the group up to about 40 square miles. The trunk glacier from its most distant source to the tongue is almost exactly nine miles long.

In the summer of 1922, the writer in company with Dr. J. Monroe Thorington and Edward Feuz, Swiss guide, visited the Freshfield group mainly for the purpose of ascending some of the unclimbed peaks. At the same time, however, it was felt that advantage should be taken of the opportunity to make such observations on the glacier itself as conditions might permit. Accordingly the writer brought along a small light telescopic level reading to 5' of arc on both vertical and horizontal circles, a prismatic compass, a clinometer, a 100-foot steel tape for baseline measurements, white paint for marking stations, white cotton cloth and wire for erecting signals etc., in addition to the usual aneroids and thermometers employed in mountaineering. As it turned out, we were able to spend only eleven days at the glacier, and of these only three were exclusively devoted to observations on it, so that the results presented herewith cannot claim to be more than of a preliminary and tentative nature. We did, however, familiarize ourselves with nearly every part, for in the course of our five ascents (Mts. Gilgit, Nanga Parbat, Trutch, Barnard, and Freshfield) we travelled, on the ice itself, some 40 miles besides obtaining excellent views from the summits.

The work attempted falls under the following headings: (1) measurement of the rate of surface velocity of the ice; (2) instrumental triangulation for the location and measurement of a line of stones and for effecting connection with the government map; (3) observations on the tongue and its retreat; (4) observations on general features of the glacier.

I. MEASUREMENT OF THE RATE OF SURFACE VELOCITY

We established our base camp 683 yards from the forefoot on July 10, altitude 5300 feet. The site, on the top of a high bank, commands an excellent view of the broad flat tongue completely filling the valley bottom, and of the sharp peak of Mt. Freshfield (10,945 feet) rising over it in the background five miles away. Around the trunk of an evergreen tree on the edge of the bank a white band was painted to serve as a station in the instrumental triangulation. A stream of clear water lies at the foot of the bank.

After a trip up the three-mile tongue, a suitable location, 1250 yards above the end of the glacier, was chosen for establishing a line across the surface of the ice. The mark for the northern end was a rectangular slab of rock a rod square, perched on the inner slope of the north lateral moraine 50 yards above the glacier. It is one of the most prominent boulders anywhere on that side of the valley and is visible from nearly all parts of the northern half of the lower glacier. It is also visible from Camp Station, being about one and one-quarter miles distant therefrom. It is tilted towards the glacier and is the largest stone to be seen near the top of the lateral moraine from that standpoint. It is designated Station A. Owing to lack of time it was not painted. The mark for the southern end of the line was a much smaller boulder 125 feet above the edge of the ice on the crest of the south lateral moraine near the base of a prominent gully that scars the valley wall. A vertical reference line was painted on the side towards the glacier. It is designated Station B.

On July 13, Station A was occupied with the instrument. Fourteen numbered flat stones were carried out on the glacier and set in flat-bottomed niches chipped in the ice, 50 paces apart, on the line indicated by the vertical hair of the telescope, in accordance with signals from the observer. Such stones, particularly if dark in color, have a tendency to become fixed in the ice through melting. The writer has set out three of these lines, and has never had reason to suspect that any stone slipped from its original position. If one side of the stone is straight, it gives a good fiducial edge upon which to sight with the instrument. The azimuth and angle of depression of each stone were determined from a second station on the north moraine, later ascertained to be 320 feet distant. On line A–B the ice was 1133 yards wide.

The positions of the stones are shown on the accompanying cross-section of the glacier (fig. 1, [page 132]). The estimated thickness of the ice is based upon the assumption that the gradient of the valley floor obtaining below the forefoot continues uniformly back under the ice. According to the configuration of the valley hereabouts, this does not seem unwarranted. The slope is about 125 feet to the mile and the maximum thickness of the glacier at the line of stones works out at 400 feet. The longitudinal section is also constructed on the assumption that the valley bottom continues back at the same gradient of 125 feet per mile, the surface slope being plotted from the contours of the government map. Although this basal gradient is purely hypothetical, it probably is fairly approximate to the truth on this particular tongue, where the evenness of the surface and its comparative freedom from crevasses are strong indications of a smooth, regular valley floor beneath. The average slope of the similarly situated Forbes Brook valley adjacent, is 160 feet per mile.

Six days later (July 19) Station A was occupied again and the line redetermined on the ice, which had meanwhile moved downward. The amount each stone had advanced was measured directly with a tape. The results are given in the table on [page 254].

The increased average velocity of the southeasterly portion of the glacier as compared with the northwesterly portion is doubtless due to the fact that on the former side the ice is sweeping through a broad arc, which normally has the effect of deflecting the zone of most rapid motion away from the middle. When, as here, the curve is associated with a reversed curve further upstream, the deflection, following the analogy of running water, naturally would be more pronounced. And so, in fact, we find it here, the zone of maximum velocity being thrown far over towards the southeasterly margin. Actually it occurs about half-way between the center and the side instead of at the center.

The weather during the period of our stay was generally warm and pleasant, although windy and smoky, the smoke at times settling down in a dense pall almost obscuring the sun and hindering both mountaineering and photography.

OBSERVATIONS ON A LINE OF STONES SET ACROSS THE FRESHFIELD GLACIER, JULY 13, 1922

Stations		Distance from north margin of glacier (Ft.)	Motion from July 13 to July 19 (In.)	Average daily motion for six days (In.)	Remarks
On north lateral moraine	A.	255	0	0	Superficial moraine extends from ice margin out on glacier about 400 ft.
	1	420	24	4.00	
	2	610	18	3.00	
	3	775	25	4.17	
	4	950	26	4.33	
	5	1125	18	3.00	
	6	1305	26	4.33	
	7	1450	22	3.67	
	8	1620	27	4.50	
	Center of Glacier				
	9	1800	26.5	4.42	
	10	1990	24	4.00	
	11	2175	28.5	4.75	
	12	2285	28.5	4.75	
	13	2500	29	4.83	Maximum motion.
Superficial moraine begins and extends 850 ft. to margin of glacier.					
	14	2600	23	3.83	
On south lateral moraine	B.	3600			200 ft. from ice margin.
Approximate width of glacier on line of stones, 3400 ft. Distance between stations marking the line, 3855 ft.					

2. INSTRUMENTAL TRIANGULATION FOR LOCATION AND MEASUREMENT OF A LINE OF STONES AND FOR EFFECTING CONNECTION WITH THE GOVERNMENT MAP

Conditions for the laying off of a base-line on the surface of the ice were not very favorable in the neighborhood of the line of stones, but after some search a location was finally chosen, 400 yards upstream, and a level line 270 feet long was measured with a steel tape. Observations from this gave the distance (3855 feet), between Stations A and B at the ends of the line.

From these the position of the great boulder on the surface of the ice near the center of the glacier was determined. On July 19 the downstream edge of the boulder was 2440 feet distant from Station A, and 2510 feet distant from Station B, the elevation of its base being 6000 feet. The azimuths between the boulder and the ends of the line were: from A, 39° 10´, and from B, 38° 10´. It is visible from Camp Station.

This boulder is the largest of many sizable erratics that are scattered over different quarters of the tongue. They occur singly and sometimes in pairs, surrounded by clean white ice. This gives them good visibility from a distance and will render them valuable markers for studies of the ice motion. The stone in question was doubtless noticed by Dr. Collie in 1897, for it appears to be shown in the illustration opposite page 62 in his *Climbs and Exploration in the Canadian Rockies*. He writes (page 55), "We noticed them within a mile of the snout of the glacier, and in 1902 when the glacier was again visited they did not seem to have moved much." The rock is now exactly a mile from the end of the glacier. Its dimensions are estimated to be 36 feet long, 18 feet wide, and 16 feet high. The cubic contents would be about 10,000 cubic feet. With some difficulty, it was climbed by Feuz, who erected a little cairn on the downstream point out of loose fragments found on the top. It was not otherwise marked.

Another of these stones was utilized as a marker for one end of the base line. It was painted "1922" with white paint, and lay 350 feet distant from the block just mentioned. The distance to Station A was computed to be 2080 feet, and to B, 2580 feet, the elevation being 5960 feet. The azimuths between this boulder and the ends of the line were: at A, 38° 45', and at B, 30° 25'.

From Stations A and B, Mt. Freshfield, Mt. David, and other points on sheet 18 of the Boundary map were observed as controls.

3. OBSERVATIONS ON THE TONGUE AND ITS RETREAT

It was originally intended to make a detailed photographic survey of the terminal ice tongue and the area adjacent, but this had to be abandoned on account of the density of the smoke. A local secondary triangulation, however, was carried out by the writer from a 305-foot base, measured on the out-wash plain near camp. By this means a boulder at the ice lip was located, together with several other features of importance, including a large stone on the north lateral moraine to serve as a station for test views of the tongue.

This rock is designated Station C. It was marked on the side towards Camp Station, from which it is distant 505 yards, with a three-foot cross (X) in white paint. The cross is visible from Camp Station, but only upon careful scrutiny and with glasses. The stone rests on the only sizable exposure of bed-rock on the north side of the valley, about 45 feet above the flat ground moraine. It lies just to the left of and above an oval-topped reddish stone plainly to be seen from Camp Station. It was occupied with the camera July 20.

There is no question but that the glacier is retreating. The actual end is a thin, semicircular, concave lip, furrowed with the typical longitudinal depressions almost universally associated with this condition. The frontal slope varies between 20° and 30°. As regards the rate of retreat, there seems to be no precise data available. However, a view of the tongue, secured by the late Hermann Woolley on the occasion of his visit in 1902, almost certainly taken very close to Camp Station, when compared with a similar photograph of 1922, exhibits a marked shrinkage and recession. The view of 1902, taken in connection with another of that year, leaves little doubt but that a certain pile of moraine was then in process of formation at the ice lip.[112] Assuming this to be true, this pile of moraine being 925 feet distant from the most advanced ice in 1922 allows an estimate to be made of an average retreat of 46 feet per year for the 20 years intervening. A distant photograph by the Boundary Survey (pl. 1, fig. 1 [page 122]) taken in 1918 plainly shows the presence of this same moraine pile, although the exact position of the ice front in relation to it cannot be satisfactorily fixed.

The inner slopes of moraine and gravel bounding the open space below the tongue have not had sufficient time, since the ice was near, to develop any forest. A scattering of trees and bushes is growing up, but none have reached large size and there is far from being a continuous mat of vegetation. The 1902 picture above referred to indicates that there has been only a slight increase in the amount of vegetation on these slopes in the score of years intervening. One is probably safe therefore in estimating a lapse of at least half a century since the ice abutted against the banks in question. It was regretted that opportunity was wanting for a detailed study of this question by the cutting of trees. No growth whatever was noticed on the ground moraine of the valley floor below the tongue. The rapid cutting of the migratory glacial streams would perhaps account for this.

In the test photograph taken from Station C, three fair-sized stones may be noted near the edge of the ice. These should constitute helpful markers for the future. The one most advanced lies exactly at the ice margin and is located on the accompanying map of the glacier-tongue. It is distant 683 yards from Camp Station and is marked H on the map (fig. 2 [page 132]).

Drainage streams emerging at several points along the forefoot soon unite in a powerful torrent which cuts off the southeasterly side of the valley and prevents access to the surface of the ice except at the extreme right. Apparently the tongue does not produce a terminal ice arch or cavern.

The vertical shrinkage of the three mile tongue has been enormous, according to the indications of the most recent lateral moraines. In the lower portions of the valley these moraines rise more than 100 feet above the ice. There is no terminal moraine, properly speaking. The tongue, as well as the upper plateau of the glacier, is singularly free from superficial moraines. The medial moraines of the trunk mingle with the northwesterly lateral and do not extend within a mile of the forefoot.

4. GENERAL FEATURES OF THE GLACIER

The main reservoir or collecting area of the glacier is a broad, fan-shaped basin with a flat floor that occupies a distorted synclinal fold on the axis of the main range of the Rockies. The dissipator tongue discharges at right angles in the position of the handle of the fan. The dip and direction of the northeasterly limb of the syncline are remarkably constant, so that the ice flows along a nearly straight line on this side. The inner slopes of the basin here are practically snowless, affording little, if any, nourishment to the trunk stream. The southwesterly limb is a loftier and more abrupt folding, with a greater shattering of the strata and a greater irregularity of sculpture. Here are the culminating summits of the group, and from them descend in broken ice falls many smaller tributary glaciers.

The trunk glacier takes its source on the inner slopes of the southerly wall of the basin, a ridge 9500–10,000 feet high, stretching for six miles between mounts Barnard and Low. Here, broad, unbroken, gently tilted inclines afford ideal conditions for glacier alimentation. In the first three miles the snowfields descend to 8000 feet, where, as nearly as may be judged, the snowline occurs. The next three miles are a wide icy plain, flat and level to the eye, but really descending a thousand feet, designated on the map the "Freshfield Icefield"[113] ([Fig. 3, page 119; see also] pl. 1, fig. 2 [page 122] and pl. 2, figs. 1 and 2 [page 123]). Hereabouts the medial moraines, so prominent half-way down the tongue, begin to appear along the westerly side. On the diagram, figure 2 [page 132], they have been sketched in from photographs, giving a graphic picture of the relative importance of the tributaries as sources of ice supply. Compared to the size of the ice system, they are small and scanty (pl. 3, figs. 1 and 2 [page 124]). They do not anywhere pile themselves up into lofty continuous ridges. Their prominence is due chiefly to their lineal distinctness and lack of wide dispersion over the surface of the ice.

The northerly segment of the basin, beyond the discharge tongue, contributes scantily to it (pl. 4, fig. 1 [page 125]). Owing to various causes, but chiefly to a more direct exposure to the sun, melting has exceeded the snow supply and the ice is in an essentially stagnant condition. Three commensal streams occur here: the Niverville and Pangman glaciers, and another without a name which issues from a deep, precipitously walled cirque on the north side of Mt. Freshfield. Judging from its position and length, this is the most vigorous of the trio. At the corner where the main tongue issues from the basin, the Niverville and Pangman glaciers, in receding to the higher slopes, have uncovered a portion of the trough floor and a little upland valley filled with rushing streams and bordered with ice tongues. (See pl. 4, fig. 2 [page 125] and pl. 1, fig. 2 [page 122].) Thus there has been produced a lateral U-shaped alcove, across the open end of which the main body of ice flows, exposing a section about 75 feet thick and 500 yards wide. Its position has been indicated on the map (fig. 3 [page 119]).

Such depressions are not uncommon features of valley glaciers. They often give rise to marginal lakelets, as the Marjelen See on the Aletsch Glacier. But this particular one possesses the peculiarity of occasionally being filled by an offshoot from the main icefield in the shape of a secondary tongue. Although at the time of our visit in 1922, it was entirely bare of ice, in July 1918, the Boundary Survey photographs show that it was filled to the brim with shattered ice fragments in the nature of icebergs or séracs. (Note even line of vegetation at level of main glacier in pl. 4, fig. 1 [page 125]. This would seem to be an "ice-line" corresponding to the waterline in the case of a lake.) The accompanying photograph, taken in August 1913 (pl. 5, fig. 1 [page 126]), indicates that not long before an ice invasion had also occurred here, as many wasting pillars of glacier ice were scattered about on the floor of the alcove. Thus, the place appears to serve as a kind of safety valve, which relieves pressure on the constricted dissipator whenever the snow-fall on the mountains to the south and west has accumulated beyond the dissipator's capacity for prompt discharge.

The writer spent an afternoon visiting the locality and in photographing the ice wall at close quarters. Another secondary tongue seemed to be forming, for the wall had thrown forward several blocks of ice, a distinct nose projected at the center, and a push moraine four feet high had been raised along the base of the wall (pl. 5, fig. 2 [page 126]). Another push moraine was noted 150 feet in front of the ice, apparently indicating the termination of the last advance preceding.

We thus have evidence that advances occurred here in about 1912 and 1918 and that another might soon be expected, perhaps in 1923. Can it be that this is a periodic phenomenon? It would be a very interesting matter to determine.

The floor of the alcove consists of comminuted shingle and well-broken ground moraine (see pl. 5, fig. 1 [page 126]). A ridge of slaty, well-scored bed rock occurs in the center where the nose is advancing. The drainage stream from the upper glacier basin flows under the ice wall here. No signs of a lake in the alcove were to be detected.

For so great an expanse of ice, there are singularly few large crevasses and ice falls. One can wander about almost at will without serious hindrance. At the easterly corner where the tongue leaves the basin, occurs the only notable ice fall in the glacier proper. Here a 300-foot cliff breaks the floor of the basin and gives rise to a steep and interesting ice cascade of this height (pl. 6 [page 127]).

No considerable drainage streams were noted on the tongue or upper icefield, although small brooks of course run everywhere. The water soon finds its way beneath the ice through numerous moulins.

The rock surrounding the Freshfield Glacier is mainly dark, slaty limestone, fossiliferous in places. About two miles above the forefoot a crushed and crumpled anticlinal arch is very well displayed in the rocks of the gorge on both sides of the valley.

SUMMARY OF GLACIER MEASUREMENTS AND OBSERVATIONS IN THE CANADIAN ALPS, WITH REFERENCES

This note aims to present a brief digest of what has been done in the way of glacial measurements and study in the Canadian Alps. Not every individual report has been listed, but the titles here brought together represent the main body of the literature and will supply materials for an exhaustive study by anyone interested.

The most complete and comprehensive single publication dealing with the glaciers of the Canadian Alps is the monograph entitled "Glaciers of the Canadian Rockies and Selkirks," by W.H. Sherzer, published by the Smithsonian Institution in 1907. (*Contributions to Knowledge*, Vol. XXXIV, Publ. No. 1692.) It is handsomely illustrated and contains 135 pages. The glaciers studied were the Victoria, Wenkchemna, Yoho, in the Rockies, and the Illecillewaet and Asulkan in the Selkirks, the period covered being between 1902 and 1905. About half the space is devoted to the Victoria Glacier. See also "Nature and Activity of Canadian Glaciers," by W.H. Sherzer, *Canadian Alpine Journal*, Vol. I, No. 2, pp. 249–263. Another general discussion of the glaciers in the Canadian Rockies and Selkirks is contained in the paper "Notes on Glaciers," by A.O. Wheeler, *Canadian Alpine Journal*, 1920, Vol. XI, pp. 121–146.

Detailed studies of the surface velocity and frontal retreat of the Illecillewaet Glacier were made over a long period by Messrs. George and William S. Vaux, and continued by Miss Mary M. Vaux. See the following articles: "Glacier Observations," by George Vaux Jr. and William S. Vaux, *Canadian Alpine Journal*, Vol. I, No. 1, 1907, pp. 138–148, with map; "Observations on Glaciers, 1909," by George Vaux Jr., *Canadian Alpine Journal*, Vol. II, No. 2, pp. 126–130; "Observations on Glaciers, 1910," by Mary M. Vaux, *Canadian Alpine Journal*, Vol. III, p. 127; "Observations on Glaciers," by Mary M. Vaux, *Canadian Alpine Journal*, Vol. V, p. 59. These papers also report observations on the Asulkan Glacier.

The surface velocity and retreat of the Yoho Glacier were observed continuously between 1906 and 1919 by A.O. Wheeler, and reported in the pages of the *Canadian Alpine Journal*, Vol. I to Vol. XI. See Vol. XI (1920), p. 182, for a summary of these observations and measurements.

The only other glaciers that have been studied are the Robson, the Sir Sandford, and the Freshfield. Descriptions and measurements of the retreat of the first named are reported in the following papers: "Geology and Glacial Features of Mt. Robson," by A.P. Coleman, *Canadian Alpine Journal*, Vol. II, No. 2, pp. 108–113; "Robson Glacier Measurements," by A.O. Wheeler, *Canadian Alpine Journal*, Vol. IV, 1912, pp. 44–45; "Robson Glacier," by A.O. Wheeler, *Canadian Alpine Journal*, Vol. VI, 1915, p. 139; "Motion of Robson Glacier," by A.O. Wheeler, *Canadian Alpine Journal*, Vol. XIII, 1923, p. 158. No measurements of surface velocity have been performed on the Robson Glacier.

The Sir Sandford was mapped and observed by the writer in 1910. The next year its surface velocity was measured. See "Observations on the Sir Sandford Glacier, 1911," *Geographical Journal*, May 1912, Vol. XXXIX, pp. 446–453. Work was continued in 1912, the surface velocity being redetermined on the same line. See *Mountaineering and Exploration in the Selkirks*, by H. Palmer, Putnam, 1914, pp. 376–391.

TABULAR SUMMARY OF GLACIER OBSERVATIONS IN THE CANADIAN ALPS, 1899–1922

ROCKIES

Glacier	Frontal Recession	Surface Velocity (Inches per diem)		Remarks
		Maximum	Minimum	
Victoria	1899–1912 14 ft. per year	2.165	.005	Period of 423 days, 1904–1905.
Yoho	1906–1918 33 ft. per year	5.03	3.09	Average, 1906–1918.
Freshfield	1902–1922 Estimated at 46 ft. per year	4.83	3.00	Summer motion for 6 days, 1922.
Robson	1911–1922 22.1 ft. per year			No measurements.

SELKIRKS

Glacier	Frontal Recession	Surface Velocity (Inches per diem)		Remarks
		Maximum	Minimum	
Illecillewaet	1898–1906 33 ft. per year	5.65	3.21	1899–1903. Summer motion for 12 days, 1906.
	1898–1912 40 ft. per year	11.33	7.00	
		6.73	2.45	Period of 396 days, 1906–1907.
		5.13	1.34	Period of 342 days, 1909–1910.
Asulkan	Intermittent	3.13	1.13	Period of 398 days, 1906–1907.
		8.90	2.40	Summer motion for 10 days, 1906.
Sir Sandford	1909–1910 25 ft.	6.73	1.36	Summer motion for 15 days, 1911.
	1910–1911 37.3 ft. in 50 wks.	6.25	3.15	Summer motion for 11¾ days, 1912.
	1911–1912 54 ft. in 51 wks.	...	...	

(NOTE.—The writer estimates the total frontal recession of the Illecillewaet Glacier between 1887 and 1923 as upwards of 2000 feet.)

So far as the writer can ascertain, all the glaciers in the Canadian Alps are now in a phase of retreat. Certainly all that he has personally observed in the last 15 years are in this condition. Among them may be mentioned the following:

Swift Current
Fraser
Columbia
King Edward
Serenity

Victoria
Sir Sandford
Adamant
Goldstream
Palmer

Coronet	Illecillewaet
Unwin	Asulkan
Nameless (at S. end Maligne Lake)	
Geikie	Bishops
Conway	Deville
Freshfield	Battle

The Wenkchemna Glacier has been reported to have exhibited signs of advance during this period, but the writer has not seen it. The Clemenceau, a very large glacier situated southwest of Fortress Lake, is recently reported to be essentially stagnant at an advanced stage, close up to its terminal moraine. It does not appear to have receded at all for a long period.

APPENDIX E

DAVID THOMPSON AND THE FIRST CROSSING OF HOWSE PASS

There is no known portrait of David Thompson, Explorer of the North-West Company, existing, but Bigsby,[114] the naturalist of the International Boundary Commission, who first met him in 1817, tells us, "He was plainly dressed, quiet, and observant. His figure was short and compact, and his black hair was worn long all round, and cut square, as if by one stroke of the shears, just above the eyebrows. His complexion was of the gardener's ruddy brown, while the expression of deeply furrowed features was friendly and intelligent, but his cut-short nose gave him an odd look. ... I might have spared this description of Mr. David Thompson by saying he greatly resembled Curran, the Irish orator. ... Never mind his Bunyan-like face and cropped hair; he has a very powerful mind, and a singular faculty of picture-making. He can create a wilderness and people it with warring savages, or climb the Rocky Mountains with you in a snow-storm, so clearly and palpably, that only shut your eyes and you hear the crack of the rifle, or feel the snow-flakes melt on your cheeks as he talks."

The pass by which Thompson crossed the Continental Divide in 1807 came to be and still is mapped as the Howse Pass. Engineers who selected the route for the Canadian Pacific Railroad explored this pass at a later date and some preferred it to the Kicking Horse which was actually used. The stream down which Thompson travelled is the Blaeberry; he refers to it merely as the portage river.

In outlining Thompson's itinerary during 1807, Tyrrell says:[115] "On May 10, accompanied by his wife and family, Thompson started from Rocky Mountain House to cross the mountains. Finan McDonald took a canoe with provisions up the Saskatchewan River, while Thompson himself travelled on horseback on the north side of the river. On June 3 they reached the Kootenay Plain, a wide, open flat on the north side of the river within the mountains, in latitude 56° 2' 6" N.; and on June 6 they reached the Forks. They then turned up the south branch of the stream; but after ascending it for three miles were obliged to stop, as they could take the canoes no further. They remained here till June 25, when they started across the mountains, packing all their supplies with them on horses. At 1 p.m. on June 25 they reached the height of land in latitude 51° 48' 27" N. Thence they descended along the banks of a mountain torrent (Blaeberry River) to 'Kootanie' (Columbia) River, which they reached on June 30, in latitude 51° 25' 14" N., longitude 116° 52' 45" W., a mile or two north-west of Moberly station on the Canadian Pacific Railway."

The earliest reference to a crossing of Howse Pass appears to be in a manuscript now in the possession of the Archives Department of the Canadian Government.[116] It was written by David Thompson, and is entitled, "Narrative of the Expedition to the Kootanae and Flat Bow Indian Countries, on the Sources of the Columbia River, Pacific Ocean, by D. Thompson on behalf of the N. W. Company, 1807."

Thompson writes as follows: "On June 6th (1807) at Noon we left the main Stream coming from the N.N.W^d. and followed a Rivulet for ab^r. 4 Miles, where it becoming too shoal, we put the Goods on shore, and I staid in care of them; the Men and Canoe immediately went off for the remainder, and by June 10 all was landed at my Residence the People returned to live at

Kootanae Plain, 'till I should send for them. Here among the stupendous and solitary Wilds covered with eternal Snow, and Mountain connected to Mountain by immense Glaciers, the collection of Ages and on which the Beams of the Sun make hardly any Impression when aided by the most favorable weather. I staid 14 Days more, impatiently waiting the melting of the Snows on the Height of Land. During this Time we arranged all the Goods and whatever could receive Harm by Shocks against the Trees, Rocks, etc., in Boxes of thin Boards sewed together. The Weather was often very severe, cloathing all the Trees with Snow as in the Depth of Winter, and the Wind seldom less than a Storm we had no Thunder, very little Lightning, and that very mild; but in return the rushing of the Snows down the Sides of the Mountains equalled the Thunder in Sound, overturning everything less than solid Rock in its Course, sweeping the Mountain Forests, whole acres at a Time from the very Roots, leaving not a Vestige behind; scarcely an Hour passed without hearing one or more of these threatening Noises assailing our Ears. The Mountains themselves for half way down, were almost ever covered with Clouds; in the chance Intervals of fair Weather I geometrically measured the Height of 3 of those that were most eligible, and found their perpendicular Height above their Bases, or the level of the Rivulet to be 4707 ft., 5200 ft. and 5089 ft. The Peakes of a few Mountains rose ab^t. 500 to 700 ft. above these; and considering their elevated Situation on the Globe, they fall little short of the most celebrated in Height above the Level of the Ocean. Wearied with waiting and anxious to proceed, contrary to the Opinion of every one, I set off with Bercier, my Guide to examine if the Portage was passable. We started very early on 2 good Horses and by 10 a.m. we were at the Head of the Defile or Ravine where the Springs send their Rills to the Pacific Ocean; the Sight overjoyed me. We held our Route along the Brook, which was continually increasing its Stream, our Road was very bad: by 1 p.m. from the view of the Country I considered that part of the Defile as passed in which the Snow was most likely to remain; my Guide affirmed not but as all the Snow that lay direct in our Road noways incommoded us, being only Patches, altho' every Thing was dreary Winter about us. I determined to return immediately and send for the Men and Horses from the Kootanae Plain—June 24 in the Evening all the Men and Horses arrived."

The foregoing is of no little historical interest as describing one of the earliest overland crossings, within Canadian territory, to the Pacific. But fourteen years had elapsed since the memorable journey of Alexander Mackenzie, and the great northwestern wilderness was as yet scarcely known to white men.

Thompson's camp appears to have been situated along the middle course of the present Howse River, not far from the entrance of the stream from Glacier Lake. His measurements are among the very first made of Rocky Mountain peaks in the main chain and are accurate within reason—the valley of Howse River being 4500 feet and the present Mt. Outram 10,600 feet. None of his measurements corresponds with the height of Mt. Forbes (11,902 feet) and it is unlikely that he measured this mountain.

Thompson's statement that the mountains "fall little short of the most celebrated in Height above the Level of the Ocean," can, therefore, only be interpreted as indicating that he overestimated his valley level. This may be an original source of the error which perpetuated itself as a *Tradition of Height*, and which crops out again and again, notably in the Athabaska Pass area, in the journals of Thompson and of later *voyageurs*. It is upon this error, copied from one narrative into the next, that the overestimated elevations of Mount Brown and Mount Hooker have their most plausible foundation.

APPENDIX F

THE PANORAMA FROM MT. COLUMBIA, 12,294 FEET

(Second Elevation: Rocky Mountains of Canada)
The mountaineering results of an expedition to the Columbia Icefield, made, in 1923, in company with Dr. W.S. Ladd and the guide Conrad Kain, have already been presented in Chapters V–VII.

On July 14, in fine weather, we accomplished the second ascent of Mt. Columbia, and for several reasons interest has centred in a photographic panorama obtained from its summit.

In the first place, there are but four peaks—Robson, Columbia, North Twin, Clemenceau—of the Rocky Mountains of Canada exceeding 12,000 ft. in elevation. Mt. Columbia was first ascended in 1902 by Sir James Outram and Christian Kaufmann. Mt. Robson, 12,972 ft., succumbed in 1913 to Messrs. MacCarthy and Foster, with Conrad Kain. North Twin, 12,085 ft., fell to our party in 1923, while later in the same season Mt. Clemenceau, 12,001 ft., was captured by the guideless party of Messrs. de Villiers-Schwab, Hall, Durand, and Harris.

Outram was favoured by clear weather on Mt. Columbia and has graphically described the view. The summit was reached shortly after two o'clock and an hour was spent on top. ..."Thirty miles to the southeast Mt. Forbes (as yet unconquered) towered high above everything in that direction, and alone challenged comparison with our elevation. But at twice that distance to the north-west Mt. Robson showed up grandly and is perhaps the one mountain in the Canadian Rockies that exceeds 13,000 ft. ...Some old friends in the distant south, fully eighty miles away, Mts. Temple, Goodsir, Hungabee, Dawson and Sir Donald, and more recent acquaintances of the past fortnight, gave one great pleasure to recognize amongst the myriads of peaks of every shape and size." Outram never published his summit views.[117]

The first party to reach the summit of Mt. Robson arrived after five o'clock, and, although the prospect was fair, they had no camera and could stop for only a moment.

Our own group attained North Twin, in weather that was far from ideal, and so our pictures from Mt. Columbia are the first to give a comprehensive idea of a Canadian Rocky panorama from above 12,000 ft. It is, therefore, of some interest to determine just what and how far one can see. It will be quite evident, however, that while the eye can perceive things beyond the range of photography, the camera preserves the record permanently and more accurately than the mind. The after-cogitation—"Now just what did we see?"—led to some remarkable delusions in the days before photography: witness the prevalent pre-Alpine Club opinion that the Mediterranean was visible from the summit of Mont Blanc.

It is the purpose of the present communication briefly to outline what was revealed from the summit of Mt. Columbia, 12,294 feet, the second elevation of the Canadian Rocky Mountains. The photographs were snap-shots, 4 by 5, taken on roll-film, without filters other than a cloud filter which did not alter the exposure time. The complete, drafted panorama has been made from tracings from the prints, plus additions obtained by lens examination of the negatives and from enlargements.

The central position of Mt. Columbia is emphasized if one draws on a map—with the mountain as a centre—a circle of radius approximating forty-two miles. The circumference will nearly pass through the tip of the Columbia loop, the Columbia River–Canadian Pacific intersection at Beavermouth, Howse Pass, and Whirlpool Pass. Within the circle are included Kinbasket, Glacier, Brazeau, Maligne, and Fortress lakes, and headwaters of the Columbia, Saskatchewan, and Athabaska river systems. Within it are found the most important icefield groups of the Continental Divide, together with the notable Maligne and Wood River mountains, and the crest of the Selkirks in the Sir Sandford area.

From the summit of Mt. Columbia, the foreground of icefield is perhaps the most impressive thing. The Columbia field is a tri-oceanic watershed, nearly 150 square miles in extent, from whose snows drain head-sources of the Athabaska, through the Peace–Mackenzie system to the Arctic; through the Bush–Columbia to the Pacific; and by way of the Saskatchewan–Nelson system to Hudson Bay.

Northward, one has The Twins and Mt. Alberta almost in line; The Twins above the deep gorge of the banded Columbia Glacier, an Athabaska source. On either side of North Twin are peaks of the Maligne Group, Mt. Brazeau (11,385 feet) standing out prominently although twenty-five miles distant.

In the northeast are many unnamed peaks—one does not have to wander far from the Continental Divide to find unnamed peaks—several of which, south of Brazeau River, exceed 10,000 ft. and may be much higher.

Eastward, one looks across the icefield toward Snow Dome, the hydrographic apex of the field, and Mt. Athabaska, the latter rising above Sunwapta Pass—the Athabaska–Saskatchewan divide—with Athabaska Glacier on its northern flank and the Saskatchewan Glacier on its southern.

In the southeasterly direction, Mt. Castleguard is seen, low-lying on the margin of the icefield, with Mt. Saskatchewan towering above and flanking Alexandra River—the old "West Branch"—down which one glimpses mounts Wilson and Murchison, between which the North Saskatchewan emerges to the eastern prairie. Across Thompson Pass are massed the peaks of the Continental Divide: Alexandra, Lyell, and a host of others. Mt. Forbes, 11,902 ft., the fifth elevation of the chain, lies in Alberta, but, due to a bending of the Divide, it appears just over Peak 3 of Mt. Lyell. It is this irregularity of the Divide, in the vicinity of Howse Pass, which makes the Freshfield Group show up across the western shoulder of Mt. Alexandra, and between the latter and Mt. Bryce.

In the south, Mt. Bryce—a veritable Finsteraarhorn—its eastern shoulder on the Divide, projects into British Columbia to flank the gloomy gorge of Bush River. One traces the river with certainty past the junction of the North and South Forks, but it cannot be followed to the Columbia.

Southwesterly, across Tsar Creek, are extensive snowfields and, more distant, high peaks: presumably within the tip of the Columbia loop. The foreground is a sea of unnamed peaks.

The western foreground is dominated by Mt. King Edward, icefields mantling the Divide, and, except when broken into different levels by crossing ridges, continuous for miles toward the Wood River area. The distant named point in the west is Mt. Tsar.

In the northwest, thirty miles away, is the Wood River Group, on the British Columbia side: most impressive, with Mt. Clemenceau looming hugely. One looks across the glacier-hung Athabaska–Chaba Divide to ranges in the direction of Fortress Lake.

So much the camera identifies as a permanent record; now of what the eye could reach. Outram mentions the peaks of the Lake Louise district; we looked for them in vain. Temple was nowhere to be seen; although, of course, from Mt. Temple, on a clear day, especially if one looks with binoculars, there is not much trouble in finding Mt. Columbia. But from Columbia, in the south and southeast, the Continental Divide is seen in a foreshortened line: the peaks are massed, and of such an average height that it is exceedingly difficult to locate distant individuals from an unfamiliar point. Even Mt. Forbes was not a conspicuous summit, although little more than thirty miles away. It will then be recalled that Lake Louise is seventy-five miles in air-line from Mt. Columbia. It should be remembered that Outram was exceedingly familiar with this topography, having mapped a considerable portion of it.

Taking it for granted then that Lake Louise peaks are visible from Mt. Columbia, or vice versa, let us lay out a circle from Mt. Columbia, on a seventy-mile radius. It will cut Lake Louise; it will cross the southern Selkirks just north of the Beaver–Duncan Pass and the Battle Range. Following on, the circumference just touches Clemina station on the North Thompson River and again cuts the Canadian National Railroad, midway between Yellowhead Pass and Moose Lake. Fraser sources and all of Jasper Park are included in the circle.

Our party spent nearly an hour and a half on the summit of Mt. Columbia; we had arrived at 1.30. In the southeast the most distantly identifiable points were peaks of the Freshfield Group—Mt. Forbes, and Mt. Chephren near Howse Pass. If we had known exactly where to look between summits, we *might* have located a peak in the Lake Louise area.

In the south and southwest, the horizon was sharper and the peaks not so massed as on the Divide. Sir Sandford was distinct, although it does not show in photos. We thought we recognized Mt. Rogers; one can, of course, see Mt. Columbia and even the Wood River area from Mt. Rogers. Conrad, ever optimistic, attempted to show us the Purcells and even identified the Howser Spires. We were not entirely convinced. In the west, we saw high snowfields which are possibly in the Gold Range.

The question arose as to Mt. Robson. Conrad had been on the first ascent of it; the writer had camped north of it in a former year. We had no small-scale map with us. The mountain should appear between the Wood River Group and the direction of Fortress Lake. Mt. Clemenceau was splendidly in view and there were fine peaks beyond, outside of photographic range. But we were never sure of Mt. Robson; we felt that we *should* have seen it; Outram had seen it.[118]

A remaining fact is this: if one draws from Mt. Columbia as a centre a circle seventy miles in radius it will include the Lake Louise area. From Mt. Temple, the highest peak of this area, Mt. Columbia is visible; but with some difficulty and only in the best of weather. On the other hand, peaks on the Divide, massed in line, are exceedingly difficult to identify individually. The position of Mt. Robson, almost due northwest of Mt. Columbia, falls at least twenty-five miles beyond the seventy-mile radius already laid down as approximately the limit of visibility. Outram speaks of Mt. Forbes as being thirty miles to the southeast, just about correct. But when he states that Mt. Robson showed up grandly at "twice that distance to the north-west," he is nearly forty miles short of his mark.[119]

From the direction of Mt. Columbia, Mt. Robson would present an acute Λ-shape, narrow and sharp, and easily overlooked, even by an observer with binoculars. Local conditions, such as light, shadow, smoke, cloud, and heat-haze, have often more to do with visibility than mere distance. A small peak in line with a greater one may hide it at such a distance.

Mt. Robson often has a cap of cloud which might easily render it invisible; and, from Mt. Columbia, many high peaks of the Continental Divide intervene. One concludes, therefore, that, while Mt. Robson—under very exceptional circumstances—might be picked up from the summit of Mt. Columbia, no one has yet done so. It would certainly not "show up grandly"; and it is barely possible that Outram was looking at Mt. Clemenceau.

It used to be quite traditional to make high level panoramas in the Alps. Here is an interesting problem and a chance to amplify and carry on a bit of investigation in the newer Alps of Canada.

APPENDIX G

A NOTE ON THE ORIGINAL JOURNALS OF DAVID DOUGLAS

(A Re-examination of the Problem of Mount Brown and Mount Hooker)

"... the researches of many antiquarians have already thrown much darkness on the subject, and it is probable, if they continue, that we shall soon know nothing at all."

—MARK TWAIN

Few problems more interesting have arisen in the mountaineering history of the Canadian Alps than that occasioned by the Scots botanist David Douglas, who, in 1827, incorrectly ascribed tremendous elevations to the peaks of Athabaska Pass, which he named Mount Brown and Mount Hooker. For nearly three-quarters of a century they were considered the highest mountains of North America, and only recently has the legend been dispelled.

Douglas' journals, the earliest documents describing the ascent of a peak in the Canadian Rocky Mountains, were published almost a century later by the Royal Horticultural Society in a most carefully edited monograph[120] which has been the standard work referred to by commentators. The original journals, strangely enough, appear never to have been consulted by anyone with mountaineering experience—a fact that induced me, during a visit to London, to investigate the problem at its source.[121] It is my intention here to record the results of my examination of these manuscripts and to show their inter-relation with other data concerned in the origin of the mythical heights of the Athabaska Pass region.

In the preface to the Royal Horticultural Society's monograph it is stated in regard to the journals that:

1. The handwriting is nowhere easy to read, and in places most difficult, occasionally if not quite impossible.

2. In the course of nearly one hundred years the ink has faded and become in places very hard to decipher.

3. After the diary of his journey in North-Western America had been prepared for the press and set up in type, a second manuscript was discovered which at first sight was taken to be a duplicate, but which on closer examination was found to contain a great deal of additional information. It had therefore to be compared word for word with the diary and the additions inserted in their proper places.

Both the diary, often spoken of as the "Longer Journal," and the manuscript discovered later, the "Shorter Journal," contain accounts of Douglas' crossing of the Athabaska Pass in the spring of 1827. Only the "Shorter Journal" contains the names, Mount Brown and Mount Hooker, and makes mention of the supposedly great height of Mount Brown. The "Longer Journal," while describing the ascent of a peak, leaves it unnamed and gives estimates which more nearly agree with modern surveys.

The passages which concern the Brown–Hooker problem have already been quoted in Chapter X (at pages 161–163) where the two versions may be contrasted.[122]

It has been suggested[123] that the Longer Journal was the original journal and that the Shorter Journal was written later, after Douglas' return to London, and that names and heights were added at that time. No proofs were advanced for this supposition and there remained doubt as to which of the journals was the earlier.

I. GENERAL COMPARISON OF THE TWO JOURNALS

1. The Shorter Journal consists of fifty-six pages, 8 × 13 inches, written on each side of each sheet, with two-inch blank margin at the left. It bears the caption, *"A Sketch of a Journey to the North-Western Parts of the Continent of North America During the Years 1824, 1825, 1826, and 1827,"* is signed with the initials, "D.D.," and is apparently a prepared paper. The writing is in a large, bold, even, legible hand, and the manuscript is fresh in appearance. [See facsimiles at page 120.]

It was thought by some that the altitude given for Mount Brown in the Shorter Journal might possibly have become illegible with time and therefore incorrectly copied during the preparation of the Royal Horticultural Society's monograph. This is not so: on page 47 of the original, the passage, "... exceeds 6000 feet 17000 above the sea," is exceedingly clear and legible, and no mistake has been made in copying.

2. The Longer Journal consists of 131 pages, 8 × 13 inches, closely written on each side of each sheet, without margins, and with occasional notes written vertically at the left-hand edge. The handwriting throughout is smaller and more compressed than in the Shorter Journal; the paper is the worse for wear, and entries appear to have been made over a long period of time.

II. RELATIVE DATES OF THE TWO JOURNALS

A decisive clue to the dates of the two manuscripts is given in the watermarks of the paper.

On the page of the Longer Journal may be found the mark, "J. & T. Jellyman *1824*" while on the facing page is a crowned seal with the figure of Britannia seated.

On the page of the Shorter Journal one finds the mark, "C. & H. *1828*," and on the facing page a crowned seal with a lion rampant.

Douglas left England in July 1824, and crossed Athabaska Pass, eastward bound, in the spring of 1827, arriving at York Factory on August 28, 1827. He, therefore, could not have had with him the paper, watermarked "1828," on which the Shorter Journal is written. The watermark, "1824," on the pages of the Longer Journal is quite consistent with Douglas' period in the field.

From these facts we see that:

1. The Longer Journal is the field journal, in which entries were made from July 1824, until August 1827.

2. The Shorter Journal was written after Douglas returned to England, probably during the latter part of 1828, during a period of comparative leisure, as shown by the large, even handwriting and broad margins—men in the field do not do things so neatly. The manuscript was possibly prepared for reading before the Royal Horticultural Society, which had sponsored his journeys.

3. In the Longer Journal, Douglas speaks of the mountain which he ascended as being "on the left hand or West side" of Athabaska Pass; in the Shorter Journal he describes Mount Brown as "the highest peak on the North or left hand side." This may have been a slip of the pen during transcription. Mount Brown is on the western side of Athabaska Pass, and Douglas has given its correct position in his 1829 map. This point will receive further consideration.

4. The names, Mount Brown and Mount Hooker, were not given in the field, but were added later when the Shorter Journal was written, no doubt as much out of compliment to Douglas' patrons as to distinguish topographical features. This would also account for the alteration of the statement in the Longer Journal, "…mountains such as I was on, and many higher," to "the highest

yet known in the Northern Continent of America," as it reads in the Shorter Journal.

5. Mount Hooker is not mentioned in any way in the field journal. The Shorter Journal contains the name but no figure for elevation; nothing save the statement that it is a peak "nearly of the same height [as Mount Brown] rising more into a sharp point." The figure for elevation appears first on the 1829 map.

6. The altitude of 17,000 feet for Mount Brown[124] was not given in the field. It is unlikely that Douglas himself made such a measurement. In the *Proceedings of the Royal Society,* under the date April 27, 1837, it is recorded that Mr. Sabine received from Douglas several volumes of lunar, chronometrical, magnetical, meteorological and geographical observations, together with a volume of field sketches. It is known that the geographical observations referred to the Columbia River and its tributaries; but the volumes are not in the possession of the Royal Horticultural Society and cannot be traced.

Certain it is that Douglas met men at Fort Vancouver, Jasper House, and at Carlton House who may have given him the figure. At Fort Vancouver, in November 1826, Douglas mentions[125] his acquaintance with Lieut. Simpson, officer of the Royal Navy, who surveyed south of Jasper House during the winter 1825–26, and whom Thomas Drummond, Assistant Naturalist to the Second Franklin Expedition, quotes as having obtained a figure of about 16,000 feet for the elevation near Athabaska Pass.[126]

Douglas may have been confused by the winter conditions under which he himself crossed Athabaska Pass. More likely, it would appear, he was influenced by the prevalent idea of high altitude, arising from the journals of the *voyageurs,* from the time of David Thompson onward.[127] Douglas no doubt was able to consult this material in London, and elsewhere, before his own Shorter Journal was ever written.

With these data at hand we may inquire further into the Brown–Hooker problem, with the interesting progress of events conveniently grouped as follows:

1. Douglas kept a field journal in which entries were made, 1824–27. In this he describes his ascent of a mountain on the western side of Athabaska Pass. No names or altitudes are given, other than the estimate that the mountain rises about 5500 feet above its base.

2. In a second journal, written after his return to England, probably late in 1828, Douglas describes his mountain ascent, names his peak Mount Brown and gives it an elevation of 17,000 feet. He mentions a peak a little to the south and attaches to it the name of Mount Hooker; no altitude is given, nothing except the implication that it is nearly as high as Mount Brown and rises to a sharper peak.

3. In a map appearing during October 1829, which Douglas supervised, we find the name Mount Brown, altitude 16,000 feet, placed on the western side of Athabaska Pass, and Mount Hooker, 15,700 feet, on the eastern side of the pass, approximately southeast of Mount Brown.

To summarize: Douglas ascends a mountain in May 1827, which remains without altitude or name for more than a year, when, in 1828, it becomes Mount Brown, 17,000 feet. Mount Hooker appears at this time without elevation being given. Yet another year passes and Douglas, in 1829, approved the publication of a map giving the relative positions of the two peaks, one on either side of Athabaska Pass. Reducing his original figure, he now gives Mount Brown an elevation of 16,000 feet, and Mount Hooker—for the first time honoured with a figure—15,700 feet.

The further juggling with fact: that in the field journal Douglas speaks of "...mountains such as I was on, and many higher," and alters it to "the highest yet known in the Northern Continent of

America" in his manuscript of 1828, makes it certain that the pre-eminent height of Mount Brown was created in England.

If one descends Pacific Creek for a half-mile below Athabaska Pass summit and, supposing Ermatinger's camp on the morning of May 1, 1827, to have been made near this point (the field journal indicates four miles' progress from the Big Hill), if one looks northward toward the pass, the present Mount Brown is on the left-hand side of the pass. Further, it is "north" from this supposed camp-site, as well as "west" from the pass summit—a neglected fact which may reconcile Douglas' varying statements of the local topography.

The station Mount Brown Ridge does not especially attract one's attention from this viewpoint, and the present Mount Hooker is invisible. On the eastern side of the pass, McGillivray's Rock is the outstanding feature; it rises to a sharper point than Mount Brown and is not so high, thereby agreeing with Douglas' description. The actual difference in elevation between Mount Brown and McGillivray's Rock is 376 feet (9156 - 8780, Boundary Survey),[128] while the difference between Mount Brown and Mount Hooker, as given on Douglas' map of 1829 is 300 feet (16,000 - 15,700).

It is probable that Douglas obtained figures for elevation from Lieut. Simpson, R.N., whom he met at Fort Vancouver. Douglas is approximately correct for estimations above the level of the Athabaska Pass but is misled by an incorrect base.[129]

Now Douglas distinctly states in his field journal that there were many peaks higher than the one he was on; yet he singled out a lower one to name Mount Hooker—no doubt the peak east of the pass which seemed the loftiest in that direction as seen from his camp. He might well recognize this mountain and keep it in view as a landmark as he ascended Mount Brown. His map indicates that Mount Hooker is east of Athabaska Pass; that it is lower than Mount Brown.

Therefore, if the present Mount Brown be the peak which Douglas climbed—and it is the easiest mountain, and hence appears most logical, whether he went to the very top or not—then the Mount Hooker of Douglas is on the eastern side of the pass and lower than Mount Brown. Nothing fills these requirements more satisfactorily than McGillivray's Rock. This is the theory originally proposed by Professor Coleman, in 1893, and to which one is inevitably drawn by a consideration of the facts.

McGillivray's Rock was named before Douglas crossed Athabaska Pass. Franchère mentions it and ascribes its origin to Henry.[130] It is a name worthy of preservation, and, in this respect, the Boundary Commission is perhaps justified in applying the name Mount Hooker in its present location; but the present Mount Hooker is not likely the peak which Douglas so designated.

I have followed the problem as far as seems humanly possible. My field work included an examination of the Athabaska Pass area, the ascent of Mount Brown, a close inspection of McGillivray's Rock, and the first ascent of the present Mount Hooker. In London I studied and photographed the original journals of Douglas. In various libraries I searched every available source-book which could possibly contain additional information. With this work as a basis I have arrived at the following conclusions:

1. Douglas ascended or partially ascended the present Mount Brown, as being apparently the highest mountain in view from his camping-place.

2. He also singled out the loftiest point on the other side of the pass, noticed that it was rather lower and somewhat sharper, and subsequently named it (the present McGillivray's Rock) Mount Hooker.

3. His figure of elevation for Mount Brown is based on Lieut. Simpson's survey figure for the general height of the region, and on David Thompson's incorrect figure for Athabaska Pass. The

latter is Thompson's own error and should not be attributed to Sir George Simpson.

4. The elevation of Mount Hooker is Douglas' own figure based on estimated difference of elevation.

5. Finally, while the Brown–Hooker problem may never be completely solved, the facts of the case are best satisfied by considering the present Mount Brown to be the peak Douglas climbed and McGillivray's Rock to be Douglas' Mount Hooker.

Personally I am more than a little uncertain about this young botanist of a century ago. A more competent psychologist than myself would be required to decide whether or not Douglas was a borderline case of what Gamaliel Bradford has termed a "damaged soul"—one whose ambition, the sin by which the angels fell, occasionally led him to add fiction to actuality. Certainly the progressive changes in his journals are difficult to explain on any other basis.

David Douglas was born in 1793, and was in his twenty-eighth year when he crossed Athabaska Pass. Men of his day wrote more light-heartedly about alpine regions than we do now; moderate exaggerations were not then considered so sinful. So it is extremely probable that Mount Brown and Mount Hooker, and their altitudes, did not weigh too heavily on his conscience. What we should remember is that Douglas was one of our greatest and most successful exploring botanists, and that his sad and tragic death in the Sandwich Islands, in 1834, brought to a close a career of immense promise. His journals, although puzzling in their details, have been a factor of no little importance to the incidence of Canadian mountaineering; his story of the wonders of Athabaska Pass altogether an influence for good. If we attempt to judge Douglas after nearly a century, we can perhaps do no better than to accept his own words, written at Fort Vancouver on New Year's Day 1826: "I can die satisfied with myself. I never have given cause for remonstrance or pain to an individual on earth."

NOTES

1. The following is a partial list of the author's publications dealing with the Rockies:

   A Climbers Guide to the Rocky Mountains of Canada, PALMER AND THORINGTON (G.P. Putnam's Sons, The Knickerbocker Press, New York, 1921).

   Alpine Journal:

   xxxiv, Nov., 1922, "The Freshfield Group."

   xxxv, Nov., 1923, "The Mountains of the Columbia Icefield."

   xxxvi, May, 1924, "The Panorama from Mt. Columbia."

   xxxvi, Nov., 1924, "The Mountains of the Whirlpool."

   xxxvii, May and Nov., 1925, "Side Valleys and Peaks of the Yellowhead Trail."

   Bulletin of the Geographical Society of Philadelphia:

   xx, Oct., 1922, "Old Trails and New Peaks."

   xxii, Jan., 1924, "The Topography of a Canadian Watershed."

   xxii, Oct., 1924, "Heights of Athabaska."

   Canadian Alpine Journal:

   xiii, 1923, "The Freshfield Group, 1922."

   xiv, 1924, "A Mountaineering Journey to the Columbia Icefield."

2. Lake Louise was named in 1884 in honour of Princess Louise, Duchess of Argyll; it was known to the Indians as the Lake of Little Fishes.

3. Major-General Sir John Henry Lefroy (1817–90), was head of Toronto Observatory, 1843–53.

4. Lake Agnes, the upper lake, was visited, about 1886, by Susan Agnes, Baroness Macdonald of Earnscliffe.

5. The Indians formerly came to the valley to gather wood for bow-making.

6. Sir George Stephen, Baron Mount Stephen, was first president of the Canadian Pacific Railroad.

7. *The Journals, Detailed Reports and Observations Relative to the Exploration by Captain Palliser* (Eyre & Spottiswoode, London, 1863), p. 105.

8. While the entire body of snow and ice is more or less continuous, it is arbitrarily divided into two portions—the Waputik Icefield, extending along the crest of the continental watershed from Bath Creek to Balfour Glacier; and the Wapta Icefield, triangular in shape, continuing from Balfour and

8. Yoho glaciers to Baker Glacier and other tongues at its northern apex.
9. Cree Indian word meaning "beaver tail."
10. *Col*—the depression on a ridge connecting two mountain peaks.
11. For a description of the first crossing of Howse Pass, by David Thompson in 1807, see Appendix E.
12. *Cirque*—the semicircular amphitheatre of a glaciated mountain, caused by lateral plucking of the rock wall through ice agency.
13. Chapter III.
14. Cree Indian word meaning "grizzly bear."
15. *Icefall*—a fall in a glacier caused by any abrupt increase in the gradient of its bed. Ice, when tension is applied, on account of its brittleness, is riven into pinnacles called séracs.
16. *Névé*—accumulated snow in the highest parts of a mountain, while it is still in granular condition before its downward movement in the form of ice.
17. The family name of the Marquess of Aberdeen and Temair, Governor-General of Canada, 1893–98.
18. *David Thompson's Narrative of His Explorations in Western America, 1784–1812* (The Champlain Society, Toronto, 1916), p. lxxxvi.
19. *The Journals, Detailed Reports and Observations Relative to the Exploration by Captain Palliser* (Eyre & Spottiswoode, London, 1863), p. 150.
20. *Alpine Journal*, xxi, p. 367; *Climbs and Exploration in the Canadian Rockies*, H.E.M. STUTFIELD and J.N. COLLIE (Longmans, Green & Co., London, 1908), pp. 251, 266. The first climbing party in the group was that of Collie and Baker, with the guide Sarbach, in 1897. The only climbing accomplished was a partial ascent of Freshfield, made for topographical purposes. It was at this time that the group and its peaks were named. Collie returned to the group in 1902.
21. *Moraine*—broken or eroded rock fragments fallen upon glacial ice and transported by the ice motion.
22. *Crevasse*—a fracture or break in glacial ice due to brittleness and tension.
23. *Moulin*—a circular shaft in glacial ice, usually at a crevasse, formed by swirling streams.
24. Joseph Boucher, Chevalier de Niverville, whose party of men in two canoes went up the Saskatchewan River from The Pas, Manitoba, built Fort La Jonquière in 1751.
25. Howard Palmer has published the results of this work, as "The Freshfield Glacier, Canadian Rockies" (Smithsonian Miscellaneous Collections, Vol. 76, No. 11; publication 2757. Washington, 1924), a paper which is here reprinted as Appendix D.
26. Sir Frank S. Barnard, K.C.M.G. (1856–), Lieut.-Governor of British Columbia, 1914–19.
27. *Bergschrund*—the large crevasse marking the line where névé separates from the unpacked snow.
28. *Arête*—a sharp ridge of a mountain.
29. *Couloir*—a steeply ascending

ravine or gully in the side of a mountain.

30. Sir Joseph Trutch (1826–1904), first Lieut.-Governor of British Columbia, 1871–76.

31. Near the mouth of Waitabit Creek, travellers descending the Columbia were accustomed to rest and adjust the loads in their canoes before entering the rapids.

32. In 1918 members of the Boundary Survey ascending from Bush Pass occupied a station at 10,380 feet on the western ridge of the mountain. We noticed this at the time of our ascent, but did not find a cairn on the actual summit. This day Palmer spent on the glacier completing work of our survey.

33. John McDonald of Garth, fur-trader, was in charge of Fort George in 1793, and of Fort de l'Isle on the Saskatchewan in 1805. Rocky Mountain House was built under his direction in 1799. He crossed Howse Pass during the winter of 1811 to bring supplies to David Thompson on the Columbia.

34. Peter Pangman, an original partner of the North-West Company, ascended the Saskatchewan as far as the location of Rocky Mountain House in 1789.

35. *Massif*—a mountain mass or group of mountain heights.

36. *The Journals, Detailed Reports, and Observations Relative to the Exploration by Captain Palliser,* p. 110.

37. In his journal, under date of February 8, 1811, Alexander Henry (the younger) makes the following entry: "... we came to the forks, where the river spread to about half a mile wide, free from islands; but as usual in such places, the bed was choked with bars of sand and gravel. Here a branch of the Saskatchewan comes in from the N. opposite a smaller branch from the S.; both appear contracted, winding their courses through mountains. The main channel, up which our course lay, is still wide, and comes from the W. At the junction of these forks we had a grand view of the mountains, more elevated and craggy than any we had before seen. The upper parts of some of them are curiously formed, some closely resemble citadels, round towers, and pinnacles rising to a great height, with perpendicular summits, so steep that no human being could ascend them. Some of the highest remained all day enveloped in clouds, which were not dispersed for several hours after the wind arose, and even then hovered upon the summits as if loath to leave, until torn away by the violence of the wind, which increased to a gale from the W. Upon the top of a mountain N.W. of us, whose summit appeared level, I observed an immense field of snow, of which a part seemed lately to have separated and fallen down. This frequently happens during winter, when vast quantities of snow accumulate till the mass projects beyond the rocks and then gives way. The noise occasioned by the fall of such a body of snow equals an explosion of thunder, and the avalanche sweeps away everything movable in its course to the valleys. On the sides of some of the mountains S. of us, where the rays of the sun never reach, are vast beds of eternal snow, or, more properly, bodies

of eternal ice, their bluish color plainly distinguishing them from the snows of this season; some parts have recently given way and fallen into the valleys, while the remainder presents a perpendicular face of ice in strata of different thicknesses. Here we saw the tracks of several herds of buffalo, which had crossed the river." "New Light on the Early History of the greater North-West," *Henry–Thompson Journals*, 1789–1814, Elliott Coues (F.P. Harper, New York, 1897), Vol. II, p. 689.

38. Ross Cox, in 1817, found Jasper House in charge of "a man by the name of Klyne, a jolly old fellow, with a large family." Michel Klyne was still postmaster in 1834.

39. "The Rockies of Canada," W.D. Wilcox (G.P. Putnam's Sons, New York, 1909), pp. 139, 152.

40. During the summer of 1900, Messrs. Collie, Spencer and Stutfield attempted to penetrate to the Columbia Icefield by way of the Bush Valley and the western slope of the mountains. C.S. Thompson at the same time went north by the Saskatchewan Valley, hoping to locate Collie's party by way of the pass at the head of the "West Branch."

The hardship of pack-train travel on the British Columbia side of the Divide is amusingly set forth in a letter, dated Dec. 31, 1902, from Collie's outfitter, Fred Stephens, to Mr. Walter D. Wilcox:

"Better late than Never so as i Promised you; would Rite and tell you something of our Bush River trip i will just give you a Pointer to Pass it By. We left Donald and followed an old trail whitch Led through a Dence forest to the mouth of Bush River. We apparently followed the Columbia but was out of sight of it most of the time; never saw sutch undergrowth mud and wet, with mosquitoes that would stop a syclone, the poor Englishmen looked like Plum Puddings walking around with their faces swoolen up to twice their Natural size. Well we wanted to get to the head of the Bush River but found it in high water to be impossible to follow up the Bank. We took the trail back 6 miles then climbed up over a mountain with the outfit and struck the River 7 or 8 miles up. It was raining 7 days out of 6, to make it more Pleasant. The Pack horses got covered with Brittish Columbia mold, the oat meal soured, the hard tack swelled up so we had to Pack our saddle horses. The wood would not burn and a few more things went Rong. We finally got up the River far enough so it commenced to get deep and the valley was Narrow and filled with Burnt fallen timber. We nearly drowned Harry Long because he could not ride a raft of water soaked logs. We found it impossible to follow up the valley to the foot of Mt. Bryce and Columbia so we took to the hills and camped 7000 above sea Level. Here it snowed for 4 days and the wind blowed so we had to tie down the Pack Saddles to keep them in camp. I suppose this would be Delightfull to you But somehow it dont catch me. This was as far as we got although i could go mutch farther but the weather was so cloudy that it was useless to go farther. Here we turned and came Back to Donald. I think we were about Due west of the west Branch whitch comes into the west fork of the Saskatchewan.

"I will wind this interesting slip to a close; have no Doubt you would find this a very interesting country to go to as the mountains are verry high and craggy. The whole country is verry Rough and the weather in July will freeze a kyote so I am sure you would call it Grand."

41. In the moraines we found balls of iron pyrite, similar to those reported by Outram and found by us, in 1922, on the Freshfield Glacier. We saw none in either the Saskatchewan or Athabaska moraines.

42. *Climbs and Exploration in the Canadian Rockies*, p. 107.

43. Fatigue mirages—momentary illusions—began to appear; for an instant I was convinced that the dark line of a distant crevasse was a staff planted on the summit of North Twin; and I berated Conrad for bringing us so far only to let us be cheated of a first ascent. Mr. Osgood Field, whose party crossed the icefield during the next summer, reported a similar experience—bushes and trees at various places on the icefield, and groups of people pitilessly watching the slow progress across the snow. (*Appalachia* xvi, p. 144.)

44. The first ascent of Mount Alberta was accomplished during July, 1925, by a party of six Japanese, led by the well-known climber Mr. Yuko Maki, and accompanied by the guides Heinrich Führer and Hans Kohler, with a Swiss named Weber. These nine took sixteen hours to reach the summit from a bivouac at about 7000 feet. The night was spent on the summit ridge, some 800 feet below the top. Coming down next day they roped off three times, descent occupying the same time as ascent.

45. See Appendix F, "The Panorama from Mt. Columbia."

46. Mr. Brazeau was a highly respected officer of the Hudson's Bay Company, in charge of Rocky Mountain House, 1858–59, and later, of Fort Edmonton.

47. To identify the route, and because of the dominating peak, the name "Castleguard Pass" is suggested for the pass between the head of Castleguard Valley and the Saskatchewan Glaciers.

48. Stoney Indian word meaning "turbulent water."

49. *The Canadian Rockies, New and Old Trails*, A.P. COLEMAN (T. Fisher Unwin, London, 1911), p. 252.

50. For the relative importance of the Athabaska Pass route compared with other trans-continental routes, consult chapter on "Routes to British Columbia," in R.C. MAYNE's *Four Years in British Columbia and Vancouver Island* (John Murray, London, 1862), chap. xiii, p. 353.

51. *Description and Guide to Jasper Park* (edited by E. DEVILLE, Department of the Interior, Ottawa, 1917), p. 16.

52. "New Light on the Early History of the Greater North-West," *Henry–Thompson Journals*, 1789–1814, ELLIOTT COUES (3 vols., F.P. Harper, New York, 1897), I, 253; II, 652.

53. *David Thompson's Narrative of His Explorations in Western America, 1784–1812* (The Champlain Society, Toronto, 1916), pp. 445 et seq.

54. Note 90, Chap. XI.

55. *Voyage à la Côte du Nord-Ouest de l'Amérique Septentrionale* (Montreal, 1820). English translation and edition by J.V. HUNTINGTON, *Narrative of a Voyage to the North-West Coast of America*, Gabriel Franchère. (Redfield, New York, 1854), pp. 120 and 288.

56. Mackenzie, in the journal of his voyages, states: "... we came to the Peace Point; from which, according to the report of my interpreter, the river derives its name... . When this country was formerly invaded by the Knisteneaux, they found the Beaver Indians inhabiting the land about Portage la Roche; and the adjoining tribe were those whom they called the slaves. They drove both these tribes before them; when the latter proceeded down the river from the Lake of the Hills, in consequence, of which that part of it obtains the name of the Slave River. The former proceeded up the river; and when the Knisteneaux made peace with them, this place was settled to be the boundary."

57. *Adventures on the Columbia River*, ROSS COX (J. & J. Harper, New York, 1832), p. 246.

58. *The Fur Hunters of the Far West*, ALEXANDER ROSS (2 vols., Smith, Elder & Co., London, 1855), Vol. II, p. 189.

59. "Sketch of a Journey to the Rocky Mountains and to the Columbia River in North America," THOMAS DRUMMOND, Assistant Naturalist to the Second Land Arctic Exploring Expedition, under the command of Captain Sir John Franklin, R.N., in *Hooker's Botanical Miscellany*, Vol. I, pp. 178–219.

60. "York Factory Express Journal," EDWARD ERMATINGER. Reprinted in *Transactions of the Royal Society of Canada*, section ii, 1912, p. 67.

61. *Douglas' Journal*, 1823–1827. (Royal Horticultural Society, London, 1914), p. 257.

62. This is an early, accurate description of the present Scott Glacier and its bordering peaks.

63. *Douglas' Journal*, 1823–1827, p. 71.

64. *Oregon Missions and Travel over the Rocky Mountains, in* 1845–46, FATHER P.J. DE SMET (Edward Dunigan, New York, 1847), pp. 191, 197, 201.

65. The glacier described by de Smet is the present Scott Glacier, descending from the Hooker Icefield. It is quite probable that the Indians of that day knew of Fortress Lake and had visited it. According to the Indians there was once a trail, now in disuse, from the Whirlpool Valley over a pass of the Continental Divide to Alnus Valley, from whence the lake could be reached.

66. *Sketches in North America and the Oregon Territory*, HENRY JAMES WARRE (Dickinson & Co., London, 1849), p. 4. The plates in this very rare book are of unusual interest.

67. *Wanderings of an Artist Among the Indians of North America*, PAUL KANE (Longman, Brown, Green, Longmans & Roberts, London, 1859), pp. 151, 160 and 340.

68. *The Journals, Detailed Reports and Observations Relative to the Exploration by Captain Palliser*

(Eyre & Spottiswoode, London, 1863), p. 125.

69. Richard Hardisty was chief factor of the Hudson's Bay Company, in charge of Fort Carlton, 1857–58.

70. William J. Christie was chief factor of the Hudson's Bay Company, in charge at Edmonton, 1858–59.

71. *The Rocks and Rivers of British Columbia*, WALTER MOBERLY (H. Blacklock & Co., London, 1885), pp. 52, 81, 83. For a condensed parallel account, see *Blazing the Trail through the Rockies: The Story of Walter Moberly and His Share in the Making of Vancouver*, NOEL ROBINSON (*Vancouver News Advertiser*, Reprint 1914), p. 79.

72. Moberly's route from Athabaska Pass was apparently across the present Canoe and Fraser passes.

73. "Canadian Pacific Railroad. Report of Progress on the Exploration and Surveys, up to January 1874," WALTER MOBERLY. Appendix G, pp. 162–73.

74. *David Thompson's Narrative of His Explorations in Western America, 1784–1812*, pp. 402–03.

75. *Astoria*, WASHINGTON IRVING (Philadelphia, 1836), Vol. II, p. 275.

76. See *Hooker's Botanical Miscellany*, Vol. I, p. 190.

77. *Voyage à la Côte du Nord-Ouest de l'Amérique Septentrionale*, p. 299.

78. *Adventures on the Columbia River*, p. 255.

79. *Douglas' Journal*, 1823–1827, p. 71. (The transcription as here given is my own, made in London from the original journals. See Appendix G.—J.M.T.)

80. Robert Brown, F.R.S. (1773–1858), British botanist, served as naturalist to Captain Flinders' expedition which surveyed portions of the Australian coast, 1801–05. He was president of the Linnaean Society, 1849–53. In 1827 he observed by the microscope the continual non-organic movement among minute particles suspended in a liquid—the so-called "Brownian movement."

81. Sir William Jackson Hooker (1785–1865) was appointed Regius professor of botany at Glasgow University in 1820, and director of the Royal Botanical Gardens at Kew in 1841.

82. *Douglas' Journal*, p. 258.

83. *Companion to the Botanical Magazine*, WILLIAM HOOKER (1836), Vol. II, p. 136.

84. "Peace River. A Canoe Voyage from Hudson's Bay to the Pacific, by the late Sir George Simpson, in 1828." *Journal of Archibald McDonald*, edited by MALCOLM MCLEOD (J. Durie & Son, Ottawa, 1872), p. 66, note xxxv.

85. *Oregon Missions and Travel over the Rocky Mountains in 1845–46*, p. 198–99.

86. *The Journals, Detailed Reports, and Observations Relative to the Exploration by Captain Palliser*, p. 149.

87. *The Canadian Rockies, New and Old Trails*, A.P. COLEMAN (T. Fisher. Unwin, London, 1911), pp. 79, 147, 170, 207.

88. "At the Western Sources of the Athabaska," JEAN HABEL, *Appalachia* x, p. 28.

89. "The Whirlpool (1913)," G.E. HOWARD and A.L. MUMM, *Canadian Alpine Journal* vi, p. 74.

90. "The Location of Mts. Brown and Hooker," A.O. W‍HEELER, *Canadian Alpine Journal* xii, p. 163. Yet the Survey Commissioners, at the time of publishing their decision, were apparently unaware of the existence of Douglas' longer journal—a document of fundamental importance in any attempt at solving the problem. (See Chapter X and Appendix G.)

   One should also consult the interesting paper, "New Light on Mounts Brown and Hooker," E.W.D. H‍OLWAY, with supplementary note by J‍AMES W‍HITE, *Canadian Alpine Journal* xi, p. 45.

   Those interested in the region should also consult two additional papers:

   "Athabaska Pass to Tonquin Valley, via Goat and Fraser Rivers," D. P‍HILLIPS, *Canadian Alpine Journal* xiii, p. 209.

   "Characteristics of Passes in the Canadian Rockies," R.W. C‍AUTLEY, *Canadian Alpine Journal* xiii, p. 155.

   Mr. Cautley describes, among other things, the discovery, just north of the pass summit, of the musket-balls lost by David Thompson 110 years before. (See Chapter VIII at page 75.)

91. The altitude of Mount Edith Cavell is 11,033 feet, usually considered the highest point within the Park. This is, however, not true, since the southern boundary of the Park now includes higher peaks of the Columbia Group.

92. It is a pleasure to acknowledge the many courtesies extended to our party by Colonel S. Maynard Rogers, Superintendent of Jasper Park. We are also indebted to Warden P.H. Goodair for assistance rendered during our stay in Area No. 10.

93. This is the probable site of Campement de fusil, mentioned by Ermatinger in 1828.

94. A similar and independent conclusion was arrived at by the first party to ascend Mount Serenity. Mr. Carpe informs me that "both Palmer and myself were very much surprised when the survey map came out showing Scott to be higher than Hooker. It definitely did not make that impression from Serenity. I should say that it (Mount Scott) seemed lower than Serenity. On subsequent examination of photographs taken from the Fraser Group the previous year, however, Scott appears to hide Serenity. Owing to the late hour at which we reached the top of Serenity, I did not take instrumental levels on anything. I have no reason to question the Boundary Commission's figures."

95. The unselfish sportsmanship of Mr. Fynn, who unhesitatingly threw over his own plans on hearing of our supposed difficulties, compels our admiration and remains a cherished memory.

96. *David Thompson's Narrative of His Explorations in Western America, 1784–1812*, p. 445.

97. A Cree Indian name meaning "where there are reeds," referring to the muddy delta of the river. On the 1785 map of Peter Pond, an original partner of the North-West Company, the name is written *Arabosca*.

98. *Douglas' Journal*, 1823–1827, pp. 73, 261.

99. *The North-West Passage by Land*, M‍ILTON AND C‍HEADLE (First edition, Cassell, Petter & Galpin, London, 1865), p. 296.

100. *Ocean to Ocean: Sandford Fleming's Expedition*, G.M. GRANT (Campbell & Son, Toronto, 1873), pp. 230, 235.

101. Simon Fraser (1776–1862) was born in Bennington, Vermont. The Fraser River was named for him late in 1808, by officers of the North-West Company, at which time he was Superintendent of New Caledonia. His wife was the daughter of Col. Allan McDonell, of Dundas County, Ontario.

102. We ourselves had at no time any real designs on the mountain, Mr. Wates having written to me requesting that a professional guide should not be taken on an attempt until after his party had had another try.

103. In the summit cairn we found the following record:
    "Aug. 16, 1919—Carpe, Chapman, Palmer.
    "Aug. 23, 1923—D.B. Durant, B. Durant.
    "Sept. 13, 1923—J.J. Landry, F. Krahnstover."

104. *The North-West Passage by Land*, first edition, page 257.

105. "Jasper Park, Yellowhead Pass and Mt. Robson Expedition," A.O. WHEELER, *Canadian Alpine Journal* iv, p. 42. Mr. H.J. Moberly, factor of the Hudson's Bay Company, gives the following information in regard to the name of the mountain: "Years before the Hudson's Bay Co. and the Nor'-West Co. joined (1821), it was the custom for the Nor'-West Co. to outfit a party for a two years' trip, hunting and trading. They went west and north, even as far as the border of California. One party, under the charge of Peter S. Ogden, some two hundred men, chiefly Iroquois and French Canadians. When west of the Rockies, he scattered his hunters in different parties under the charge of a foreman, to hunt for the season. One of his camps, under the charge of a man named Robson, was somewhere in the vicinity of this mountain, and it was the rallying point where all other parties came together for their return east."

106. "Report of the Geology and Resources of the Country Traversed by the Yellowhead Pass Route from Edmonton to Tête Jaune Cache," JAMES McEVOY, *Report of the Geological Survey of Canada*, 1898, vi, Part D (Ottawa, 1901). A parallel account will be found in this paper.

107. "The Shuswap People of British Columbia," G.M. DAWSON, *Transactions of the Royal Society of Canada*, 1891, ix, Sect. II, p. 37 (Ottawa, 1891).

108. Viscount Milton (1839–77) was the son of the 6th Earl Fitzwilliam.

109. Mr. Val A. Fynn supports my view, in stating (*Alpine Journal*, xxxvi, p. 321), the "ridge runs into the ice-cap of the mountain, and in its highest portion is absolutely dominated by part of that ice-cap. All the parties passed under and over hanging ice-walls, or séracs, and were exposed to ice-falls for at least half an hour. It seems to me that this route is unnecessarily risky."

110. I have at least made climbing contact with the first three of the 12,000 ft. peaks of the Rockies of Canada. I wonder if some energetic climber will ever have all four peaks—Robson, Columbia, North Twin, Clemenceau—on his list?

111. A summary of glacier measurements and observations in the Canadian Alps, with references, will be found at the end of this paper, page 261.

112. It is possible that the moraine may have been formed in 1897, with almost no retreat between 1897 and 1902, for Professor Collie, at page 56 in his book already cited, states (referring to his visit in 1897), "The snout of the glacier was advancing and plowing up the débris before it."

113. The writer deprecates the use of "icefield" as commonly employed in connection with valley glaciers. It tends to obscure the fact that the "icefield" is only a portion of an advancing body of ice. Emphasis needs to be laid on the fact that a glacier is a distinct entity, with a definite locality of origin and a definite place of termination, between which the ice mass moves in an orderly progression. We do not so easily or so harmfully call the slack water of a river, "lake."

114. *The Shoe and Canoe*, JOHN J. BIGSBY, M.D. (2 vols., Chapman & Hall, London, 1850), p. 113.

115. *David Thompson's Narrative of His Explorations in Western America, 1784–1812* (The Champlain Society, Toronto, 1916), p. lxxxvi.

116. "David Thompson's narrative, 'The discovery of the source of the Columbia River'" (*Quarterly of the Oregon Historical Society*, March 1925, pp. 23–49). This is possibly the document cited, under different title, by Elliott Coues: see *Henry–Thompson Journals*, 1799–1814, Vol. II, p. 748.

117. During August, 1924, I had the pleasure of meeting Sir James, with whom I had corresponded for a number of years. He informed me that his summit photographs from Mt. Columbia were failures; he could not be certain that he had really seen Mt. Robson.

118. See note 117.

119. Mr. Howard Palmer has favoured me with notes of several observations made on distant Canadian views, which are tabulated below with estimates of the mileage from the small-scale Key Map (Index Sheet, 1 : 792,000) of the Interprovincial Boundary Commission.
It is understood that Binoculars were used in identifying peaks.
Mt. Wheeler from
    Abbot Pass.................65 miles.
Mt. Assiniboine from
    Mt. Sir Donald.........82 miles.
Mt. Clemenceau from
    Mt. Rogers................70 miles.
Mt. Robson from
    Mt. Unwin................75 miles.

120. *Douglas' Journal*, 1823–27. (Royal Horticultural Society monograph. William Wesley & Son, London, 1914.)

121. Thanks are due the Council of the Royal Horticultural Society for allowing pages of Douglas' Journals to be photographed. The pages, here reproduced in facsimile, are on an equally reduced scale for the two journals, and give a clear idea of the comparative appearance of handwriting, spacing and margination.

122. R.H.S. monograph, pp. 71 and 258. The quotations in Chapter X of the present volume are, however,

from the original journals, with alterations of punctuation only where necessary to clarify the narrative.

123. "New Light on Mounts Brown and Hooker," E.W.D. HOLWAY (*Canadian Alpine Journal* ix, 1918, p. 47).

124. On the map appearing in Vol. I of *Flora Boreali Americana*, WILLIAM JACKSON HOOKER, 1840, the elevations for Mount Brown and Mount Hooker are given, respectively, as 16,000 and 15,700 feet. The map is on a small scale (1:1,500,000), in conical projection. Mount Hooker is indicated as exactly S.E. of Mount Brown, with Athabaska Pass, unnamed, between the two mountains. This map, the earliest on which the names and altitudes appear, was issued in October, 1829, under the superintendence of Douglas. In two years, therefore, Douglas reduced his original estimate of Mount Brown by 1000 ft., arriving at a figure similar to that obtained by Lieut. Simpson.

125. R.H.S. monograph, p. 239.

126. *Hooker's Botanical Miscellany*, Vol. I, p. 190; see Chapter X, page 159.

127. See Chapter X.

128. Interprovincial Survey Sheet 27.

129. See note on David Thompson, Appendix E. Douglas estimated Mount Brown to be about 5500 feet above the pass (actually it is less; 9156-5724 = 3432), and subtracting this from his lowest figure for Mount Brown (16,000 feet, on the 1829 map) we have remaining an elevation of 10,500 feet for Athabaska Pass—almost double that of modern surveys—a figure approximating Thompson's boiling-point determination of 11,000 feet.

130. See Chapter VIII at page 75.

INDEX

Agnes, Lake   289.
See also Lakes in the Clouds.

Alberta, Mt. (11,874 ft.)   48, 50, 54, 63

Alcove Mtn. (9219 ft.)   203

Alexandra Glaciers   42

Alexandra, Mt. (11,214 ft.)   40, 41

Alexandra River   xlix, 34, 40, 41, 49, 57

Alnus Pk. (9673 ft.)   171

Amethyst Lakes   195, 203, 206

Amiskwi River   10

Angle Pk. (9547 ft.)   203

Ascents, Summary of Author's (1922–24), Appendix A   237

Athabaska Glacier   53, 66, 67

Athabaska, Mt. (11,452 ft.)   47
    Third Ascent   67–68

Athabaska Pass (5741 ft.)   xlviii, 19, 47, 71–75, 139, 158–159, 168–169, 172–173

Athabaska River   46, 47, 50, 137, 142, 144, 198–199

Ayesha, Mt. (10,026 feet)   11

Baker, Mt. (10,441 feet)   11

Balfour, Mt. (10,741 ft.)   5, 9

Banff   2, 168

Barbican Pk. (10,100 ft.)   203

Barlow, Mt. (10,320 ft.)   24

Barnard, Mt. (10,955 ft.)   xlix, 22

First Ascent   xxiii–xxiv, 25–27

Bastion Pk. (9812 ft.)   203
    ascent attempted   211

Beacon Pk. (9795 ft.)   204

Belanger, Mt. (10,200 ft.)   171

Bennington Glacier   204, 209, 211

Bennington Pk. (10,726 ft.)   203, 204

Berg Lake   221

Bergne, Mt. (10,420 ft.)   22

Big Hill   141.
See also Grande Côte (Athabaska Pass).

Blackrock Mtn. (9580 ft.)   202

Blaeberry River   12

Boat Encampment (Columbia River)   137, 138, 150, 153, 157

Bow Lake   15, 16, 38

Bow Pass   15, 16, 38

Bow Peak   5

Bow River   10

Bow Valley   2, 3, 6, 15

Brazeau Lake   273

Brazeau, Mt. (11,385 ft.)   273

Brazeau River   16, 62

Brown, Mt. (9156 ft.) xvii, xxxviii–xl, 48, 71, 153, 163, 164, 169–170, 180, 195–196
    Appendix G   279
    named by David Douglas   xxxviii, 161

Brussels Pk. (10,370 ft.) 171
Bryce, Mt. (11,507 ft.) 43, 48, 49, 63
Bulyea, Mt. (10,900 ft.) 22, 27
Burgess, Mt. (8463 ft.) 9
Burgess Pass 10
Bush Mtn. (10,827 ft.) 39.
See also Icefall Pk.; Rostrum Pk.
Bush Pass (7860 ft.) 14, 20, 23, 34
Bush River 21
Bush Valley 63, 292
Cairnes, Mt. (10,120 ft.) 12
Cambrai, Mt. (10,380 ft.) 40
Canoe River 76, 133, 134–135
Cardinal, Jacques 198
Cariboo Range 220, 228
Carpe, Allen 296, 297
  ascends McDonnell and Paragon pks. 204
  ascends Mt. Serenity 169
Casemate Mtn. (10,160 ft.) 204
Castleguard Camp 50
Castleguard, Mt. (10,096 ft.) 49, 50
  First Traverse xxx, 51
Castleguard Pass 293
Catacombs Mt. (10,800 ft.) 171
Cathedral Mt. (10,463 ft.) 7
Cavell, Mt. Edith. See Edith Cavell, Mt.
Chaba Pk. (10,540 ft.) 49
Cheadle, Dr. W.B. 199, 216
Chephren, Mt. ("White Pyramid") (10,715 ft.) 13, 15, 275
Christie, Mt. (10,160 ft.) 171
Christie, William J. 154
Clearwater River 5
Clemenceau, Mt. (12,001 ft.) 62, 191, 271

Cline River 40, 62
Coleman, Mt. (10,285 ft.) 40
Coleman, Prof. A.P. 36
  Athabaska Pass 168
  canvas boat 68–69, 168
  Mt. Robson 226
Collie, J. Norman 169
  Bush Valley 292
  Columbia Icefield 47–48
  First Ascent of Mt. Freshfield 21
Collie, Mt. (10,315 feet) 11
Columbia Icefield 33, 37, 46–48, 49–50, 52–53, 54, 68, 273
Columbia, Mt. (12,294 ft.) 33, 37, 48, 49, 271–273
  panorama from: Appendix F 271
  Second Ascent xxxiv, 60–63
Columbia River 46–48, 149, 154
Committee Punch Bowl 69, 137–138, 138, 146, 149–150, 150, 153, 168, 172, 177–178
Conway Glacier xxii, 13, 20
Conway, Mt. (10,170 ft.) 13
Coronation Mt. (10,420 ft.) 14
  First Ascent from Freshfield Glacier xxiv, 30
Cox, Ross 76, 134, 160
Crowfoot Glacier 16
Dent, Mt. (10,720 ft.) 22
De Smet, Pierre Jean 146–148, 149, 164
De Smet, Roche 146
Diadem Pk. (11,060 ft.) 50
Divergence Pk. (9275 ft.) 171
Dolomite Peak 16
Douai Mtn. (10,236 ft.) 40
Douglas, David xxxvii–xxxviii, 139–144, 170, 198
  Appendix G 279
  ascends Mt. Brown 160–163

Drummond, Thomas	138, 159	discovered by Dr. Hector	19–20
Dungeon Pk. (10,000 ft.)	203	surveyed	xxiii, 24–25
Eaton, J.E.C.		Freshfield Group	19–30
ascents in Freshfield Group	22	Freshfield Icefield	xlix, 21
Edith Cavell, Mt. (11,033 ft.)	171, 174, 201, 204, 207, 296	Freshfield, Mt. (10,945 ft.) Fourth Ascent	xxiv, 22, 30
Emerald Lake	7, 9	Fresnoy, Mt. (10,730 feet)	40
Erebus, Mt. (10,234 ft.)	203	Fryatt, Mt. (11,026 ft.)	171
Eremite Mtn. (9500 ft.)	203	attempt to reach	174–175
Ermatinger, Edward	138–140, 148	Fynn, Val A.	xliii, 194, 296, 297
Ermatinger, Mt. (10,039 ft.)	171, 185	ascends Freshfield	22
Evans, Mt. (10,460 ft.)	172, 177	ascends Mt. Geikie	209–210
Fairview Mt. (9001 ft.)	xxi, 2, 3, 6	Garth, Mt. (9970 ft.)	31
Farbus, Mt. (10,550 ft.)	40, 42	Geikie, Mt. (10,854 ft.)	203, 209, 211
Feuz, Edward (Swiss Guide)	xx, 10, 19	Gilgit, Mt. (10,300 ft.) First Ascent	xxiv, 24, 29
ascends Mt. Barnard	xxiii–xxiv, 25–27	Glacier Lake	15, 34–35, 273
Coronation Mtn.	xxiv, 30–31	Gordon, Mt. (10,336 ft.)	9, 17
Mt. Freshfield	xxiv, 30	Grande Côte (Athabaska Pass)	135, 139, 141, 143, 148, 150
Mt. Gilgit	xxiv, 29		
Mt. Nanga Parbat	xxiv, 28	Habel, Jean	12, 37, 60, 168
Mt. Trutch	27–28	Hardisty, Richard	153
Field	xxii, 7, 9	Headless Indian	199–200
Fleming, Sir Sandford	200–201	Hector, Dr. James	151, 157, 164
Forbes, Mt. (11,902 ft.)	29, 39	discovers Kicking Horse Pass	8
Forks. See Saskatchewan Forks.		Freshfield Glacier	19–20
Fortress Lake	36, 49, 273, 294	Lyell Glacier	35–36
Fortress Mtn. (9908 ft.)	171	Roche Miette	152
Fortress Pass (4388 ft.)	49, 171	Hector Lake	5, 16
Franchère, Gabriel	75, 76, 133–134, 160	Hector, Mt. (11,135 ft.)	5, 16
Fraser, Mt.	204.	Height of Land	149
See also Simon, McDonell and Bennington pks.		Helmer, Mt. (10,045 ft.)	31
Fraser Pass	295	Henry, Alexander Athabasca Pass, and	73
Fraser, Simon	199, 297	at Saskatchewan Forks	291
Freshfield Glacier	xxv, xlix	Hooker, Dr. William Jackson	162–163
Appendix D	249–265	Hooker, Mt. (10,782 ft.)	xvii, 48, 71, 153, 163, 170
crevasses	25–26		

Appendix G	279
ascent	xl–xliv, 187–196
named by David Douglas	162
Howse, Joseph	19
Howse Pass (5010 ft.)	xxii, xlviii, 10, 12, 19, 20, 21
Appendix E	267–270
Howse Peak (10,800 ft.)	13
Howse River	14, 15, 21, 29, 34
Hudson's Bay Company	19, 136, 138, 139, 151
Icefall Pk. (10,420 ft.)	40
Illecillewaet Glacier	262
Itinerary, Summarized, Appendix B	241
Jasper	153, 217
Jasper House	150, 151, 157
Jasper Park	xix, 71, 146, 197–198, 205, 296
Kain, Conrad (Austrian Guide)	xix, xxi, xxvii–xxix, 173, 201–202, 212
ascends Mt. Gordon	17
attempts Bastion Pk.	211
McDonell Pk. traverse	210
Mt. Athabaska	67–68
Mt. Brown	xxxviii–xl, 180–181
Mt. Castleguard	xxx, 51
Mt. Columbia	xxxiv–xxxv, 60–63
Mt. Hooker	xl–xliv, 187–194
Mt. Kane	xxxviii, 179–180
Mt. Oates	185
Mt. Resplendent	224–225
Mt. Robson	229–232
Mt. Saskatchewan	xxxiv, 58–61
North Twin	xxxi–xxxiii, 54
Simon Pk.	207–209
Terrace Mtn.	xxxi, 52
Kane, Mt. (10,000 ft.)	xxxviii, 172, 177
Kane, Paul	149–151
Kaufmann Pks.	15
Kicking Horse Pass (5329 ft.)	
discovery by Dr. Hector	8
Kicking Horse River	
naming of	8
Kinbasket Lake	154, 155, 168, 273
King Edward, Mt. (11,400 ft.)	49
Kinney Lake	220, 226–227
Kinney, Rev. G.B.	
First Ascent of Mt. Robson	226
Kitchener, Mt. (11,500 ft.)	49
Kohler, Hans (Swiss Guide)	xliii, 194
ascends Mt. Alberta	293
Mt. Resplendent	223–225
Kootenay Plain	39, 47, 268
Ladd, Dr. William S.	xxvi–xxviii, 33
ascends Mt. Gordon	17
Mt. Athabaska	67–68
Mt. Castleguard	51–53
Mt. Columbia	xxxiv, xxxiv–xxxv, 60–63
Mt. Saskatchewan	58–60
North Twin	xxxi–xxxiii, 52–54
Lake Louise	3, 5, 37, 168
Lakes in the Clouds	5
Lambe, Mt. (10,438 ft.)	22
Lapensée, Mt. (10,190 ft.)	171
Laussedat, Mt. (10,035 ft.)	12
Leather Pass. See Yellowhead Pass.	
Lyell Icefield	39
discovered by Dr. Hector	35–36
Lyell (No. 3), Mt. (11,495 ft.)	
attempted ascent	42
Lynx Mtn. (10,471 ft.)	225
Mackenzie, Alexander	134, 294
Mackenzie River	46, 222
Maki, Yuko	
ascends Mt. Alberta	293
Maligne Lake	54, 63, 273
Mastodon Mtn. (9800 ft.)	202
McArthur, Mt. (9882 ft.)	11

McDonald, Archibald 164
McDonell Pk. (10,776 ft.) 195, 203, 204
   traverse 210
McEvoy, James 297
   triangulates Mt. Robson 217
Messines Mtn. (10,290 ft.) 40
M'Gillivray, Simon 158
M'Gillivray's Rock 133, 136, 168, 170, 180, 285
M'Gillivray, William 136
Miette's Rock. *See* Roche Miette.
Milton, Viscount 199, 216
Mistaya River 15, 34
   forded 38
Moat Lake 204
Moberly, David Washington xxxvii, xliii, 173
Moberly, Walter xxxvii, 151, 152, 153, 154–155, 155, 174, 295
Mons Icefield 39
Mons Pk. (10,114 ft.) 40
Mumm, A.L. 22
   ascends Mt. Freshfield 22
   Athabaska Pass 169
   attempts Mt. Robson 226
   Scott Glacier 185
Mummery, Mt. (10,918 ft.) 12, 22, 29
Mumm Pk. (9,718 ft.) 222
Murchison, Mt. 15, 34, 70, 165
Nanga Parbat, Mt. (10,780 ft.)
   First Ascent xxiv, 28
Needle Pk. (9668 ft.) 174, 202
Nigel Pass (6906 ft.) 16
Nigel Peak (10,535 ft.) 68
Niverville Meadow Camp xxiii, xxiv, 24
Niverville, Mt. (9720 ft.) 24

North Fork 34.
   See also Saskatchewan River.
North Twin. *See* Twin (North).
North-West Company 19, 47, 72, 75, 136
Oates, Mt. (10,220 ft.) 171
   First Ascent 186
Oppy, Mt. (10,940 ft.) 40, 42
Ostheimer, Alfred J. 173, 198, 210
   ascends Mt. Kane xxxviii, 178–179
   attempts Mt. Robson xxxvii, 229–232
   McDonell Pk. 210
   Mt. Brown xxxviii–xl, 180
   Mt. Hooker xl–xliv, 187–193
   Mt. Oates 186
   Mt. Resplendent 224–225
   Simon Pk. 207–211
Ottertail Group 9, 17
Outpost Pk. (9449 ft.) 203
Outram, Sir James 37, 42, 60, 271, 298
Palliser Expedition 8, 19, 151
Palmer, Howard xxi, 10, 22, 296, 298
   ascends Mt. Barnard xxiii–xxiv, 26–27
   Freshfield Group 19
   Mt. Freshfield xxiv, 30
   Mt. Gilgit xxiv, 29
   Mt. Nanga Parbat xxiv, 28
   Mt. Serenity 169
   Mt. Truth 27–28
   Paragon and McDonell pks. 204
   survey of Freshfield Glacier:
      Appendix D 249–265
Pangman Pk. (10,420 ft.) 31
Paragon Pk. (9800 ft.) 203, 204
Parker Ridge xxxvi
Patterson, Mt. (10,490 ft.) 16
Peace River 134, 136
Peyto Glacier 34
Peyto Lake 16
Phillips, Donald ("Curly") 173, 194, 219
   First Ascent of Mt. Robson xxxvii, 226

Pilkington, Mt. (10,720 ft.)	22
Pinto Pass	40
Pipestone Valley	5
Postern Mtn. (9720 ft.)	204
Presidential Range	9, 10
Quesnel, Jules	199
Ramparts, The	198, 201, 203, 205
Redoubt, Mt. (10,200 ft.)	203
Renwick, Prof. James	158–159
Resplendent, Mt. (11,240 ft.)	224–225
Richardson Group	3
Robson, Mt. (12,972 ft.	xxxvi, 49, 179, 199, 215–232, 271. See also McEvoy, James.
Robson Pass (5417 ft.)	222, 224
Roche de Smet	146
Roche Miette	149, 152
Rocky Mountains, Canadian, List of Loftiest Peaks, Appendix C	247–248
Ross, Alexander	136–137
Ross Cox, Mt. (9840 ft.)	171
Rostrum Pk. (10,770 ft.)	40
Rufus Pk. (9053 ft.)	204
Saddle Mtn.	3
Sarbach, Mt. (10,351 ft.)	15, 34, 39
Saskatchewan Forks	39–40, 69. See also Saskatchewan River.
Saskatchewan Glacier	47, 51
first passage with pack-train	xxxv–xxxvi, 65–66
Saskatchewan, Mt. (10,964 ft.)	49
First Ascent	xxxiii, 58–60
Saskatchewan River	15, 29, 33, 38, 47, 57
Scarp Mtn. (9900 ft.)	202
Scott Glacier	138, 169, 177, 184, 191, 294
Scott, Mt. (10,826 ft.)	171, 296
Serenity, Mt. (10,573 ft.)	168, 169, 172, 186
Siffleur River	5
Simon Creek	174, 176, 202, 203
Simon Pk. (10,899 ft.)	195, 198, 203, 204
First Ascent	207–210
Simpson, James	xxi, xxix, 10, 37, 43, 68
ascends Mt. Castleguard	51
Mt. Columbia	xxxiv–xxxv, 60
Saskatchewan Glacier	xxxv–xxxvi
Simpson, Lieut., R.N.	159
Simpson, Sir George	136, 149, 159–160, 164
Sir Sandford Glacier	263
Sir Sandford, Mt. (11,590 ft.)	273, 275
Skene, Mt. (10,100 ft.)	25
Smoky River	222
Snow Dome (11,340 ft.)	48, 53
Solitaire, Mt. (10,800 ft.)	25, 31
South Twin. See Twin (South).	
Spring Rice, Mt. (10,745 ft.)	40
Stephen, Mt. (10,485 ft.)	7
St. Nicholas Pk. (9744 ft.)	16, 17
Streich, Alfred (Swiss Guide)	xliii, 194
ascends Mt. Resplendent	223–225
Strumia, Max	xxxvii, 173, 206
ascends Mt. Kane	xxxviii, 178–179
attempts Bastion Pk.	211
McDonell Pk.	210
Mt. Brown	xxxviii–xl, 180
Mt. Hooker	xl–xliv, 187–193
Mt. Oates	186
Simon Pk.	207–210
Surprise Point	206–207
Stuart, John	199
Stutfield Pk. (11,320 ft.)	50
Sunwapta Pass	34, 66

Sunwapta River	67	Vulture Col	17
Surprise Point (7873 ft.)	204	Walker, Mt. (10,825 ft.)	22
ascent	206	Wapta Icefield	289
Takakkaw Falls	9	Waputik Icefield	5, 289
Temple, Mt. (11,626 ft.)	4, 16, 274	Waputik Range	5, 10, 13
Ten Peaks, Valley of the	2	Warre, Capt. Henry J.	148
Terrace Mtn. (9750 ft.)	50	Watchman Pk. (9873 ft.)	40, 43
First Ascent	xxxi, 52	Whirlpool Pass (5936 ft.)	171, 202
Tête Jaune	200, 215.	Whirlpool River	138, 153, 155, 169, 172
See also Yellowhead Pass.			
Thompson, C.S.	41, 292	Whirlpool Valley	172, 180
Thompson, David	19, 134	Whitecrow Mtn. (9288 ft.)	202, 204
Athabaska Pass	47, 72–75, 158–160	Whitehorn Mtn. (11,100 ft.)	220, 221, 222, 231
Howse Pass, Appendix E	267–270		
Thompson Pass (6511 ft.)	34, 40, 43, 50	"White Pyramid". *See* Chephren, Mt.	
Thompson River (North)	199	Wilcox Pass	54, 67
Tonquin Pass (6393 ft.)	203	Wilcox, Walter D.	36, 168
Tonquin Valley	198, 205, 206	Wildfowl Lakes	15, 38
Trutch, Mt. (10,690 ft.)	27	Wilson, Mt. (10,696 ft.)	16, 34, 39, 40
Turret Pk. (10,200 ft.)	203	Wood River	172, 191
Twin (North) (12,085 ft.)	49, 271	Wood River Group	179, 180, 274
First Ascent	xxxi–xxxiii, 52–55	Woolley, Mt. (11,700 ft.)	50
Twin (South) (11,675 ft.)	49, 54	Yellowhead Pass	21, 199–200.
Unjigah. *See* Peace River.		*See also* Tête Jaune.	
Van Horne Range	11		
Vavasour, Lieut. M.	148	Yoho Glacier	18, 262
Vermilion Pass (5376 ft.)	2, 8	Yoho Valley	10
Victoria, Mt. (11,355 ft.)	3, 5, 16	York Factory Brigade	140, 147